汉英对照 Chinese-English

中 国 古 代 爱 情 故 事

The Peacock Flies Southeast

孔雀东南飞

徐 飞 编著

NEW WORLD PRESS
新 世 界 出 版 社

First Edition 2003

Translated by Paul White
Edited by Zhang Minjie
Book Design by He Yuting

ISBN 7-80005-923-5

published by
NEW WORLD PRESS
24 Baiwanzhuang Road, Beijing 100037, China

Distributed by
NEW WORLD PRESS
24 Baiwanzhuang Road, Beijing 100037, China
Tel: 0086-10-68994118
Fax: 0086-10-68326679
E-mail: nwpcn@public.bta.net.cn

Printed in the People's Republic of China

刘兰芝

焦
仲
卿

焦
母

前　言

　　《孔雀东南飞》，又名《焦仲卿妻》，又名《古诗为焦仲卿妻作》，是中国古代最著名的一首长篇叙事诗，描写的是东汉末年庐江郡（治所在今安徽省潜山县）小吏焦仲卿与其妻刘兰芝的爱情悲剧故事。

　　这首诗的作者是谁，早已不得而知。南朝徐陵编《玉台新咏》收录此诗时，便在题下注明："不知谁氏作此也。"据我们的推测，它很可能是一段长期流传于民间的传说，后经文人加工，最终形成了颇具艺术感染力的文学作品。《玉台新咏》在此诗之前有个小序说："汉末建安中，庐江府小吏焦仲卿妻刘氏为仲卿母所遣，自誓不嫁。其家逼之，乃投水而死。仲卿闻之，亦自缢于庭树。时人伤之，为诗云尔。"仔细阅读这首三百五十多句、一千七百余字的长诗，我们可以发现，其故事情节很简单，并没有什么曲折离奇之处。既是如此，此诗又为何流传甚广，至今仍为家喻户晓的古典名作呢？这就要从它的思想意义和艺术技巧来分析了。

　　先来说说这个故事的思想意义。全诗通过东汉末年一对年轻夫妇不堪封建礼教的重压，为了纯真的爱情以死相殉的故事，反映出封建礼教吃人的本质。诗中的女主人公刘兰芝是一个很有素养的少女，她"十三能织素，十四学裁衣，十五弹箜篌，十六诵诗书"，这样的女孩子原本应该拥有十分幸福的爱情生活，然而在那个黑暗的年代里，她嫁到焦家，便成了一个供人驱使的奴隶，成了一个没日没夜纺线织布的纺织娘，"鸡鸣入机织，夜夜不得息。三日断五匹，大人故嫌迟"。作为封建家长制代表人物的焦母，对新过门的媳妇行使着不可抗拒的专制权。在焦母的眼里，儿媳就是一个生产机器和延续后代的工具，不管儿子焦仲卿如何哀求，她也丝毫不能改变对刘兰芝的绝对支配权，最后竟把刘兰芝休回娘家，使她的支配欲得到了最大限度的满足。作为儿子的焦仲卿，眼看着爱妻遭遣，除了哀求之外，却没有任何能力为自己的爱情抗争，他只能眼睁睁地看着心上人乘上回娘家的车子。而刘兰芝作为特定时代的一位年轻妇女，誓不二嫁的观念在她的头脑中也根深蒂固。当自己被焦家折磨得心力交瘁时，她仍旧恪守着自己的诺言，矢志不移地等待着有朝一日仲卿再与她破镜重圆。之所以如此，固然有着刘兰芝对焦仲卿难以割舍的爱，但更重要的是从一而终的封建礼教支配着她的行动。在那样的时代里，女子被遣回娘家，是一件很不光彩的事。刘兰芝回娘家之后，她的母亲和哥哥并没有给予她更多的同情，而是埋怨她不能取悦于婆母，为刘家丢了脸面。后来母亲、哥哥逼迫她改嫁县令之子、太守之子，这样做的本意主要是出于遮丑，想把被休回来的女儿赶快嫁出去，这就使本已脆弱的刘兰芝雪上加霜，她抗住了一次，但抗不住一次又一次的逼嫁，最后只得用投湖自尽向焦仲卿、向世人表白她忠贞不二的爱情。刘兰芝的死对焦仲卿无疑是致命的打击，失去了这世界上惟一的所爱，他感到自己的生命也黯然失色，为了反抗母亲的专横，更为了纯真无价的爱情，他也选择了"自挂东南枝"的最终归宿。从表面上看，二者都是为情而死，而其更深层的意义则在于以死反抗那扼杀人性、泯灭良知的罪恶社会。这对青年男女虽然是弱者，但他们所采取的极端行为，却表现出一种对社会叛逆的强大力量。

在艺术处理上，全诗主线分明，人物并不多，除主人公刘兰芝与焦仲卿外，旁及到的只有焦母、刘母、刘兄，还有影影绰绰侧面表现的"东家贤女秦罗敷"和县令、太守，线条明朗而简单，简单到几乎没有故事情节，人物的性格大多是通过对话和大段集中描写来表现的，如开篇，在略述刘兰芝不堪焦母驱使后，立即进入到焦仲卿与其母的对话中，焦仲卿哀求母亲不要休回兰芝，且为刘兰芝作了无罪的辩解，这一方面表现出焦仲卿温厚的性格，另一方面也表现出他对刘兰芝专注的爱情。而焦母的一番话，则活灵活现地把她蛮横强硬的性格显露殆尽："吾意久怀忿，汝岂得自由！"在这个家庭里，她就是至高无上的权力代表，任何人都不能违抗她的意志。随后写兰芝离开焦家前的言谈举止，也是颇费笔墨，尽管兰芝被遣全是婆母专断所为，但她还是对婆母尽了最后的礼数："昔作女儿时，生小出野里。本自无教训，兼愧贵家子。受母钱帛多，不堪母驱使。今日还家去，念母劳家里。"这是一个多么善良的妇女形象！自己受尽了婆婆的羞辱和折磨，临行时却还惦记着自己一走，有劳婆婆操持家务，增添她的劳累。这一席话，把刘兰芝善良的品性刻划得十分到位。

矛盾发展到后来，焦仲卿与刘兰芝二人的临终诀别，也是催人泪下。刘兰芝被逼改嫁太守家，焦仲卿有些埋怨之词，而通晓大义、早已准备以死抗争的刘兰芝却十分冷静地向所爱的人说了个明白："同是被逼迫，君尔妾亦然。黄泉下相见，勿负今日言。"这是多么凄凉而美丽的语言，又是多么凄凉而美丽的情感。

这个故事在流传当中，也曾经有人试图将它改编为戏曲或小说，但均因缺乏较为丰富的故事情节和略显单弱而未果。我们这次改编，在基本忠实于原著的前提下，将诗中凡提到的人物，如秦罗敷、县令家的三郎、郡太守及太守公子等，均赋予其新的内容，使整个故事情节更加曲折，矛盾冲突更加复杂。这些内容的插入，是我们经过长时间的思考而精心设计的。另外，东汉建安时期是历史上一个动荡不安、战乱频仍的时期。为了烘托这个大背景，我们也适当地插入一些情节，如魏别驾与焦仲卿出使中原、王县令的三公子山中遇险、二公子死于战乱等，其目的在于将这个爱情悲剧置于全民族大悲剧的背景之下，读者阅读时，不知能否体察我们的苦心。

本书从选题策划到编辑出版，都得到新世界出版社张民捷先生的悉心指教，在此谨表衷心的感谢。

徐　飞

2002 年 6 月于盐城师范学院

古籍整理研究所

Foreword

The Peacock Flies Southeast, also known as *The Wife of Jiao Zhongqing* or *An Old Poem Written for the Wife of Jiao Zhongqing*, is the most celebrated long narrative poem of ancient China. Set in the late years of the Eastern Han Dynasty (25-220), the story tells of the tragic love between Jiao Zhongqing, a minor official of Lujiang Prefecture (in the area of present-day Qianshan County, Anhui Province), and his wife Liu Lanzhi.

The author of the poem is unknown. In the *New Recitations of the Jade Terrace*, compiled by Xu Ling of the Southern Dynasties Period (420-589), the note " It is not known who wrote this" immediately follows the title. It is probable that the story circulated as a folk legend for a long period of time, and was eventually written down and embellished by various scholarly hands until it became a literary work with powerful artistic appeal. There is a brief synopsis of the poem's story in the *New Recitations of the Jade Terrace*, as follows: " In the Jian'an reign period of the latter part of the Eastern Han Dynasty, Liu Lanzhi, the wife of the minor official Jiao Zhongqing, was expelled from the house by her mother-in-law. She vowed never to marry another. When her own family pressured her to marry again, she drowned herself. When news of this was brought to Jiao Zhongqing, he hanged himself from a tree in his courtyard. The people of the time were moved by this double tragedy, and wrote this poem about it." A careful reading of the poem, which is over 1,700 words long, in 350 lines, reveals a straightforward plot with no complications or surprises. So why did it become so widely known, until today it is a classic familiar in every household in China? The answer can be found in an analysis of its ideological message and artistry.

First of all, its ideological content. The poem tells the story of a young couple's defiance of feudal mores in the later part of the Han Dynasty, which finally leads them to sacrificing their lives for true love. It reflects the carnivorous nature of feudal ethics. The poem's heroine, Liu Lanzhi, is an accomplished young girl: " At 13, she could weave plain cloth; at 14, she learned tailoring; at 15, she mastered the *konghou* [a type of stringed instrument — Trans.]; and at 16, she could recite poetry." Such a talented girl, by rights, should have enjoyed a happy love life. But in those benighted days, she was married off into the Jiao family, where she became no better than a slave, at everybody's beck and call. She was forced to weave cloth from cockcrow to well into the night. The head of this oppressive feudal household was her mother-in-law, Lady Jiao, who had absolute authority which the new member of the household had no way to defend herself against. In the eyes of Lady Jiao, Liu Lanzhi was nothing more than an instrument for weaving cloth and producing the next generation of Jiaos. Despite all her son's pleadings, Lady Jiao would not relax her cruel tyranny; in the end, she sent Liu Lanzhi back to her parents, in a supreme gesture of contempt. Jiao Zhongqing could do nothing but watch, grief-stricken, as the love of his life mounted the carriage and went away. Liu Lanzhi, meanwhile, was a young woman of her time; a resolution never to remarry was something deeply ingrained in her psychology. Despite all the physical and mental torments she was subjected to by the Jiao family, she was adamant in adhering to her marriage vow, and steadfast in her determination to wait until she was reunited with her husband Jiao Zhongqing. This situation came about partly because she found it difficult to put aside her love for the young man, but more important was the overwhelming pressure brought to bear on her by feudal ethics. In those days, it was a terrible disgrace for a bride to be sent back to her family, and her mother and older brother bitterly resented her for not having been able to please her mother-in-law and bringing shame on the Liu family. They tried to wipe away this stain on the family honor by pressuring Lanzhi to marry first the son of the county magistrate, and then, when she refused, the son of the local military commander. Eventually, these importunities grew too vexing for the frail girl. She drowned herself in a lake as testimony to her husband and to the world of her undying love and her resolve to preserve her honor to the end. This was a mortal blow for Jiao Zhongqing too; having lost his only true love, he chose to " hang himself on the southeastern branch" as a gesture of defiance of his domineering mother and his pure and priceless love. On a superficial level, these deaths arose from thwarted love, but at a deeper level, they were caused by the rottenness of a society which extinguished noble sentiments and throttled human lives. The extreme course which the young people chose shows that even in their weak and helpless position they could still muster a kind of powerful defiance against the perverse society they lived in.

From the aspect of the artistic handling of the tale, the theme is straightforward, and the number of protagonists limited. In fact, apart from the hero and heroine — Liu Lanzhi and Jiao Zhongqing — and the supporting roles of Lady Jiao, and Lanzhi's mother and brother, we are only presented with shadowy figures, namely, the "worthy Mistress Qin Luofu," the county magistrate and the local commander. The story line is clear, and so simple as to be almost without plot. The characters of the participants are conveyed through dialogue and sweeping statements. In the opening part, immediately after a description of how Lady Jiao bullies Lanzhi, the scene shifts to an exchange between Jiao Zhongqing and his mother in which the young man pleads on behalf of his bride, showing his tender-hearted nature and his love for Lanzhi. The cruelty and ruthlessness of Lady Jiao, on the other hand, is vividly brought out in her short outburst: "My heart is full of hatred. How dare you think you can do as you please?" She is the supreme authority in this household, and nobody has the power to defy her. The description which follows, of Lanzhi's actions and words just before she departs from the Jiao home, is somewhat long-winded, a striking fact emerges: Despite all she has suffered at the hands of her cruel mother-in-law, Lanzhi is never less than most respectful and considerate toward her. She says, "You took me, a boorish and uncultured child, into your honored household, and showered me with presents. Now I am being sent away, but when I am at home it will grieve me to think of the toil you will have to endure, as I will no longer be here to help you." Truly an image of a good-hearted woman!

As the tragedy works itself out to its inevitable conclusion, the effect on the reader is powerfully moving. Lanzhi, after being forced marry another man, makes up her mind to commit suicide in protest. She addresses Jiao Zhongqing in the following chilling but magnificent words: "You and I have suffered the same oppression. When we finally meet at the Yellow Springs [the underworld — Trans.] do not forget the promise we made today."

In the course of the story's transmission down the ages, there have been attempts to make into a stage play and a novel. These efforts have been less than successful, because the plot lacks richness of content and dramatic interest. In this version, while sticking faithfully to the original, we have taken the liberty of embellishing the roles of such characters as Qin Luofu, and the county magistrate's and commander's sons, in order to add twists and conflicts to the plot. This took a lot of thought and planning. In addition, because the Jian'an reign period of the Eastern Han Dynasty was a time of great upheaval, we thought it necessary to add some episodes which would provide a suitable background of the suffering of the whole nation for the unfolding of the tragedy of the lovers. Such episodes include the ones in which Mounted Escort Wei and Jiao Zhongqing are sent on a mission to the Central Plains, the magistrate's third son meets danger in the mountains and his second son dies in battle. We hope the reader will appreciate this effort.

We would like to express our deepest gratitude to Mr Zhang Minjie of New World Press, who guided this book with the greatest care through all the stages from choosing the theme, to planning, to final publication.

Xu Fei

Yancheng Normal College

Ancient Texts Collation and Research Office

内容简介

　　东汉末年，庐江郡小吏焦仲卿娶了鸳鸯集刘兰芝为妻，二人情同鱼水，十分相得。但焦仲卿的母亲日日逼迫刘兰芝纺织，还时时表示不满，两三年中，刘兰芝受尽辛苦和屈辱，终因婆媳间矛盾不可调和，刘兰芝被休回娘家。焦仲卿一直深深爱着刘兰芝，他多次苦苦哀求母亲不要将兰芝休弃，但其母以兰芝举动自专，又不生育为由，没有听从儿子的劝阻。焦仲卿与刘兰芝相约，不久将想办法把刘兰芝接回家重续鸾胶，让兰芝在娘家暂忍一时。两人都发誓不再婚嫁。刘兰芝弹得一手好箜篌，一次偶然的机会，居巢县令的三公子王瑞琪听到了这美妙的琴声，不由对刘兰芝深有好感。当王瑞琪得知刘兰芝被休回家的消息后，亲往鸳鸯集向刘兰芝求婚，不料路遇贼寇，受伤而返。庐江郡许太守家有一公子，生性愚痴。太守命人前往鸳鸯集向刘家求婚，刘兰芝在兄长的逼迫下，应下这门亲事，但她心中所想的只有一死，她要用死来表示对焦仲卿的忠贞。与刘兰芝一同长大的伙伴秦罗敷深得焦母喜爱，焦母打算休了刘兰芝后把她娶进家门，可是焦仲卿面对罗敷的美貌全不动心，他始终不渝地爱着刘兰芝。兰芝新婚之夜投湖自尽，焦仲卿得知这个消息后，也在与罗敷结婚之前上吊自尽，二人用生命的代价圆了黄泉之下永相厮守的凤愿。

Synopsis

In the closing years of the Eastern Han Dynasty, a minor official of Lujiang prefecture, by the name of Jiao Zhongqing, takes to wife Liu Lanzhi, a girl from the market town of Yuanyang. It is a perfect love match, and the two would have lived happily ever after if it had not been for the jealousy of Jiao Zhongqing's mother. Lady Jiao forces her daughter-in-law to slave away at the loom morning, noon and night, constantly complaining about what she regarded as her poor work. Eventually, the antagonism between them comes to a head, and Lady Jiao sends Lanzhi back to her home. Despite her son's pleading, Lady Jiao insists that the girl is willful, and besides she has failed to produce a grandchild for her, and so the marriage must be annulled. Jiao Zhongqing and Liu Lanzhi make a secret pact that neither of them will remarry, and that before long they will find a way to renew their bliss. In the meantime, Lanzhi is to wait patiently at home. One day, as Lanzhi is playing the *konghou*, the third son of the magistrate of Juchao County, Wang Ruiqi, happens to be passing. Hearing the sweet tune, Wang makes inquiries as to the player, and learns that she is a young girl who has been expelled from her bridal home. On his way to Yuanyang to ask for Lanzhi's hand in marriage, Wang is waylaid by robbers, and returns to nurse his injuries. Meanwhile, Commander Xu of Lujiang Prefecture has also heard about Lanzhi, and sends to Yuanyang to ask that she be betrothed to his son. Against her will, Lanzhi is married off to the simpleton son of the commander. Lanzhi decides that only by committing suicide can she express her faithfulness to Jiao Zhongqing. Now that

Lanzhi has been married off to the commander's son, Lady Jiao sees that the way is clear to get her son to marry Qin Luofu, who is a dear friend of Lanzhi. But Jiao Zhongqing can never love anyone but Lanzhi, and refuses to countenance the match. On the night of her wedding to the commander's son, Lanzhi drowns herself in a nearby lake. When the tragic news is brought to him, the distraught Jiao Zhongqing hangs himself. The two lovers sacrifice their lives to be together for ever at the Yellow Springs.

目 录

◎第一章
少女兰芝未嫁时

　　东汉献帝即位后，中原地区已经是群雄并起，百姓流离于兵荒马乱之中，遍野尸骸无人收殓。而偏于东南的庐江郡，却因其地处山重水复之中，很少受到兵火的洗劫。在这里，官吏和百姓除了听到南来北往的商贾们说起中原战乱之惨烈之外，感觉不出这个世间还有刀光血影。也正是由于中原已乱，原本宁静的庐江潜山一带，外来的中原人明显增多，倒使过于恬静的山城增添了不少的活力。

　　离庐江郡城三十多里有一个镇子，名叫鸳鸯集，住着几百户人家，在全郡也算得是一个大镇。这个地方北、东、西三方尽是山峦，只有南面一溜斜坡平缓地向下蔓延，直延伸到前面的鸳鸯河，傍河有一条官道，官道再南，便又是陡起的青山，名叫华山。鸳鸯集的几百户人家，就世世代代安静地生活在这片平缓的坡地上。正是阳春三月间，鸳鸯河清澈见底，河水不急不缓地流淌着，发出汩汩的声音，河岸上长满缤纷的花草，飘散出沁人心脾的幽香。春风吹过河岸，花草摇曳，流水潺潺，北坡上炊烟袅袅，南山上绿树荫荫，真可

Chapter One
The Maiden Lanzhi

Emperor Xian of Eastern Han came to the throne in a time of turmoil for the Central Plains. The common people fled in droves from battles and marauders, and the ground was everywhere strewn with corpses. But one place that was too remote to be affected much by the turmoil was the prefecture of Lujiang, in the southeast. Here, the tragedies that afflicted the rest of the country were known only from accounts brought by itinerant merchants, and by refugees, who swelled the population of this quiet little district and made it somewhat more bustling than it hitherto had been.

Some 30 *li* [a *li* is a measurement of distance equal to 0.5 km — Trans.] from the prefectural seat of Lujiang lay the market town of Yuanyang, a community of only a few hundred households but considered one of the larger towns of the prefecture. Mountain ranges protected Yuanyang on the north, east and west, while on the south, the land gently sloped down to the Yuanyang River. An official highway followed the line of the river on its opposite side, and south of the road towered the massif of Mount Huashan. The local inhabitants of Yuanyang had dwelt on these gentle slopes in peace and contentment for many generations. In the spring, the Yuanyang River trickled and gurgled its way unhurriedly, its water so clear that you could see its sandy bed. The river's banks were lush with grass, thickly studded with flowers of all kinds which gave out a perfume to gladden the heart.

谓美不胜收。

太阳已经西斜了，河边上游春的姑娘们还在尽情地嬉笑蹦跳，不时发出银铃般悦耳的笑声和娇甜的叫喊声，使官道上偶尔路过的行人不由得驻足观看。一座稍显破旧的小木桥边，三个姑娘光着脚，从岸上走下河边，又从河边跑上岸来，追逐着，格格地笑着。这时，跑在最后的那个少女朝离她们很远处独立花丛的一位姑娘高声叫着：

"兰芝，兰芝，我捉到一条银鱼哎！兰芝，快来呀，我们比一比谁捉到的鱼多，好不好？你为什么偏喜欢一个人在那里掐花，不跟我们一块玩呀！"

被她们喊兰芝的姑娘生得面色红润，十分漂亮，在鸳鸯集是个十分惹眼的美女，她父亲是个郎中，十里八乡有些小名气，从小读过几年书，也颇会读几首诗。古诗里有位少妇叫秦罗敷，据说是位绝色美人，恰好他也姓秦，于是便为自己的女儿取名叫罗敷了。依这位秦郎中的意思，为女儿起这么个名儿，不仅要表明女儿生得标致，更盼望她长大成人后能嫁个五马太守，也好光耀门庭。

兰芝原是鸳鸯集里刘家的女儿，父亲刘耀先原籍在中原汝南，因做官来到庐江，不想生下一儿一女后没几年，便不幸患病去世，这使得原本殷富的刘氏母子家道中落。兰芝的母亲本想带着这一双儿女回到老家，可是听说汝南那地方匪患日多，

The spring scene, when the flowers and grass waved in the gentle breeze and the smoke from cooking fires spiraled lazily among the cool green shade of the trees was truly a feast for the eyes.

One day, just as the sinking in the west, three young girls on a spring outing were frolicking on the bank of the river. Their tinkling laughter and merry jokes caused the rare traveler on the highway to stop and gaze at them with a smile. By a decrepit wooden bridge, the girls bared their feet, and paddled in the water or chased each other on the bank. Suddenly one shouted to another, who had been attracted by a clump of flowering shrubs: "Lanzhi! Lanzhi! I've caught a silver fish. Come here, quick. Let's see who can catch the most fish. What fun is there in picking flowers all by yourself?"

The one calling Lanzhi was a pretty, rosy-cheeked girl, who turned many heads in Yuanyang. Her surname was Qin, and she was the daughter of a noted herbal doctor of the area. Because she had shown an aptitude for learning from an early age, being especially good at reciting poetry, her father had named her after a beauty, also surnamed Qin, celebrated in an ancient poem. That was how she got the name Qin Luofu, a name which her father hoped would bring her good fortune and marriage into a rich and influential family.

Lanzhi herself was the daughter of Liu Yaoxian, who had come to Yuanyang as a petty official, from Ru'nan in the Central Plains area. He had died suddenly of an illness, leaving behind a young son and an even younger daughter. Deterred from returning to Ru'nan by reports of the worsening situation there, Lanzhi's mother had decided to remain in Yuanyang and struggle to bring up her two children as best she could in the straitened circumstance she found herself in.

百姓的日子难得太平，于是便在鸳鸯集安下了家。
她原想在中原安定之后再返回故里，可是这些年
中原不但不能安定，战事反而越来越多。时间既
久，她也就打消了回乡的念头，安下心来抚养自己
的儿女了。兰芝今年已是十五岁的姑娘，虽然脸庞
不像罗敷那样光采照人，但白皙文静，不爱笑闹。
她十三岁时，母亲就亲手教她织布裁衣，这兰芝又
是个心灵手巧的孩子，还在别的女娃只会喂鸡拾
柴的时候，她已经是远近闻名的巧手少女了。她有
时也来到田里河边，甚至有时也到对面的华山里
去，因为她喜欢这美丽的自然景致。她又是个很好
动脑子的女孩，这一带生长着一种细而长的香草，
春天里开蓝色的花，花朵细瘦而长，花开时香气令
人心醉。她喜欢这种不大争艳的花，曾经问母亲这
花儿叫什么名字，母亲说这是一种无名小草。兰芝
是个十分认真的女孩，她认为世上万事万物都有
名字，为了问明这花的名字，她跑遍了全镇到处打
听，结果谁也说不清。于是她为这种香草取了个特
别雅致的名字，叫孔雀兰。并郑重其事地告诉女伴
们："这种草叫孔雀兰。"久而久之，不论大人还是
孩子，远近村落里的人们就都把它称做孔雀兰了。

罗敷喊兰芝时，兰芝正在采摘孔雀兰，此时的
孔雀兰有的刚刚长出浅兰色的花蕊，有的还含苞
未放。她听到罗敷的叫声，扭过头来，朝罗敷她们

At the time our story starts, Lanzhi was already 15 years old. While her looks were not as dazzling as those of Luofu, her complexion had a more delicate and pleasing fairness, and she was not as boisterous as her friend. From the age of 13, her mother had taught her to weave cloth and tailor garments. Lanzhi was a quick learner, and at the age when most girls can do no more than feed chickens and gather hay she was already renowned far and wide for her nimble fingers. She often came down to the riverside, and even ventured as far as Mount Huashan on the other side, as she was fascinated by the natural beauty of these places. Besides, Lanzhi had an inquiring mind. There was a long and thin type of plant which grew in the area, which produced blue flowers in the spring, with an intoxicating scent. Lanzhi was attracted to this plant, although it was not outstandingly beautiful, but when she asked her mother what it was called, her mother simply said that it had no name. The girl was astute enough to know that everything had a name, and so she inquired of wiseacres far and wide, but nobody knew the name of the mysterious plant. Lanzhi thereupon decided to christen it herself; she called it the "peacock orchid." It was not long before everyone in the district became familiar with the name.

Lanzhi was picking peacock orchids just as Luofu called out to her. The delicate stamens of the flowers were just emerging at that time of year, and on some the buds had not yet appeared. Turning her head at the sound of Luofu's voice, Lanzhi gave her a sweet smile, and said, "Girls don't catch fish; that's a boys' game. No, I don't want to join you in your rowdy antics."

"Oh!" exclaimed Luofu, who had run up to Lanzhi by this time, "So we're not allowed to play with Miss Lanzhi, aren't we?" she said, in a tone half-annoyed and half-mocking. "I suppose

嫣然一笑，说道："女孩儿家摸什么鱼，那是男孩子的把戏，我可不跟你们胡闹！"

"呦！"罗敷等人此时已经跑到兰芝面前，只听罗敷半是嗔怪半是揶揄地说："咱们可不敢跟兰芝玩呢，人家是大家闺秀，不像咱们，是山里的土丫头。"

"什么大家闺秀，我只是没你们那么大胆量罢了。"兰芝一点也没有恼，细声细气地说。

谁知另一个叫艳艳的女孩更加放肆，一边用手指划着脸蛋，一边朝兰芝喊："兰芝，采这么多孔雀兰，是不是要送给自家的相好？哎哎，相好是哪个人啊？"说完，格格地大笑。

"去你的！"兰芝扬起拿着孔雀兰的手，做出要打艳艳的样子。

"害什么羞？"罗敷赶上来圆场，"女孩家嘛，总归要有个相好嫁给他才是。我娘总是对我说：'要多些规矩，不然以后嫁到婆家，婆家会不喜欢的。'"说完，小嘴巴朝上一撇，不屑地哼了一声："婆家不喜欢有什么了不起，只要相好喜欢，那才是正经的。"

艳艳听罢，啧了一声，问道：

"罗敷，你的相好在哪儿？漂亮吗？"

罗敷有点得意忘形，依旧仰着头，迷着眼睛，伸出手漫无目的地一指，说："在那边儿！"

她原本是在与小姐妹嬉戏，谁知几个姐妹顺

you're a refined young lady of a prominent family — not like us country bumpkins?"

"Don't be silly," rejoined Lanzhi, gently. "It's just that I'm not as bold as you."

At this point, the third girl, Yanyan, stuck her oar in. Pointing an accusing finger at Lanzhi, she jeered, "I suppose you've gathered all these peacock orchids to give to your lover, haven't you? Who is he? Come on, tell us!" And she cackled with glee.

"Mind your own business!" hissed Lanzhi, waving the peacock orchids as if to hit Yanyan with them.

"What's wrong with having a lover?" said Luofu, soothingly. "Every girl's got to have a lover and get married sooner or later. My mother keeps saying to me: 'You must act with more decorum, young lady; otherwise you'll be disliked by your future mother-in-law.' " She then pouted, and snorted: "Who cares about mothers-in-law? So long as the lovers get on well together, that's all that matters."

At this, Yanyan tut-tutted. "Luofu, where's your lover? Is he handsome?" she asked, coyly.

Luofu raised her head, closed her eyes, and seemed to go into a trance. She made a vague gesture with her arm. "There he is," she said.

She was fooling about, but by sheer coincidence she had pointed in the direction of the old wooden bridge, and just as she did so a man leading a horse was crossing it in their direction. He was a young man, wearing a piece of cloth wrapped round his head, a green gown and silk boots. Lanzhi and Yanyan gazed at the stranger without uttering a word, and Luofu, noticing the sudden silence, opened her eyes and stared too.

The young man came up to the three girls, made an elegant

着她指的方向往木桥边看去，恰好有个牵马的人朝她们走过来。这是一位头戴幅巾的少年男子，一件青袍，一双丝靴，刚刚走下桥来。这情景着实让兰芝、艳艳等人愣住了，闭着眼睛的罗敷见女伴们没了声音，这才睁开眼睛。这时，那位少年渐渐走到姑娘们面前，向她们斯斯文文地施了一揖，问道："敢问诸位姐姐，往郡城朝哪个方向走？"

这声音温和细腻，几个姑娘虽然凑在一起耍嘴皮子时一个比一个胆大，真在少年面前，却谁也不敢先开口了。片刻，兰芝答道："客人只顺着这官道向西，便是郡城。"

那少年约摸十八九岁的样子，又略略一揖，说道："谢谢姐姐指教，不知还有多少路程？"

兰芝望着少年白皙俊秀的面庞，应声答道："还有三四十里路程呢，如今天色向晚，路上又不大安全，先生何不住在鸳鸯集客栈，明日一早再行。"

少年显出感激之情，这才抬起头来，注视着兰芝。当他的目光与兰芝对视的那一瞬间，似乎被兰芝的眼睛胶住了，而兰芝此时心中也怦然一动，她觉得从她记事时起，见到的男孩子都是灰头土脸，何曾见过这样斯文白净的少年。她只觉得脸上一阵阵发热，羞得把头低了又低，恨不得埋进胸前，让绣襦遮起来，两只手不住地揉着那束孔雀兰。

少年定了定神，施过礼后，便折回木桥，沿着

bow, and inquired, "May I ask you young ladies in which direction the seat of the prefecture lies?"

The girls, who normally chattered like sparrows when they were together, were struck dumb with awe at the newcomer's refined and cultured tone. Finally, Lanzhi found her tongue.

"If you follow this highway west, sir, you will come to prefectural town," she said, pointing in the direction of the setting sun.

The young man, who seemed to be about 18 years old, bowed to her.

"Thank you, miss," he said. "And may I ask how far the town is from here?"

Lanzhi, fascinated by the youth's fair-skinned and delicate features, replied, "It's a good thirty or forty //from here, sir. Might I suggest that, as the day is late and the road unsafe after dark, that you put up at the inn at Yuanyang, and continue your journey tomorrow?"

The young man's face seemed to glow as he gazed on Lanzhi, and indeed the latter's eyes seemed to be glued to his. Lanzhi's heart fluttered. Ever since she could remember, all the men she had seen had had swarthy, weather-beaten faces; she had never imagined that a young man could have such a fair complexion. She suddenly felt her own face becoming quite hot, and she drooped her head modestly, wishing she could hide it in the folds of her embroidered blouse. Her hands fidgeted nervously with the bunch of peacock orchids.

The young man got a grip on himself, bowed politely, and went back in the direction he had come from. Probably because such a bevy of beauties was a rare sight in that part of the countryside, he soon turned his head to look back. When he saw that the girls were still watching him, he gave a low bow with his

官道朝西去了。大概是这位少年也从未见过美女齐集的场面，走了不远，又回转头来，只见几个姑娘仍在望着他，连忙朝这边拱了拱手，再表谢意。兰芝突然感到少年的目光只注视着自己，那目光里像是埋藏着爱意。

姑娘们这时都没了话，直到目送少年远去，气氛才又活跃起来。这回是艳艳先开口：

"兰芝，我看你方才不住地揉着孔雀兰，还以为你要把花儿送给他呢！"

兰芝不知该怎么回答，她原本就是个内向的女子，又碰见这么件尴尬事儿，心里乱腾腾的。

艳艳转过脸又来调侃罗敷："罗敷姐，这个人可是你亲手指的相好，什么时候嫁给他呢？"

罗敷倒是颇为大方，爽爽快快地说：

"对，他就是我的相好，你们可不许跟我抢新郎呦！待我嫁他的时候，保你们每人都有喜酒喝。"

太阳终于隐在了山后，河岸也开始弥漫起淡淡的雾气，姑娘们已经玩得尽兴，各自回家去了。兰芝手里攥着那束兰花还没进镇，只见一个十八九岁的小伙子大步流星地正往镇外走，一见几个女孩，怒冲冲地盯着兰芝吼道："一出门就忘了回家，没规矩！快回去，快点！"他嚷嚷了几句，还在嘟囔："像你这样，将来嫁了人，不让人休回来才怪呢！"

罗敷、艳艳像鼠儿见了猫一样纷纷绕开他，一

hands cupped in front of his chest, in a further gesture of thanks. As he did so, Lanzhi was sure that his eyes were looking at her alone, and, moreover, that those eyes were filled with love.

Not until the young man was out of sight did the girls break their unusual silence. Yanyan was the first to speak.

"Lanzhi," she teased, "I noticed that you were stroking those peacock orchids the whole time. I think you wanted to give them to him, didn't you?"

Lanzhi was at a loss what to say. She was by nature a reserved person, and this banter left her agitated.

Yanyan then turned her attention to ribbing Luofu:

"Luofu, you pointed at him, and said he was your lover. When are we going to hear wedding bells?"

But, unlike Lanzhi, Luofu was a match for her. Without any hesitation whatsoever, she shot back, "Yes, that's right. He's my fiancé. And I don't want either of you stealing him. I'll invite you to the wedding."

The sun had almost vanished behind the western hills, and a thin mist was beginning to creep from the river. The three girls walked slowly homeward, tired after their outing. Lanzhi was still holding her bunch of peacock orchids. Suddenly there loomed up on the path before them the figure of a youth in his late teens striding toward them. As soon as he caught sight of the girls, he shouted at Lanzhi:

"What sort of behavior is this? Did you forget to come home? Get back home right now!" He then mumbled to himself: "You'll lead your husband a merry dance some day, gallivanting around all the time."

Luofu and Yanyan scurried around the threatening figure like mice which have seen a cat. When they were at a safe

边往镇里溜一边窃窃笑道："老天！但愿我们将来别嫁给这样的粗汉！"

这个"粗汉"是兰芝的哥哥，名叫继宗。这是兰芝的父亲为他取的名，希望他长大后能出人头地，光宗耀祖。谁知继宗生性粗朴，虽然母亲自小教他读书，又专门为他觅了一位先生教授五经，可是他读了后面忘了前面，把先生气得没办法。这位先生也是中原流落到此地的，有家难回。日子一久，就在这里成了亲，东家教两天书，西家写两封信。说是"教书"，其实不过是哄几钱银子养家糊口罢了。

兰芝没吭一声，跟在哥哥后面回到家里，娘把晚饭给她蒸热，端到她面前，说："吃罢，以后记着早点回来。"

"她哪懂得女孩家的规矩！"继宗怒气未消，打断了母亲的话。

"好啦，姑娘家该由娘来管束，你当哥哥的怎么能这么训斥妹妹。"母亲打断了哥哥的话，又说："该掌灯了，去读你的书吧。"

"还读书？我都读了一后响了！"继宗像是受了多大的委屈，气得直跺脚。

"你急什么？"兰芝娘没有再说兰芝，却把话头转到继宗身上了，"女孩儿家成人出嫁是娘操心的事，男子汉不认真读书，将来怎么立身？"

继宗嘴里不知嘟囔些什么，一扭身进了自己

distance, they started giggling. "I'm definitely not going to marry an ogre like that," said Luofu. Yanyan agreed that that was the last thing in the world she would do too.

The "ogre" was Lanzhi's elder brother. His father had named him Jizong [meaning "a credit to the ancestors" — Trans.] in the hope that when he grew up he would make a name for himself and bring glory on the family. Jizong, however, was boorish by nature. His mother had tried to educate him from an early age, and later hired a tutor, but knowledge was not something that the lad seemed capable of acquiring. He was the despair of his tutor, a refugee from the Central Plains, who himself was not a qualified teacher but someone who peddled his meager knowledge of writing and the classics to make ends meet.

Lanzhi said nothing in her own defense, but simply followed Jizong home. Once she arrived, her mother hurriedly served her a hot meal. "Lanzhi dear, make sure you come home early in future," was her gentle admonishment.

"She has no idea how to behave," snarled her brother.

"Let me take care of bringing up my daughter, Jizong," their mother said pointedly to the boy. "What would you know about such things? Take a lamp, and get on with your studies."

"More studying?" wailed Jizong, stamping his foot in a temper. "But I've been studying all afternoon."

"A girl has to prepare for marriage, and a boy has to study in order to get along in the world," said his mother.

Grumbling, Jizong shuffled off to his bedroom.

After taking only a few mouthfuls of supper, Lanzhi went to her bedroom. There, she sat for a while staring vacantly into the bronze mirror on her dressing table. Then she carefully arranged the peacock orchids so that they framed the mirror, setting off the

的厢房。

兰芝草草地吃了几口饭，便回到了自己的绣房，她呆呆地坐在榻前，面对铜镜，心不在焉地看了两眼，又小心翼翼地把那束孔雀兰放在妆台镜子的前面，兰草映在镜子里，像是在烘托她秀丽的面容，灯光轻轻地摇曳，一闪一闪，把兰芝带进了一片遐想之中，她在努力地搜寻刚才在河边见到的那位少年俊秀的面庞和潇洒的风致，特别是那双善解人意的眼睛，她又在细细地体味自己目光与少年对视那一刻的感觉，这种感觉是从来没有过的，想到这里，她觉得胸口跳得厉害，方才的满脸灼热似乎又袭上来了。她不由自主地用双手捂住脸，可是心跳得更快了。

鸳鸯集属居巢县，但处在该县的东南，从鸳鸯集到县城，比到郡城还要远些。按照当时的制度，县令要按时巡察属镇。尤其是在春季里，不论哪个县的长官，都十分关注庄稼的长势，为的是到夏收时能缴足租税。只有这样，才能保住自己头上的纱帽。

这一天，居巢县令王居安前呼后拥地来到鸳鸯集，这是他此行的最后一个镇子了。镇上的里正胡坎早已率数位耆旧恭恭敬敬地伺候在官道路口，还没等王县令的车子停稳，胡坎便快步上前，一手揭开车帘，一手搀扶着县令下了车。

prettiness of her reflected features. Sitting there in the flickering light of the oil lamp, Lanzhi passed into a reverie, conjuring up a vision of the young man with the aristocratic and refined features and poise she had encountered earlier that evening by the river. His eyes, especially, were vivid in her memory. Again she felt the thrill of his eyes meeting hers. It was a sensation she had never experience before, and she felt her heart flutter. At the same time, a hot flush suffused her face. Instinctively, she hid her face with her hands, but her heart throbbed all the more.

The market town of Yuanyang lay under the jurisdiction of Juchao County. But, being located in the extreme southeast of that county, it was actually nearer to the capital of the prefecture surrounding the county than to the county seat itself. According to the administrative system of the time, the county magistrate would make regular tours of inspection of all the towns under his authority, usually in the spring. All local officials, in fact, had an interest in how the farming work was going on in these districts, because it was on the basis of the conditions of the crops that the summer harvest taxes were levied, and this in turn determined how much went into the officials' pockets.

One morning, the magistrate of Juchao County, Wang Ju'an, approached Yuanyang as the last leg of a tour of inspection, in the midst of a large retinue. Village Head Hu Kan had stationed himself early at the head of all the elders and other worthies of Yuanyang on the road, eager to make a good impression on his superior. The magistrate's carriage had hardly come to a halt, when Hu Kan bustled forward, wrenched the vehicle's curtains aside, and almost dragged the magistrate bodily out of it with a great show of busy deference.

王县令抖抖双袖，又抬起一只手遮住前额，颇有诗意地说了声："好个艳阳天！"

"大人所言不甚切当。"县令身后一个年轻子弟突然出来纠正县令的话，"艳阳天乃秋天之谓，如今是阳春三月，岂能称艳阳！"

在场的人顿时鸦雀无声，胡坎见这个后生穿着一身锦绣，风度举止也与众人不同，想呵止他，又不知此人来路，所以"这，这"了两声，瞅着王县令又发出一声苦笑。

"哦，犬子有长进了！"王县令手捻胡须呵呵笑道，"为父一时失口，竟被犬子听出了破绽。"

"啊！"胡坎这才明白，原来这位后生是县令的公子，他连忙凑到公子面前，不绝口地赞道："王公子饱读诗书，天下文章无所不通，可敬！可敬啊！"说着，便要上前搀扶，公子一甩手，冷冷地问道："你是何人？"

"我，咳咳！"胡坎讨了个没趣，自我解嘲地干笑了几声。

一后响，王县令在众人拱护下巡察了长势良好的庄稼地，见到此处禾苗粗壮，他心里有数了，也不想再费劳苦，晚饭时候便回到镇上。此时胡坎已吩咐下人在镇上公馆里预备了丰盛的宴席。正北放着一张大桌，胡坎恭恭敬敬地请王县令坐上正席，又让王公子坐在左席，然后自己落座于右。

The first thing Magistrate Wang did upon being propelled so unexpectedly into the morning sunlight from his shady carriage, threw up his hands to shield his eyes from the glare, proclaiming as he did so, in poetic terms: "Oh, how radiant the sky!"

"Not quite, sir!" said a young man, appearing in the doorway of the carriage, and correcting the magistrate. "The word 'radiant' is properly used of the autumn sky. It is still spring here."

The onlookers were dumbfounded at the young fellow's presumption. Hu Kan was particularly indignant, but checked an impulse to rebuke the stranger, who was dressed in a fine silk robe and had a dignified bearing which set him apart from the throng of commoners around him. So, apart from clicking his tongue, in disapproval, he said nothing.

The magistrate merely stroked his beard and uttered a chilly laugh. "Aha, so you presume to correct your father's slip of the tongue, do you, you clever little puppy?" he said.

Realizing that the young fellow was the magistrate's son, Hu Kan hastened to help him down, gushing, "Most learned, young sir! How well versed in literature you are! Admirable, admirable!"

The other waved him aside, and asked coldly: "Who are you?"

The village head simply gave a self-deprecating chuckle.

At length, the magistrate was escorted on his inspection of the fields. It did not take him long to ascertain that a bumper harvest was in the offing, so, satisfied, he proceeded to his lodgings in the official guesthouse in Yuanyang in time for the customary welcoming banquet. Hu Kan had already given orders that a sumptuous feast be prepared, and Magistrate Wang was in high spirits. The magistrate was in the south-facing seat of the guest-of-honor, with his son on his right and the Village Head Hu

也许是此次鸳鸯集之行让王县令心中惬意，他今天的兴致特别高。全镇大大小小稍有头面的人物轮流为他敬酒，直喝到日落西山，月上梢头，他似乎仍旧余兴不尽，不觉叹道：

"想当年本县在京城时，酒宴间丝竹悦耳，颇助酒兴。可惜呀，如今在这乡壤之间，难得再听到悠悠琴声了！"

也是太凑巧了，王县令话音刚落，就听得从墙外传进缕缕琴声，这声音凄凄咽咽，好像从虚空中飘来，在公馆中回旋缭绕，又升还到虚空中去。王县令此时像是醉中初醒，耳听着这琴声，半晌，竟喊出曲子的名字：

"这是《箕山操》！"

胡坎不懂装懂连忙逢迎："是是，是《箕山操》，妙极了。"

"大人！"左席这位王公子名叫瑞琪，他今天喝得不多，又开始纠正父亲的口误了，"此曲名叫《箕子操》，其声哀怨，缕缕如诉。"

"对，《箕子操》，《箕子操》。"王县令不但没有感到尴尬，反而为儿子的博学而自豪。他瞅了瞅儿子，又端起一杯酒，大叫一声：

"为在这乡壤间能听到《箕子操》，痛饮一盏！"

"饮！""饮！"一片应和之声。

Kan dancing attendance on him on his left. All the notables of Yuanyang, of whatever degree, were present — all eager to bring themselves to the notice of the magistrate by offering toasts to his successful tour of inspection.

The party seemed to be going merrily enough as the shades of night fell, when the Magistrate Wang suddenly sighed. Instantly, a hush fell on the revelers, and they listened in consternation as the magistrate said, "You know, I was just thinking of the time I was stationed in the capital. There was always music at the feasts there, to assist the wine to go round. It's such a pity that here in the countryside I have to go without hearing the sweet strains of the zither, on such an evening as this!"

He had no sooner finished his complaint when wafting over the wall of the guesthouse compound came the notes of a zither. A haunting melody seemed to come out of thin air, and echoed and lingered around the tables. As if the fumes of wine had suddenly evaporated from his head, the magistrate listened attentively. Finally, he exclaimed, "That's *the Song of Jishan*!"

Hu Kan, who had never heard of this song, assured him that it was, indeed, the tune he had named. "Yes, Your Lordship," he cried. "That's *the Song of Jishan*, all right. And a lively piece of music it is too!"

"Sir," butted in the magistrate's son, whose name was Ruiqi, "It is *the Song of Jizi*, but, far from being a lively tune, it is a heart-rending dirge."

Far from being embarrassed by his son's impertinence, the magistrate was rather proud of his display of erudition. With a glance of approval to the boy, he raised his wine goblet and urged everyone to drink. Everyone did as he was bidden with gusto.

琴声依旧悠扬，王县令一直陶醉于乐曲声中，直到曲终半晌，才问胡坎：“弹琴者何人？”

胡坎禀道：“回大人话，这小女子名叫刘兰芝。”

“能否请这位姑娘来席间奏一曲？”王县令此时酒兴正浓。“当然，当然！”胡坎马上吆喝身边的人：“快去！”

大约一巡酒的功夫，刘兰芝抱着一张箜篌来到了公馆之中。胡坎平时从没留意过她，此时却像伺候上宾一样把兰芝请到正席之旁，还专门搬过一把椅子让她坐下，这把椅子就放在王县令与公子身后。

王县令把刘兰芝上下打量了一番，问道：

“你这箜篌弹得极好，谁教你的？”

“回禀大人，”兰芝彬彬有礼地答道：“这张箜篌是小女先父留下的，后来父亲下世，母亲时时弹奏。小女弹得不好，全是母亲教的，大人见笑了。”

“哎，无须谦逊。老夫为县几年，也没有听到过这样的琴声，想不到僻壤之间，仙音犹在，这真是天涯何处无芳草啊！”王县令见兰芝言谈乖顺，不由得更加高兴，不绝口地夸赞她。

王瑞琪是个有心人，问兰芝道：“你父亲既然有这等雅兴，想必也非田夫野老之辈，他生前是为官之人吗？”

“是。”

The sound of the lute continued, and Magistrate Wang listened to it enraptured. When the notes at last died away, he turned to Hu Kan, and asked, "Who is the player?"

"A young girl named Liu Lanzhi, Your Honor," replied Hu Kan.

"Could you invite her to join our feast?" asked the magistrate, by this time intoxicated both by wine and music.

"Certainly, Your Honor," Hu Kan assured him, turning without delay to an attendant and issuing the necessary order.

Presently, Lanzhi appeared, holding her *konghou*. Hu Kan, who at ordinary times would not have deigned to take the slightest notice of her, now ushered before the guests as if she were an honored guest herself, and seated her immediately behind the magistrate and his son.

Magistrate Wang looked the girl up and down, and said, "You play that instrument well. Who taught you?"

"Your Honor," Lanzhi replied, demurely, "this *konghou* was bequeathed to me by my late father. After he passed away, my mother taught me how to play it. The little skill I have is entirely due to her. I am sure I do not play well enough to please Your Honor."

"Oh, you are too modest, my dear," Magistrate Wang guffawed, pleased with the girl's respectful demeanor. "In all my years as a magistrate, I have never heard such a sweet sound, I assure you. I certainly never expected to hear such exquisite playing in a backwater like this."

Wang Ruiqi was an astute young man, and he remarked to Lanzhi: "Since your father was a talented musician, I presume that he was no ordinary fellow, but held some official rank?"

"Yes, sir, he did."

"身为何职？"

兰芝只知道父亲在世时官职不卑，但问到身为何官，她却是答不上来。没想到胡坎倒是对此类事记得清楚，他替兰芝答道："大人，这小女子的父亲是十年前本郡的刘督邮。"

"哦！"王县令不等胡坎说完，便打断了他的话，"怪不得呢，此女也是大家闺秀了！"他自斟了满满一盏酒，高举过头，说道："我为刘督邮饮了此盏！"

兰芝从未经历过这样的场面，不知所措地点了点头，说了声"谢大人"，其实连她自己也不知道要谢王县令什么。

"我也来敬兰芝姑娘一盏！"王瑞琪紧随其父，也饮过了，然后说："列位，我提议全场肃静，请兰芝姑娘为大家再奏一曲。"

"好！好！"一片捧场之声。

"兰芝姑娘，看我父子的薄面，不知能为镇上父老奏上哪一曲？"瑞琪像是在考兰芝，但他那目光久久盯着兰芝的面庞，分明是有三分情意在其中了。

刘兰芝双手抱住这张二十三弦的箜篌，略一沉吟，说道："就奏一曲《孔雀东南飞》吧，各位先辈见笑了。"

全场安静下来，兰芝运筹着纤纤十指，左推右拢，美妙的乐声从她的指间流淌出来，其声也哀，

"What rank?"

Unfortunately, Lanzhi was not clear exactly which rung of
the official ladder her late father had mounted to, and so she was
at a loss how to reply. But just at that moment, Hu Kan came to
the rescue, saying, "Your Honor, ten years ago her father was a
local inspector in our prefecture."

"Oh, no wonder!" Magistrate Wang responded, not giving
Hu Kan a chance to explain further. "So this young lady is the
daughter of a respectable family." And with that he filled his gob-
let once more, held it aloft, and proclaimed, "A toast to Local
Inspector Liu!"

Lanzhi, who had never been present at such a gathering
before, was at a loss how to behave at this point, and simply
nodded her head in confusion, saying, "Thank you, Your Honor,"
although she had no idea what she was thanking Magistrate Wang
for.

"I propose a toast to Miss Lanzhi!" cried the magistrate's
son, in swift succession to his master's toast. As soon as he had
swigged this toast down, he called upon the assembly for silence,
while he turned to Lanzhi and asked her to play another tune.

This was greeted with uproarious approval from all the
guests.

As Ruiqi made his request, his eyes gazed lovingly into those
of the fair musician.

Lanzhi took up her instrument, fingered its 23 strings, and
murmured, "Perhaps you gentlemen would like to hear *The Pea-
cock Flies Southeast*?"

A hush fell on the company as Lanzhi's slender fingers pro-
duced a flow of subdued and graceful notes. The ethereal tune
quavered in the air, following cadences that now quickened and

其情也婉，幽幽渺渺，飞绕于空，随着曲调的舒张疾徐，她自己也像是深深地陷入了无尽的凄怨之中，曲终之时，脸上早已挂上了两串闪着晶光的泪珠。

光阴荏苒，春去秋来，兰芝又长了一岁。常言道：女大十八变，此言不虚，去年尚显娇弱的兰芝，今年又长高了些，脸庞儿也越发显得清丽，一颦一笑之间，已看出是个大姑娘了。说来也怪，自从去年春天她与罗敷、艳艳在古桥边见过那位书生之后，不但不能把他忘怀，反而越来越放他不下，他那文质彬彬的风度，那双黑亮传情的眼睛，像个影子一样，在兰芝心中扎下了根，拂之不离，挥之不去。她知道女孩儿家长大后是要嫁人的，但她不知将要嫁的人是否能像这位少年一样举止翩翩，言容可亲。女孩儿家一旦撩起春心，那就是瓢泼的大雨也难以浇灭。这春心的萌动，使她夜夜面红耳赤，那真是再愉悦不过的一种美妙感觉。然而日积月累，这种美妙的感觉就变了滋味，它让人焦灼、让人发痴，像丢失了魂魄一样，变成一种煎熬。此时的兰芝是长高了，但那细瘦的腰肢，就像风一吹就要断开一样。她也很少再与罗敷等女伴出外游耍，宛如变了一个人。去年秋天，秦家搬到居巢县城行医，罗敷临走时专门跑到兰芝家里与她话别，

now slowed. The girl herself, meanwhile, seemed to have fallen into some sort of mournful trance. When the tune finished, two crystalline tears were observed on Lanzhi's cheeks.

Another years slipped by, and the old proverb about a change coming over a girl when she reaches the age of 18 seemed borne out once again: The delicate girl of a year before had become a comely young woman. Strangely enough, though, despite her new maturity, she didn't seem to be able to get the young man she had met the previous year, together with Luofu and Yanyan at the old bridge, out of her head. In fact, she seemed to be thinking of his refined manner and shining black eyes more and more. His image had struck roots in Lanzhi's heart, and no matter how hard she tried, she could not dislodge it. She pondered her future marriage, not able to imagine that any other young man could be so beguiling or so ideal as a husband, with his cultured bearing and speech. Alas, once the spark of springtime starts to flicker within a young woman, not all the rains of Heaven are able to extinguish it! Night after night, the stirring springtime caused Lanzhi's face and ears to burn. But, as the days and months passed, the joy of this new emotion changed to anxiety and a distressing torment.

At this time, although Lanzhi had grown taller, her waist was still so slender that it looked as if a puff of wind would snap it. She seldom associated with her two friends, as if she had become a changed person altogether. Then, the previous autumn, Luofu's family had moved to the Juchao county seat, where her father had set up a medical practice. Just before they left, Luofu had run over to say goodbye to Lanzhi. The two girls had wept copious tears over their parting, but it was not long before Lanzhi had

两姐妹为此次分别还哭了一场。罗敷搬走,兰芝虽然也有几天感到凄凉,但没过多久,她的心又被那少年的影像完全占据了。

当母亲的当然也能把女儿的心事猜出几分,她知道女大不中留的道理,所以前些天里,她就已经答应了媒人的说合。这个媒婆是居巢县里最有名的一位,绰号"说破天",据她自己说,她一生走南闯北,撮合过几百对男男女女,几乎没有一对落空的。

兰芝母亲答应下的这门亲事,男方姓焦,名仲卿,家境与兰芝家有些相似:仲卿的父亲原来也是地方官宦,后来死于恶疾,身后留下两儿一女,没想到父死未一年,大儿子伯卿也得了同样的病,不久便命赴黄泉。焦仲卿自幼喜好读书,由于父亲生前与郡太守有旧,所以成年后便在庐江郡里谋了一个小吏的职位。虽说官职卑微,总算是在官府里执役的人,这在一个县城里,也算是件光彩的事儿了。据"说破天"称,仲卿的妹妹也很懂事,那焦母更是个见过世面的人,做事说话干干脆脆,把个家撑得十分像样。兰芝的母亲思前想后,觉得门户也算相当,女婿又在官府当差,日后或许能搏一个好出身,也不算埋没了女儿,便应下了这门亲事。

没想到当她把此事告诉兰芝时,兰芝却像受了天大的委屈,眼泪像断了线的珠子一样扑簌簌

got over the loss of her friend, the place of the latter in her thoughts being usurped completely by thoughts of the mysterious young man.

Guessing the reason for Lanzhi's sudden absent-mindedness, her mother had already got in touch with a match-maker to arrange her marriage. This old woman had a reputation throughout Juchao County for her persuasive tongue. Her nick-name was "Talk Even Heaven into Anything," and she herself boasted that she had brought hundreds of young couples together, and never let a single match slip through her fingers.

Lanzhi's mother was quite pleased with the first young man that the matchmaker suggested. His name was Jiao Zhongqing, and his family circumstances were similar to those of the Lius: His father had been a local official who had died of illness, leav-ing two sons and a daughter. The elder son, Boqing had soon followed his father to the grave, carried off by the same disease. Zhongqing had been an attentive student from childhood, and when he came of age, with the help of his father's old friend, the prefect of Lujiang, he had obtained a minor official post. Being a prefectural official, no matter how junior, counted for a great deal in the county. Moreover, according to the old matchmaker, the boy's sister was a clever girl, and his mother was a sensible and worldly-wise woman who ran the household in an exemplary manner. Zhongqing obviously had bright prospects, Lanzhi's mother thought, and so she decided that he would be a most suitable match for her daughter.

However, when she confidently put the proposal to Lanzhi, to her consternation the girl burst into a fit of weeping. Lanzhi buried her head in her mother's breast, and sobbed her heart out. Her mother was flabbergasted: What had she said that had

地连串滚落，她一头扎在母亲的怀里，呜呜地哭起来，越哭越伤心，越哭越凄切，倒让母亲满心疑惑，不知哪句话刺伤了女儿的心。

"娘！我不愿嫁！"兰芝好不容易止住了哭声，抽抽答答地说出这么几个字。

"为什么？兰芝，女大当嫁你是知道的。说给娘听听，你为什么不愿意嫁？"

在堂屋里听着她们母女说话的哥哥继宗越听心里越烦，怒冲冲地撩开门帘走进屋来，嚷道：

"哪有女大不出嫁的？焦仲卿年轻轻就在官府里当差，还配不上你吗？胡闹！"

"没你事！"母亲护着兰芝，喝斥继宗道："看你像个当兄长的样子吗？"

"怎么啦？"继宗更气恼了，急得在屋里转了个圈儿，"娘，你把妹妹惯坏了，这样的好人家还不愿嫁，我要是个女孩，巴不得呢！"

母亲也不理他，又低下头抚摸着兰芝满是泪水的脸颊，问道：

"兰芝，我倒不是护着你哥哥，可你哥哥说得也不错啊，焦家也算是个好人家了，你何必这么任性呢？"

"娘，我，我……我不认识的人，怎好把一辈子交付给他呢？"

"傻孩子！"母亲微微笑了两声，我和你爹爹

been so devastating to the girl?

"Oh, mother, I don't want to get married!" Lanzhi managed
to say, jerkily through her sobs.

"What? But, Lanzhi, you know that all girls get married when they grow up," protested her puzzled mother. "Tell me, why don't you want to get married?"

Jizong had heard this commotion from the corridor, and he now flung back the beaded curtain that veiled the inner room and came striding in, snorting with rage.

"Who ever heard of a girl not wanting to get married?" he bawled. "Jiao Zhongqing is a fine young man just starting out on a splendid career. Do you think he's not good enough for you or something? What rubbish!"

"This has nothing to do with you," his mother snapped. "What kind of an elder brother are you, making your sister even more upset?"

"What?" yelled Jizong in fury. He stamped around the room a few times until he could find words to express his indignation, and then said. "Mother, you're spoiling Lanzhi. She's just being awkward, saying that she doesn't want to get married! If I were a girl I'd be all too eager to get married."

This enlightening diatribe fell on deaf ears, as his mother bent once more over Lanzhi, and wiped her tear-stained cheeks. Then, when the girl had calmed down somewhat, she said soothingly: "Lanzhi, I know your brother's a busybody, but he's right. The Jiaos are a very respectable family. Why are you being so willful?"

"Ma...." Lanzhi began wailing again. "I don't know this young man. How can I spend the rest of my life with him?"

"You silly girl!" Her mother gave Lanzhi a benign smile. "Your

没成亲前谁认得谁呢？祖宗立下的规矩就是父母之命，媒妁之言，难道当母亲的还存心想把自己的女儿推进火坑里吗？"

兰芝母亲说到这里，像突然悟到了什么，她慢慢扳起偎在自己怀里的兰芝，问道："莫非你自己有意中的人？"

这句话既点中了兰芝的痛处，又使她无法回答母亲的询问：说没有意中人吧，明明是一年前与少年书生的邂逅占满了她的心；说有意中人吧，他姓甚名谁？何方人氏，自己一点也不知道呀！她没有回答母亲的话，又哽哽咽咽地哭了起来。此时她真想让母亲继续追问她的意中人，哪怕是无法回答，那也是甜美的。谁想母亲的话却不像方才那么温和了："兰芝，父母之命是不能违抗的，女孩儿家若是自己相中夫婿，那可是件丢人的事，我可不愿意你真有自己意中的人！"

兰芝何尝不知道自己一年来的心跳耳热只能是一场梦，何尝不知道自己最终还是要按照母亲的意愿嫁给一个陌生的人，她嘴里纵然说上一万句"不嫁"，也是徒劳的。再说，自己那个意中人也太飘渺了些。她认命了，她止住抽泣，仰起脸来，无奈地说："娘，就听你的吧！"

father and I had never met each other before we were married," she said. "Our ancestors laid down the rule long ago that the matchmaker carries out the will of the parents. You don't think that I would do anything but what is best for you, do you?"

As she said this, it seemed that a troublesome though struck her. Holding her daughter at arms' length, she said, in a stern tone of voice: "I don't suppose you have somebody else in mind, have you?"

This unexpected dart struck home, and landed Lanzhi in a painful dilemma: How could she deny that there was somebody else, when her heart had been captured by the young man she had met by chance the previous year; on the other hand, if she admitted that there was another in her thoughts, her mother would demand to know what his name was, and want to know all about his family — and she wouldn't be able to answer, because she knew nothing about him.

As she hesitated, her mother spoke again, and this time in a voice that had no hint of kindness in it: "Lanzhi, a girl must not disobey her parents by choosing a husband for herself. That goes against all human decency. I certainly hope that you don't intend to try anything like that!"

Deep down, Lanzhi knew that what had made her heart flutter and her ears redden for the past year was all an idle dream, and that in the end she would have to bow to her mother's wish, and marry a stranger. No matter how many times she said no, she knew, it would make no difference. The man she had set her heart on was no more than a misty shadow. She stopped weeping, lifted her head, and said, "I will do what you say, mother."

◎第二章
新婚燕尔蒙愁思

　　且说上次跟随王县令巡察乡镇的王瑞琪，是县令的第三个儿子，县里人都称他"三郎"。王县令的大儿子瑞珏十来岁上不慎落水而死。二儿子瑞瑜生性粗鲁，孩童时便好打打斗斗，时常给他惹些祸，为此，县令夫妇没少给别人赔笑脸，说好话，特别是当瑞瑜与自己上司家的子弟发生殴斗时，王县令更是气恼万分。看着他渐渐长大，又不好读书识字，夫妇二人着实为他发愁。正当父母对他无计可施时，一位亲戚路过此地来看望他们，言谈间说起自己在军中任职，需要一个贴身的少年护卫，那位亲戚见瑞瑜长得虎背熊腰，倒有几分喜欢。王县令听出亲戚话语的意思，很爽快地同意让瑞瑜跟着亲戚走马从戎去了，那一年瑞瑜十六岁。一晃几年过去了，书信虽然稀少，但王县令知道二子现已担任了军校，倒也庆幸他走对了路。

　　俗话说，一龙九种，种种各别。王县令这第三郎却与兄长截然不同，一是人物清秀，与二哥全然不像一母同胞，二是天资聪颖，读书过目成诵，小小年纪，已经粗通诸子百家。正因为如此，县令夫

Chapter Two
A Gloomy Newlywed

Ruiqi, who accompanied Magistrate Wang on his tour of inspection, was actually the magistrate's third son. The people of the county referred to him as "Third Master." The magistrate's eldest son, Ruijue, had died in a drowning accident at the age of ten. His second son, Ruiyu, showed himself to have a boorish nature from an early age, and was always getting into fights. His scrapes had caused his parents a great deal of expense, especially when they involved the sons of Magistrate Wang's social superiors. As Ruiyu grew older, he proved to be as poor at studying as he was good at getting into trouble, and his parents were at their wits' end what to do with him, until one day a relative of the Wangs who was an army officer happened to drop by. Impressed by the 16-year-old Ruiyu's sturdy build, this man mentioned that he needed a bodyguard and why didn't the magistrate steer his unruly son in the direction of a military career? Magistrate Wang jumped at the chance to get rid of Ruiyu in this respectable way. After a couple of years had passed, the magistrate learned from one of his son's rare, short and almost illegible letters, that Ruiyu had been commissioned an officer. Magistrate Wang thereupon breathed a sigh of relief, convinced that he had pointed the scamp in the right direction after all.

As the saying goes, "A dragon has nine offspring, and every one is different." Third Master was as different from his elder brother as could be — so much so that people used to wonder if

妇把瑞琪视如掌上明珠，大事小事，绝不违拗他。转眼间，瑞琪也长到十六七岁，在这居巢县里，也算得上是数一数二的风流后生了。

眼瞅着瑞琪也到了谈婚论嫁的年龄，可是这居巢县里能有几个像样的姑娘？王县令留意过衙门里大小官吏的千金，可大都看不上眼。也曾领着瑞琪跑过上司家，希望被上司青眼相中，但一时也没有合适的。

瑞琪跟随父亲巡察鸳鸯集时见到了刘兰芝。初时瑞琪对兰芝并没有什么感觉，兰芝走进公馆时已是月上柳梢，暮色昏黄之中，也没看出她有什么动人之处，直到兰芝一曲箜篌，那绕梁三日的美妙乐声才深深地打动了瑞琪的心。他还清楚地记得当时特地注视了兰芝好一阵子，那张文雅清秀的脸庞虽然说不上光彩夺目，但那略带忧郁的眼神，蕴藏着一种如芝如兰的清芬之韵，这种风韵和着箜篌之声，拨响了瑞琪的心弦。自从这次邂逅，瑞琪深为所动，那一夜他辗转反侧。

第二天，他随父亲回到县城，直接问父亲道："鸳鸯集那个弹箜篌的女娃，父亲喜不喜欢？"

"那女孩儿蛮招人喜欢。"

"如果让她做您的儿媳，您愿意不愿意？"

"什么？你打上她的主意了？"王县令颇觉意外。

they had been born of the same mother. He had a gentle and refined personality, and was intelligent and quick to acquire knowledge. He mastered the classics and works of poetry at an early age. Not unnaturally, he was the apple of his parents' eye, and they could refuse him nothing. By the time he reached the age of 16 or 17, Third Master was the most eligible young bachelor in Juchao County.

He was now at an age to be married. But where was a suitable girl to be found? Magistrate Wang gave the daughters of his colleagues a careful scrutiny, and found them all wanting in one aspect or another. Moreover, he was hoping that Ruiqi would catch the eye of the daughter of one of his superiors. However, the young man so far had won no favor in those quarters.

Then, accompanying his father on his tour of inspection, Ruiqi had met Lanzhi. At first, he had not taken much notice of the girl, because the evening shadows had largely obscured her natural charms. It was only when she had started playing the *konghou* that he had become bewitched by her. Lanzhi was not, he admitted to himself, a raving beauty, but her melancholy and flower-like air, combined with her superb playing of the instrument, struck a resounding chord in his heart. That night, sleep eluded the young man, and he knew that he had left a chance encounter smitten with love.

The following day, on their way back to the county seat, Ruiqi said: "Father, what did you think of that girl who played the *konghou* last night?"

"Rather attractive, I thought," replied Magistrate Wang.

"How would you like her for a daughter-in-law?"

The magistrate was startled. "What, do you mean to say you've fallen for her?" he asked.

瑞琪听出父亲不大赞成，便又将心思对母亲说了。王夫人一向把瑞琪视若命根子，从小到大，儿子想要天上的星，她都要想尽办法去摘，更别说这种关乎终身的大事了。这晚王县令刚刚上床，夫人便催他拿主意，说是拿主意，分明是让他同意此事。王县令想到兰芝也曾是仕宦之女，虽然如今家境不好，但是聪明伶俐，也不算辱没自家，也就答应下来。

为了避免张扬，王县令专门派了自己贴身的何主簿到鸳鸯集去。正当瑞琪满心欢喜地等待佳音时，传来的却是一个他最不愿听到的消息：刘家女儿兰芝已经与县南焦家订婚，不久就要成亲了。

又是一个阳春三月天，住在居巢县南门的焦家里里外外喜气洋洋，大红双喜字贴在门前，门楣两侧挂着两盏大红灯笼，灯笼上也用金箔写了喜字。院门进去，影壁墙上是红纸金字的"百年好合"，绕过影壁，满院都挂满了灯笼，贴满了吉祥的条幅。大门外面，来看热闹的大人孩子围了许多，院子的天井里已经摆放了几张桌子，一切都准备就绪。

时近中午，县南大路上传过吹吹打打的声音，送新娘的人来了。

As his father showed no enthusiasm for the idea of his marrying Lanzhi, the young man then broached the matter to his mother. It was a smart move, for his mother doted on Ruiqi, and would have plucked a star from the sky if he had expressed a wish for one. The same night, she used all her powers of persuasion on her husband, reminding him that Lanzhi came from an official's family, and although the family fortunes were at a low ebb, the girl was intelligent and would be a suitable match for their son.

Magistrate Wang decided to find out more about Lanzhi before he gave his consent to the marriage, and sent one of his secretaries to Yuanyang to make inquiries. This man, He by name, brought back most unwelcome news for Ruiqi, who had been tingling with impatience in the few days the secretary had been gone: Lanzhi was already engaged to a young man called Jiao, and the wedding was to take place in a few days' time.

The spring day on which Lanzhi was to be married dawned bright and clear. The Jiao family residence, near the south gate of the Juchao county town, had been a hive of activity from early morning. A large red poster bearing the "double happiness" symbol was pasted to the front gate, and two large red lanterns hung from its lintel, with the "double happiness" symbol written in gold letters. Gazing at them was an eager crowd of sightseers, old and young. On the screen wall, just inside the courtyard, was pasted a red paper poster with the words "One Hundred Years of Harmonious Togetherness." The courtyard beyond the screen wall was festooned with lanterns and hanging scrolls on which were written auspicious slogans. In the center of the courtyard a number of tables had been arranged for the wedding feast.

As noon drew near, the sound of trumpets and drums was

随后自然是一番热闹，当新娘的花轿落在焦家门前时，人们都围了过来，新郎焦仲卿在邻家张二哥的陪伴下来到轿前，掀开轿帘，满身艳装的刘兰芝蒙着盖头，莲步轻移，由仲卿搀扶着进了大门。

围观的人们嘻笑着，啧啧赞赏着新娘衣着的艳丽和身段的窈窕。人群中只有一个人的眼神与众不同，从兰芝下轿时起，他的目光就痴痴地盯住兰芝的脚步，一直目送她走进院中，消失在影壁墙内，他像是傻了一样，当人们跟随着新娘拥进院子时，门外只剩他一个人，他就是王家三公子瑞琪。

闹腾了一整天，喜宴终于结束，客人们也渐渐散去。

焦仲卿虽然略显疲倦，但在这大喜的日子里，他还是十分兴奋。他早就想揭下新娘的盖头，一睹这位将与他厮守终身的新娘究竟是什么模样。他看着坐在床沿的新娘，突突跳动的心使他的胳膊抖动得十分厉害，以至几次想揭开红盖头，胳膊不听话，又颤抖着放了下来。

此时的兰芝却全然是另外一种心境。新婚不但没有使她感到丝毫幸福，倒像是掉进了见不到底的深渊。不过她是个懂事的孩子，不想让母亲生气，所以哭了一次之后，一切都顺从了母亲的安

heard at some distance down the road. The news that the bride was coming spread like wildfire through the crowd.

The bride's sedan chair drew up to the gate of the Jiaos, amid a hubbub of excited voices, as the crowd pressed forward, everyone eager to get a better look. Jiao Zhongqing, escorted by a neighbor, proceeded to the sedan chair, lifted the curtain, and helped Lanzhi out. Lanzhi, draped in a long veil, tottered on her tiny feet to the house, leaning on Zhongqing's arm.

The bystanders all noted with approval the dainty figure of the bride and her tasteful costume. There was one person in the throng, however, who showed no joy as his eyes dully followed Lanzhi as she stepped from her carriage and disappeared behind the screen wall, into the festive courtyard. And when the gaily chattering guests had all been ushered inside to witness the ceremony and spend the rest of the day in merriment, those glazed eyes remained fixed on the gateway bedecked with wishes for happiness and good fortune. When the last of the idlers and loungers had shuffled away, those tortured eyes did not so much as flicker. They were the eyes of Third Master Wang Ruiqi.

It was late when the revels drew to a close. The wedding guests, sated with the best food and wine, trickled away, hoarsely murmuring congratulations to the happy couple.

It had been an exhausting day for Jiao Zhongqing, but excitement overcame his fatigue. He had been waiting all day for the moment when he would lift the veil of the bride he had never met, and at last gaze on the face of the woman he was destined to spend his life with. As he entered the bridal chamber, and approached the girl seated demurely on the edge of the bed, his heart beat like a hammer, and his hands trembled. He made several attempts to reach out to lift the veil, but his arms would not

排。婚礼结束后，她独自静静地坐在新房中，等待那一刻的到来。她不知道将要面对的是个什么样的男子，越想心中越害怕，不觉眼中噙满了泪水。

决定二人一生命运的大红盖头终于被仲卿颤抖的双手揭了下来，在大红蜡烛的映照下，兰芝虽然闭着双眼，脸颊上还残挂着晶莹的珠泪，但她娇美的脸庞还是让焦仲卿的心跳得更厉害了。就在他遏止不住嘭嘭心跳的同时，他突然感到面前的美人儿有点眼熟。他终于想起来了，禁不住惊愕地叫了一声：

"是你！"

与此同时，兰芝也睁开了眼睛，看着眼前的丈夫，同样失口叫道：

"是你！"

一年前的鸳鸯集，夕阳下的古桥旁，清水岸边，香草坪上，那个探路的翩翩少年，那个让兰芝魂牵梦绕了几百个日日夜夜的情景，此刻一下子又格外清晰起来。她几乎不敢相信自己的眼睛，上苍真的如此成全自己的心愿吗？上苍真的会如此巧妙地把一个少女内心的祈求变成现实吗？此刻，兰芝的目光片刻也不敢离开仲卿那张清秀的脸，她生怕自己一眨眼，就会使眼前的欢喜变成梦境。

obey him, and every time fell limp by his sides.

Lanzhi's feelings were far different from those of her new husband at that moment. This wedding was by no means an occasion of happiness for her; instead, she felt as though she were gazing into a bottomless pit. But she was a sensible girl. So as not to upset her mother, she had wiped her tears away, and done exactly as her mother instructed her in this matter of her marriage. And now here she was, sitting in the bridal chamber, not making a sound — awaiting that fateful moment. She had no idea what sort of husband she would be looking at once the red bridal veil was lifted, and this uncertainty filled her with dread and her eyes with tears.

Finally, Jiao Zhongqing managed to master himself sufficiently to lift the veil which masked the fate of two people. His heart leaped when he saw, in the light of the large red ceremonial candle, a comely face, the eyes tightly closed and the cheeks ornamented with crystal tears. He had seen this girl somewhere before! In utter amazement, he cried out, "It's you!"

At that very moment, Lanzhi opened her eyes, saw her husband, as she thought for the first time, and uttered a shrill cry: "It's you!"

Suddenly, it all came back to Lanzhi: the old bridge at Yuanyang beneath the setting sun, the limpid water of the river, and the fragrant grass of the riverbank — and the charming young man who had haunted her thoughts night and day for a whole year. The scene flashed in front of the girl's eyes, as vivid if she had been transported back in time. She could hardly believe that Heaven had fulfilled her wish, had made a young girl's dream come true in such a magnificent way. Lanzhi was afraid to blink, lest this divine vision vanish, and turn out to have been an illu-

仲卿不由自主地用双手紧紧地攥住了兰芝的双臂，深情地望着兰芝，他也回忆起了刚刚去庐江郡当差时，在鸳鸯集向几位女孩问路的情景。没想到那个为他指路的姑娘，那个邀他在鸳鸯集权住一夜的姑娘，如今竟成了自己的新娘！

兰芝在这一瞬间仿佛变成了另一个人，原先已经灰冷的心突然变得炽热无比，已经灰暗的生命此刻一下子充满幸福的活力。她实在是无法控制自己的感情，眼泪扑簌簌地流下来，她一头扎在仲卿跳动的胸膛上，呜呜地哭出声来。

仲卿的身体像被电击了一样，因为他从来没有感受过少女的爱，没有接触过少女的身躯，他几乎一动也不能动了。

不知过了多长时间，兰芝止住了哭泣。此刻的世界静得出奇，仲卿的心跳，兰芝听得真真切切，她觉得这个世界上一切都不存在了，只有他们俩。

这一夜对兰芝来说无疑是一生中永远无法忘记的。她不知道是如何上的床，不知道是如何脱的衣，她只感觉仲卿的唇在吻她，手在抚摸她，唇手所到之处，肌肤就灼热地燃烧起来。她幸福地闭着双眼，什么都看不见，什么也不想看见，她只想感受发生在自己身上的一切。慢慢地，那肌肤的灼热变成一种渴求，一种期待被仲卿拥有的渴求。

sion after all.

Mechanically, Zhongqing reached out and took Lanzhi's hands in his. He gazed upon her with infinite tenderness. He too was remembering the time that he met the group of three girls at Yuanyang, when he was on his way to the seat of Lujiang Prefecture. And now, the girl who had pointed him in the right direction and advised him to stay the night at Yuanyang had turned out to be his bride!

In this instant, Lanzhi felt, she had changed into a completely different person. The cold dead ashes of her heart were rekindled into a glorious blaze, and what had seemed like a gloomy fate had suddenly become a future filled with joy. Unable to restrain the emotion which welled up inside her, Lanzhi burst into tears of happiness. She buried her head in Zhongqing's breast, and sobbed and sobbed.

The effect of this on the young man was akin to that brought about by a bolt of lightning. Zhongqing had never experienced love before. He had never touched a woman's body. He stood stock still.

Time passed — who knows how long? — And Lanzhi stopped weeping. The two lovers noticed that the world was eerily silent, as if only the two of them were left alive.

It was without a doubt the most unforgettable night of Lanzhi's life. She could not recollect undressing or getting into bed. All she could remember afterwards were Zhongqing's frenzied kisses and fervent caresses. His lips and hands traversed her whole body, setting her skin afire. The whole time, her eyes were tightly shut in ecstasy. She saw nothing, and wanted to see nothing: She was totally absorbed by the physical feelings that arose within her, a slowly growing thirst for possession by Zhongqing.

这一夜的云情雨意，使兰芝感到仿佛进入仙境之中，她领略了一个全新的人生，而更重要的是，她内心的甜美，远远超过了身体上的快感。这一夜她没有睡，双眼也一直没有睁开。闭着眼睛来体会幸福，才是最高境界的幸福。鸡叫了，她仰面地躺着，眼前是一片奇妙无比的幻界，焦仲卿翩翩的身影，就在这幻界中朝她微笑。突然，仲卿消失了，眼前只剩下空空的香草坪。兰芝惊出一身冷汗，连忙睁开眼睛。

看看身边躺着的心上人，她才放下心来。

"仲卿！仲卿！"她轻声呼喊着，想印证一下此刻是梦境还是现实。

焦仲卿没有睁开眼，只是伸出一只胳膊将她揽入怀中。

新婚使焦仲卿和刘兰芝双双品尝到了世间最美好的爱情，自小很少放纵情感的兰芝已经难以抑制突然降临的喜悦，一连数天，她与仲卿如影随形，寸步不离，吃罢晚饭的这段时光，更是完全属于他们两个人，喜气盈盈的新房里，两人每每相偎相抱，竟感觉不到斗转星移。

这天傍晚，两人又回到房中，刚刚关上门，焦仲卿便把兰芝搂在胸前，突然问道：

"兰芝，你嫁给我后悔吗？"

"后悔。"兰芝撒娇地说。

That night, Lanzhi felt that she had been transported to Fairyland, and had tasted a whole new dimension of life. Moreover, the bliss she felt in her heart far surpassed the pleasure felt by her body. She lay the whole night sleepless, but with closed eyes, experiencing supreme happiness. At cockcrow, she found herself lying on her back staring up at what seemed like a fantasy world. And in this fantasy world Zhongqing was smiling at her. All of a sudden, Zhongqing vanished, and all that the girl could see was the empty lawn by the river. Lanzhi broke into a cold sweat, and opened her eyes in a panic.

To her immense relief, her true love was lying beside her.

"Zhongqing! Zhongqing!" she whispered, to reassure herself that he was really there.

Without opening his eyes, Zhongqing reached out, and drew her toward him.

Jiao Zhongqing and Liu Lanzhi found their honeymoon the most blissful time of their lives. The girl, who had always been an introverted person who never gave free rein to her feelings, now found it difficult to suppress the expressions of utter joy which continually arose from inside her. Day after day, they never left each other's side.

Every evening, immediately after supper, they retired to their bedroom and clasped each other tightly until the next day, savoring all the delights of love and not noticing the passage of time.

One evening, as he closed the bedroom door behind him and enfolded Lanzhi in his arms, Zhongqing asked abruptly: "Do you have any regrets about marrying me?"

"Yes, I do," murmured his bride, sulkily.

"Really?" Zhongqing exclaimed in consternation.

孔／雀／东／南／飞

"真的？"

"我后悔为什么不早十年就嫁给你！"

仲卿激动得湿了眼眶，把兰芝抱得更紧，兰芝有些喘不上气来，可这种感觉恰恰是她最渴望的。

焦仲卿的母亲出身仕宦，是位大户人家的女儿，从小颇守闺门的规矩。出嫁后侍奉公婆惟谨惟慎，一言一行，一举一动，很难让公婆挑出毛病来，为此仲卿的父亲对她十分感激。公婆去世后，她悉心照料子女，侍奉丈夫，生活安排得有板有眼，一丝不苟。长期以来，她的生活已经形成了一套固定的模式，不论是待人接物，还是处理家事，都遵守着她认为不可变更的规矩。她对儿媳的要求，自然也是有章有法的。一连数日，新媳妇与儿子如胶似漆，这也无可深怪，新婚嘛。可是三天里倒有两天不是忘了向她问早安，就是忘了问晚安，她心中便有些不快。这一天日上三竿了，儿子和媳妇还没有起床。按照她的规矩，这时媳妇早就该到她房中请安，并去准备早饭了。她从鸡鸣时就已梳洗停当，端端正正地坐在房里，这一等就是一个时辰，心里自然有些烦躁。虽然新婚男女定然是多些疲倦，但为人妇者应当遵礼而行，黎明即起。她对儿媳开始不满起来。

好不容易盼到门帘掀起，仲卿与兰芝双双走

"Yes, I regret that we didn't get married ten years earlier."

The young man's eyes brimmed with tears of affection, as he pressed Lanzhi so closely to him that she gasped for breath. Nothing she could have said could have made him happier.

Zhongqing's mother came from a well-to-do official's family. As a young girl, she had had a very strict upbringing and training in a woman's duties. After her marriage, she had showed herself to be the epitome of an obedient wife, conceding to her husband in everything, and giving her mother-in-law not the slightest cause for complaint. Following the death of the latter, she took over the running of the household, which she managed to perfection, to the great satisfaction of her husband and children. All her life, Lady Jiao, as she was known generally known, had lived strictly according to the rules of propriety and responsibility, and she naturally expected her children to follow her example. So it was most annoying to Lady Jiao that the newlyweds were so engrossed with each other that occasionally they would forget to pay her the customary morning greeting or say good-night before she retired.

One morning found Lady Jiao sitting, washed and dressed, in her bedroom, waiting impatiently for her son and daughter-in-law to pay their morning call and hurry away to prepare breakfast. The sun was already high in the sky, and the old lady had been up for well over an hour, fuming with rage. A stickler for ceremony as she was, her resentment was chiefly aimed at Lanzhi, whose lax attitude toward her new responsibilities as a daughter-in-law struck Lady Jiao as being downright unfilial.

At long last, the door curtain was lifted, and the young couple entered. As they tendered their belated morning greetings, the

进正房,向母亲问安。焦母抬起眼皮,脸上虽然带着一丝很不自然的笑意,但话语已显出些不客气:

"这个时辰才起来,不大妥当吧?以后可要起早些啊!"

"是是。"仲卿已觉出母亲的不快,连忙抢先认错。"兰芝早就醒了,要过来为母亲请安,都是儿子困倦,起得晚了。"

焦母并不理会儿子的解释,继续对儿媳说:

"兰芝啊,女孩儿一旦嫁人,就不能像在家一样任性了,要守规矩。想必这些话你母亲在家也对你说过。"

焦母的脸色稍微缓和了一些:

"咱们家原本也是个不错的人家,可你公公下世早,如今也使不起下人了。嗨,富了富过,穷了穷过,只要咱们一心一意,万一仲卿日后再有发达之日,你我都能跟着他享些富贵。可眼下不行……"

"母亲!仲卿如今在郡里当差,已是天大的福气了,我哪敢再想什么发达?"焦仲卿打断母亲的话,"仲卿只愿一家人和和美美,也就心满意足了。"

焦仲卿这话听起来很平常,可内里却很有些含意呢,他了解母亲的脾气,就是要处处显示自己的威权。而兰芝刚刚进门,恐怕她一时接受不了母

old lady smiled coldly, and rasped:

"What time to you call this?"

Zhongqing hastened to defend Lanzhi, saying that she had risen in good time, but that he had been lazy and delayed her call on her mother-in-law.

Lady Jiao ignored his stuttering excuses, and turned on Lanzhi:

"Listen to me. When a girl marries, she may no longer do as she pleases, even if she was allowed to run wild at home. She must act with proper decorum at all times. Did your mother not tell you that?"

Lady Jiao's expression softened somewhat, as she reminisced. "We used to have a very neat and orderly household here. But my husband passed away unexpectedly, and now we cannot afford servants. Ah well, rich one day, poor the next! We will just have to get along as best we can, and then someday, when Zhongqing rises in the world, we will all share in his riches and honors. But, for the time being...."

At this, her son interrupted. "Mother!" he cried, "I have al-ready been more fortunate than I deserve to be, having gained an official position in the county government. How could I dare to aspire to any higher advancement? I will be content to live in the bosom of a happy and harmonious family. That's all I want."

There was a hidden meaning in these innocent-sounding protestations. Zhongqing knew well his mother's domineering character, and besides, he was afraid lest the inexperienced Lanzhi be intimidated by the old lady. At the same time, however, he was anxious for her to be obedient to and please his mother; he was quite aware that a comfortable and warm family life depended on good relations between his mother and his wife. But,

亲的严厉。但他又希望兰芝尽量地孝顺母亲，使母亲满意。他深知只有婆媳互谅互让，一家人才能和和美美。只是此时焦母与兰芝各有心思，谁也没有仔细体会出他话中的含义。

门外，小姑梅梅亮着清脆的嗓子喊道：

"娘，哥哥，嫂嫂，吃饭了。"

兰芝显得有些不好意思，一边上前搀扶婆婆，一边说："媳妇知错了，明日一定早起。"

"那就吃饭吧。"焦母站起身来，边走边说，"兰芝，你以后还要多织些布匹补贴家用才好。"

"是是。"兰芝满口答应，在家时她不但已经学会了织布，而且在女伴中她是织得最快最好的，因此她认为这点事对她来说并不算难。

吃罢饭，洗过碗，兰芝真想跟仲卿回到房中重享温情，但她今天没有这样做，她在梅梅的指点下，熟悉了家里的厨灶油盐，点点滴滴都记在心里。梅梅今年才十三岁，还是个小姑娘呢，她倒是很喜欢这个新嫂子，拉着兰芝的胳膊说：

"哥，嫂，咱们到后面草地去扑蝴蝶吧。"

"不懂事！"站在一旁的焦母嗔道："还不带你嫂子到织房去看看。"

梅梅撒娇地把脖子一缩，做了个鬼脸儿，说："好吧。"拉着兰芝往西边的织房去了。

晚时的饭菜是梅梅和兰芝一起做的，仲卿也

unfortunately, each of the ladies in his life had her own ideas, and neither seemed to detect the innuendo in his little speech.

Just then, Zhongqing's younger sister Meimei was heard calling out that breakfast was ready.

Lanzhi forced herself to escort Lady Jiao out of the room, saying, with rather bad grace: "I was in the wrong, mother-in-law. Tomorrow I will call on you bright and early."

"Well, it's about time breakfast was ready, anyway," said Lady Jiao, getting to her feet. "And, Lanzhi, from now on you will have to do some regular weaving, to help me out with the household expenses."

"Of course, mother-in-law," Lanzhi responded readily. In her maiden home, she had learned to weave cloth, and was reckoned the fastest and most skillful of all the local girls at this craft. This was one area, she was sure, in which the fussy old woman would be able to find no fault with her.

After breakfast, and having helped wash the dishes, Lanzhi usually returned with Zhongqing to the bedroom. But today, things turned out different; Lady Jiao ordered Meimei to make Lanzhi familiar with the kitchen and the duties appertaining thereto. Meimei, a lively child of 13, was happy to undertake this task, and when she had finished, she pulled Lanzhi by the arm, and urged her to go with her into the garden to chase butterflies.

"Oh no, you don't!" rasped Lady Jiao, overhearing this conspiracy. "You just take your sister-in-law straight to the weaving room. This minute!"

Meimei cringed and frowned. "Yes, ma'am," she said sulkily, and trudged off ahead of Lanzhi to the weaving room, on the west side of the house.

That evening, Lanzhi and Meimei prepared the supper

不时地添把柴，拉拉风箱。三个人乐乐呵呵，把焦母打发得颇为满意。天色渐渐暗下来，仲卿和兰芝向母亲道了晚安之后，便双双回到新房。这一天像是格外地长，好在终于熬过来了。兰芝把仲卿拉到床前坐定，头靠在仲卿的肩上，闭上了双眼。

"兰芝。"仲卿叫了一声。

兰芝没答应，她没听见，她又沉浸在快乐之中了。

"兰芝，兰芝。"

这一次她听见了，但这声音好像来自很远很远的地方，或许是从鸳鸯集前那座古桥边传来的，飘飘渺渺。她答应了一声，睁开眼睛，痴痴地盯住丈夫，仲卿也正用深情的目光望着她。

"兰芝，春日良宵，弹一曲箜篌好吗？我看到你嫁妆里有一架箜篌。"

兰芝点点头，不眨眼地望着仲卿，不愿起身。仲卿笑了笑，走到还没收拾过的嫁妆箱笼中，搬过箜篌，回到床前。

静夜里传出悠悠的乐声，根根琴弦都在欢快地跳动，令人心醉。兰芝瞥见仲卿听得入神的样子，更加兴奋，她把这些天的柔情蜜意都揉进了曲中，连她自己也觉得从来没有弹得这么好。

"嘭嘭嘭。"有人在敲门。"嫂嫂，是我。"

原来是小姑梅梅。

together. Zhongqing also helped, by fetching firewood and pumping the bellows to keep the cooking fire going. The three of them worked cheerfully together, and Lady Jiao seemed reasonably satisfied with their new-found relationship. Eventually, Zhongqing and Lanzhi escorted Lady Jiao to her bedroom, said goodnight, and retired. It had been a particularly long and tiring day for Lanzhi, who laid her head on her husband's shoulder as soon as the two of them had sat down on the bed, and closed her eyes.

"Lanzhi," whispered Zhongqing.

The girl made no reply, being lost in a delightful reverie.

He whispered her name again. This time, she heard him, but his voice seemed to come from very far away; in fact it seemed to come floating all the way from the old bridge at Yuanyang. She murmured something in reply, and opened her eyes. She gazed at him, unwinking, as if in a daze. His eyes were full of tender longing. "Lanzhi, why not play me a tune on your *konghou* on this fine spring night?" he urged her. "I noticed that you brought it with you in your trousseau."

She nodded in assent, but seemed unwilling to stir from the bed. Zhongqing smiled, and went and fetched the instrument himself.

The haunting rippling notes which leaped from the strings of the *konghou* were so beautiful they would send all who heard them into raptures. Lanzhi glanced at Zhongqing. She was delighted to see that he seemed to be completed entranced by the music. She then redoubled her efforts, pouring all joy and delight of the past few days into her playing. Indeed, it seemed to her that she had never played so well before.

Suddenly, the melody was interrupted by a loud knocking on the door. It was Meimei.

梅梅笑嘻嘻地走进门，眉飞色舞地说：

"嫂嫂，你弹得好听极了，我也想学，你教我好不好？"

"你个笨丫头，还能弹箜篌？"仲卿朝梅梅摆着手，半嗔半笑地说。

梅梅小嘴一撅："你怎么知道我学不会？"

转眼间十几天过去了，仲卿的婚假只有两旬。忙活了一天之后，兰芝与仲卿重回新房，因为明天一早仲卿便要回郡衙了，而且这一去可能要两个月才能回来，两人在床前对视良久，彼此都有些依依不舍的伤感。

"真不想让你离开我。"兰芝说。

"兰芝，你怎么会说出这样的傻话，我何尝愿意离开你？好在一两个月，我就会回来看你。"

"一两个月！你说得多轻巧，一两天我怕也难以忍耐。"

"兰芝，我在那里当差很安稳，一两个月肯定能回来一次。你想想那些新婚后就分别，饮马长城窟的男儿们，要是你嫁给了他们，那你心里该是什么滋味？"

"我为什么要嫁给他们？上天只让我嫁给你！"兰芝把仲卿紧紧地抱住，"仲卿，你不到郡里当差了，回家吧。你种田，我织布，我们好生伺

The girl skipped into the room, her face wreathed in smiles. "Lanzhi, you play so well," she gushed. "I want to learn to play the *konghou* too. Won't you teach me?"

"You little blockhead," Zhongqing retorted, half annoyed, half amused. "You? Learn to play the *konghou*? I never heard anything so ridiculous in all my life!"

Meimei made a wry mouth. "What makes you think that I can't?"

Another dozen days passed, and Zhongqing's leave of absence, granted on the occasion of his marriage, was drawing to a close. In the evening of the day before Zhongqing was to leave to resume his post at the prefectural seat, he and Lanzhi were sitting on the bed gazing into each other's eyes, filled with dread at the coming parting. It would be two months before they could see each other again.

"I don't want you to go away," moaned Lanzhi, breaking the silence.

"Lanzhi, how can you say such a silly thing?" the young man protested. "Do you think that I want to go? I'll be back to see you after a couple of months."

"A couple of months!" wailed the girl. "How can you say that so lightly? I won't be able to stand it, I'm sure."

"Listen, my dear. I have a steady job there," Zhongqing said, coaxingly. "And I'm lucky to be able to get leave once every couple of months or so. Think about the poor young men who are torn from their brides and sent to guard the frontier, with no guarantee when, if ever, they'll be able to return. How would you feel if you'd married one of them?"

"Well, I didn't marry one of them," retorted Lanzhi, reason-

侯母亲，这才叫和和美美呢。"

仲卿不知说什么好，沉默了许久，才又开口把话题引开：

"兰芝，我不在家，你要听母亲的话，不要违拗她。她规矩严，你要小心些才是。"

兰芝点点头，擦擦涌出的泪水。

这一夜，兰芝久久不能入睡，她迷迷糊糊地感到自己又回到了鸳鸯集前那座小桥旁，目送着翩翩少年离她远去。那少年越走越远，越走越远，她突然拔腿朝少年追去，边跑边喊："仲卿，你快回来！快些回来！"

焦仲卿回郡衙了，这座大宅院里只剩下婆母和小姑。一下子，兰芝感到了一种无情无绪的失落，时光像是停止了一般，每个时辰都显得那么漫长。好在小姑梅梅是个活泼好动爱说爱笑的女孩儿，又整天缠着她学弹箜篌，也算有些排遣。

仲卿走了三五天，兰芝除了与梅梅操持一日两餐之外，织房还没有进过，焦母的脸色开始有些不好看了。

这一日晨炊刚完，兰芝又与梅梅摆弄起箜篌，焦母推门进来：

"兰芝，织机和线都给你准备好了，你去试试呀。"

ably enough. "It was Heaven's will that I marry you." She then threw her arms around her husband. "Zhongqing," she murmured, "Don't go back to your prefectural post. Why don't you stay here? You can do farming, and I can do weaving. That way we can look after your mother properly, and we'll have a happy life!"

Zhongqing didn't know what to say for the best. He said nothing for a long time, and then finally he said, as if he had made a firm resolution: "Lanzhi, while I'm away, you must do whatever my mother tells you to do. She has very strict rules, so be very careful to observe them."

Lanzhi nodded, and resignedly dried her tears.

That night, Lanzhi lay awake for a long time. When she finally did fall asleep, she was troubled by a hazy dream, in which she was transported back to the old bridge by the river in Yuanyang. In the distance, she could see that handsome young stranger. He was moving away from her. She started to run after him, crying, "Zhongqing, come back! Come back to me!"

As soon as Zhongqing returned to his post in the prefectural seat, and she was left in the house with Lady Jiao and Meimei, Lanzhi felt an intense sense of loneliness. Time almost seemed to have stood still, as each hour dragged by. Her only diversion was teaching that livewire Meimei, who had been pestering her to do so, how to play the *konghou*.

For a week or so after her husband departed, Lanzhi had helped Meimei prepare two meals every day. But so far she had not set foot in the weaving shed. Lady Jiao's never very pleasant face grew more and more sour as the days went by, and eventually one day, after breakfast, she strode into the room where the two girls were fooling around (as she termed it) with the *konghou*,

"是，母亲，我这就去。"兰芝意识到婆婆的不满，连忙放下手中的箜篌，起身朝织房走去。

梅梅也吐了吐舌头，跟在后面。织机上经线已经挂好，织梭也绕满了。兰芝坐在机前的机凳上，右手拿起梭子看了看，觉得与自家的完全相同，便将梭子向左投去，双手扶住靠板向后拍了两下，脚下一踩，左手又将梭子向右投去。

一投、一拍、一踩，一投、一拍、一踩，兰芝虽然已有很长时间没有上机了，但几踏之后，手脚便配合得十分协调，织机的轧轧声和投梭的啪啪声好像组成了一首乐曲。不大功夫，平平整整的几寸布就已织成。梅梅不觉赞叹起来：

"果然是个巧嫂嫂，我什么时候能织出这样好的布！"

兰芝朝梅梅笑笑，说：

"织布是个死功夫，有什么难？梅梅，你喜不喜欢读书？那书里才是乐趣无穷呢！"

"嫂嫂你真了不起。"梅梅顿时对兰芝充满敬意，"又会弹琴，又会织布，还会读书！我可是个笨丫头，什么时候才能学会这么多本事！"

"梅梅，其实什么都不难，只要你肯学就行。"

"那好吧。"梅梅爽快地说："今晚吃罢饭，你就教我读书。"

"这才是，免得长成大姑娘，嫁了夫君后，人

and said, "Lanzhi, the loom and the yarn are all ready for you. It's about time you went and tried to do some weaving."

"Yes, mother-in-law. Right away!" was the prompt reply from Lanzhi, who had been becoming uneasily aware of the old woman's dissatisfaction with her. She quickly put the *konghou* away, and bustled off to the weaving shed. Meimei stuck her tongue out in annoyance, and followed her. Lanzhi sat down at the loom, inspected the shuttle and the other equipment, and decided that everything was similar to what she had been used to at home. With her right hand she threw the shuttle to the left. With both hands she pulled the bar toward her. Then she patted the weft into place twice, and pressed on the treadle with her foot. With her left hand, she then threw the shuttle to the right.

And so she continued — throw, pat, treadle, throw, pat, treadle — until she had woven a smooth and even piece of cloth several feet long. It had been a long time since Lanzhi had operated a loom, but her old skill soon came back to her, and she had the machine humming a harmonious rhythm.

Meimei gasped with admiration: "What a clever sister-in-law you are! When will I ever be able to weave cloth as finely as you do?" Lanzhi turned to her, and smiled. "Weaving is a boring occupation," she said. "Anyway, there's really nothing to it. Meimei, you should learn how to read. There is no end of interesting things in books!"

"Sister-in-law, you're such a wonderful person!" gushed Meimei in adoration. "You know how to play a musical instrument, weave cloth, and even how to read! I'm just a silly housemaid. I'm sure I'll never learn to do all these wonderful things."

"Meimei, there's nothing really hard about it. Believe me." Lanzhi said. All you need is the determination to learn.

家谈诗论赋，你一句也听不懂，能不让人日久生厌吗？"

或许是兰芝婚前许久没有纺绩，这一天她觉得很疲倦。她本想早些睡下，但梅梅端着油灯走进来。这小姑是个急性子，上午嫂嫂答应教她读书，下午她就把哥哥读过的书找了出来，一直等着嫂嫂从织房走出，也不管嫂嫂累不累，兴冲冲地让兰芝教她。兰芝虽然疲乏，但看到梅梅急切的样子，也就打起精神接过书，一看，是本《诗经》，她翻开第一页，说："好，我来教你读。"

"关关雎鸠，在河之洲。
窈窕淑女，君子好逑。"

"别忙别忙。"梅梅打断兰芝的诵读，问道："嫂嫂，这我哪能听得懂？你给我讲一讲好吗？"

"好。梅梅，这诗呀，是古代大圣人删定的，都是讲该如何做人处世的。比如这一篇，是以斑鸠打比方，说女子不但要漂亮，而且要贤慧温柔，才能得到丈夫的喜欢。诗里说有个男子爱上一个姑娘，心里再也放不下她。"说到这里，她停住了，想起自己"在河之洲"时，目送着问路的焦仲卿渐渐远去的身影。

"All right," said the spritely Meimei. "This evening, after supper, teach me how to read."

"Of course," said Lanzhi, "If you can't read, and grow up and marry an educated young man, you won't be able to understand what he and his acquaintances are talking about. And then he quickly grow tired of you, won't he?"

Perhaps it was because she had not worked so hard for a long time that her first day spinning for her mother-in-law left Lanzhi feeling fatigued. She was looking forward to retiring to bed early, when Meimei suddenly appeared before her carrying an oil lamp and an armful of her brother's old books, eager to embark on her studies. Seeing how keen the girl was to improve herself, Lanzhi tried to forget how tired she was, and reluctantly agreed to start giving her lessons.

Noticing that the volume on the top of the pile was the *Book of Odes*, she picked it out, and started reading the first poem out loud:

"Merrily the ospreys cry / on the islet in the stream.

Comely and graceful is the girl / fit wife for a squire."

"Not so fast, not so fast!" Meimei interrupted her, in consternation. "I can't understand that. What does it mean?"

"This poem," began Lanzhi patiently, "was written by a wise man in ancient times. It's all to do with right behavior. For instance, the osprey in this stanza — one of the parts into which a poem is divided — is mentioned to point out that it is not enough for a girl to be beautiful; she must be virtuous and kind too, if she wants to win the affection of her husband. The poem explains that when a man loves a woman he will never abandon her in his heart." At this point, the line "on the islet in the stream" echoed in Lanzhi's

第二天一早，兰芝没等婆婆吩咐，便早早地进了织房。她原想小姑会来陪她，可是一直快到中午，才见梅梅端着饭菜走进来。脸上的表情也不像昨天那么灿烂了，有些不自然地朝兰芝笑了一笑，说："嫂嫂，娘让我把饭给你送过来。"

"送饭？"兰芝心里略略一惊，为什么要送饭？她明白了，婆婆这样安排，无非是不给她留出回房歇息的机会，吃完饭好继续织布！她心里有些酸楚，但很快就过去了：婆婆无非是想让自己多织些布，也是为家计嘛。倒是小姑脸上的异样使她感到纳闷：

"梅梅，不舒服吗？"

"没有。"

"有心事了？"

"没有"

"娘说你了？"

"没，没有。"梅梅回答得有些吞吞吐吐。她到底是个孩子，既不会说谎，又憋不住心里话，停了停，说："娘今天说，说……"

"说什么？"

"说不让我跟你学读书。"

"为什么？"兰芝不知道自己教小姑读书识字有什么错处。

"娘说，女孩家就应该学纺织刺绣，识文断字

mind, and she suddenly thought of the image of the young man who had asked her the way on that day by the old bridge gradually fading away in the distance. She broke off her explanation abruptly.

Early the following day, Lanzhi hurried to the weaving shed without waiting for Lady Jiao to order her to work. There, she hoped to have Meimei's company, but the girl did not turn up until nearly noon. When she did, Meimei looked crestfallen. She gave Lanzhi an embarrassed smile, and said, "My mother told me to bring you your lunch."

"Lunch?" echoed Lanzhi, in surprise. "Why has she sent me my lunch here?" she wondered. Almost immediately, she realized that Lady Jiao wanted to give her no chance to go back to her room to rest, but to make her resume weaving straight after her noon-time meal. She felt a tinge of resentment, which she quickly dismissed from her mind; after all, her work was for the benefit of the whole household, wasn't it? However, the gloomy expression on Meimei's face caused Lanzhi some disquiet:

"What's the matter, Meimei? Aren't you feeling well?"

"It's nothing."

"Are you worried about something?"

"No."

"Has my mother-in-law spoken severely to you?"

"No." Meimei mumbled, as if reluctant to answer. But, being a straightforward girl, who could neither lie nor naturally hide her feelings, she eventually confessed, "Today, my mother said...."

"What did she say?"

"She said that I must stop learning to read from you."

"What?" Lanzhi was flabbergasted. She could not imagine what could possibly be wrong with teaching Meimei to read.

是男子的事。"梅梅有点嗫嚅地说,"娘还说那书全是教人怎么想男人,怎么恋女人,读书多了,人就不懂规矩了。"

"……"兰芝一时竟不知说什么好。"娘还说什么没有?"她隐隐觉得婆婆这话并不是说给小姑听的,心里有些发紧,不由得又问了一句。还没等小姑回答,只听得院里婆婆在叫:

"梅梅!梅梅!给你嫂嫂取线去。"

"哎,来了!"梅梅一边高声答应,一边又附在兰芝耳边低声加了句:"嫂嫂你别生气啊,娘说你就是读那种书读的没心思纺绩了。"说完便快步跑了出去。

兰芝实在没想到教小姑读几句诗会惹得婆婆如此不快,她心里感到很委屈,看着眼前的饭菜,她也无心下咽了。自从与仲卿成婚后,两个人除了鱼水柔情之外,更多的时间是谈诗论文。从仲卿的脸上,她可以感觉到仲卿对她的喜爱和依恋,这绝不仅仅是由于自己的年轻美貌,两人之间好像有说不完的话。兰芝还清楚地记得仲卿说过这样的话:

"谁说女子无才便是德?我倒认为女子有才胜于色。"这明明是在赞赏自己,怎么在婆婆眼里,这倒成了一堆毛病?

她眼前恍惚了一阵,又安慰自己道:"算了吧,

The girl continued, "She said that girls should learn to weave and do needlework. Reading and stuff like that is for boys." She hesitated, and then blurted out, "She said that books put silly ideas about love affairs into people's heads, and then they forget how to act with proper decorum."

Lanzhi was lost for words. Then, after a while, she asked feebly: "Did she say anything else?" She had an intuition that these words of Lady Jiao's were meant not for Meimei but really for her. As she was waiting for Meimei's reply to her last question, Lady Jiao was heard from the courtyard, calling, "Meimei! Meimei! Take your sister-in-law some more thread."

"Oh, yes," the girl cried. She then bent to whisper in Lanzhi's ear: "Don't be angry, but she said that you're neglecting your work, by spending too much time reading books." With that, she scampered out of the room.

It had never occurred to Lanzhi that teaching Meimei to read a few poems would incur the wrath of the old woman. She felt most hurt, and glancing at the dishes before her, she found that she had no stomach for food. Ever since her marriage to Zhongqing, apart from physical love-making, the two of them had spent most of their time together discussing literature. She could tell by the way that the young man looked at her that he loved her not just for her youthful beauty, but also for the heartfelt conversations they had. Lanzhi clearly remembered him saying, "Whoever said that only an uneducated woman is virtuous didn't know what he was talking about. In my opinion, a woman with a cultured mind is more to be admired that a woman who has beauty and nothing else." She knew that this was praise for her. So how, she wondered, could such a quality be a blemish in her mother-in-law's eyes?

婆婆既然不喜欢读书弹琴，那我就多织些布，哄她高兴。"她只盼着仲卿快些回来，把心中的委屈向他诉说。

喀吱、啪、啪啪，喀吱、啪、啪啪，织布机一直在响，这低沉的声音，一直持续到红日西斜。晚饭是婆婆和小姑一起送来的，兰芝并没有停下手中的活计，只是依理叫了声"母亲"，低头继续织。

焦母俯身看了看兰芝织出的布，她先摸了摸布面，说了句："还算平整。"又看了看已织好的布卷，不冷不热地加了句："就是慢了点儿。"

这分明是嫌她出活儿太少，兰芝心里一下凉了，自己从日出就坐在这里，到现在身子还没离开织机一步，倒落得这么一句评语。她的眼睛开始发潮，但还是努力地克制住情绪，不让眼泪滚出。谁知就在这时，焦母发现前晌梅梅送来的饭菜一口没动，立刻来了气，嗓门儿也高了起来：

"怎么，你这是跟我赌气不吃饭吗？还是嫌饭不好吃？"

兰芝本已觉得委屈，又听到婆婆这话，眼泪夺眶而出，倒是梅梅有些看不过去，小声说了句："娘，你看你……"

"怎么？"焦母的嗓门更高了，我当婆婆的给媳妇送饭，倒有了错了？"

She felt a spell of giddiness come over her, but soon pulled herself together. "Well, never mind," she sighed. "If my mother-in-law doesn't like me reading and playing music, I'll just have to please her with my skill at weaving." With that, she resigned herself to patiently waiting until Zhongqing returned, and pouring her heart out to him.

The clatter of the loom resumed, and continued all afternoon, as Lanzhi renewed her labors. As the sun set, Lady Jiao and Meimei together brought Lanzhi her evening meal, and found her still hard at work.

The first thing the old woman did after setting the dishes down was to feel the cloth that her daughter-in-law had woven. Straightening up, she admitted grudgingly: "It's smooth enough, I suppose." Then, glancing at the size of the pile, she remarked, "But you haven't made much, have you?"

This callous remark stung Lanzhi, who had been working flat out all day. She fought back the flood of tears threatening to cascade from her eyes. Just at that moment, Lady Jiao noticed that Lanzhi had not touched her lunch. In a rage, she berated her daughter-in-law:

"What's this? Are you deliberately trying to provoke me by refusing to eat these delicious dishes I went to so much trouble to prepare for you?"

This was the last straw for Lanzhi. As Meimei looked on, horrified, the aggrieved girl melted into a storm of weeping.

"Well, what's the matter with the food I made for you?" Lady Jiao ranted on, adding fuel to the flames.

With difficulty, Lanzhi managed to control her sobbing, and whispered hoarsely that she had been feeling dizzy at noon, and had lost her appetite.

"母亲，不是的。"兰芝用手揩去泪水，停下纺机，轻声说道，"儿媳今天中午头脑有些眩晕，不想吃饭。儿媳哪敢与婆母生气？"

"怪不得今天织得这么少，是不舒服啊！"焦母不再说什么，转身出了房门。

回到房中，兰芝啜泣不止，直到夜深，她突然又害怕起来，明天婆婆看到自己哭红的双眼，会更加恼怒的。她低低地自语了一句："仲卿，你快回来吧！"

"Oh, so that's it!" growled the old woman. "No wonder you haven't done much weaving. You're faint with hunger, I suppose!"

As soon as she got back to her room that evening, Lanzhi burst into tears. It was only the fear that the sight of her reddened eyes in the morning would give her mother-in-law another chance to scold her which finally brought her storm of weeping to an end, late in the night.

◎第三章
秦家罗敷怀春情

从这一天起，兰芝每日鸡鸣即起，粗粗梳洗一番，便坐在织机前。一日两餐，都是梅梅给她送来，晚上一直干到掌灯时分，她才挪着发肿的双脚，柔着酸痛的双腕回到房中。

倒也好，一日里难得见婆婆两面，偶尔婆婆走进织房，也是来察看一下织了多少布，婆媳二人的对话越来越少。

兰芝在家时原本是个织布的好手，在这种压力之下，自然更加卖力。

一天，小姑梅梅惊喜地跑出织房，大声地叫着：

"娘，嫂嫂织得真快，才三天就织出五匹布呢！"

焦母自然心中有数，但她可不想夸奖媳妇，所以不屑地说：

"你懂什么！娘当年三天织过六匹布呢！"其实这是没影的事，她大声嚷嚷着，故意说给兰芝听。

兰芝听到这话自然觉得十分刺耳，可她始终没弄清自己究竟如何得罪了婆婆。她也不知道新

Chapter Three
Luofu Awakens to Love

From the following day onward, Lanzhi rose at cockcrow, and after a hasty toilet hurried to the weaving shed, and sat herself down at the loom. Twice a day, Meimei brought her meals to her, and it was only with the lighting of the lamp in the evening that she at last dragged herself, with swollen ankles and aching back, off to bed. Her mother-in-law was on the rare occasions when she popped into the weaving shed to check on how much work Lanzhi had done. Much to the girl's relief, the words exchanged between them became fewer and fewer.

In her old home, Lanzhi had been used to operating a loom, but never under so much pressure as in her mother-in-law's house. One instance will suffice to illustrate this.

One day, Meimei bounced up to her mother, filled with excitement. "Ma," she cried, "Lanzhi's so quick! She's woven five rolls of cloth in only three days!"

Lady Jiao, however, although she knew quite well that such an amount was impressive, could not bring herself to show even the slightest sign of approval where Lanzhi was concerned, simply snorting, "Humph! What do you know? That's nothing. I used to turn out six rolls in three days."

This was, in fact, not true, but she said it in a loud voice deliberately so that Lanzhi would hear. Lanzhi was taken aback, and was at a loss to imagine in what way she had offended the old woman that she should make such a preposterous claim. She had

婚的幸福背后为什么是如此的痛苦。她开始怀念未嫁之前的时光，跟小伙伴不时到镇外玩耍，回到家里读读书，弹弹琴，那时虽然也纺线织锦，但从来没有人逼迫她。她想仲卿，可仲卿是千呼万唤也回不来的，她只能默默地等待。她想母亲，想扑到母亲怀中哭一场，她甚至想那个稍嫌粗暴的哥哥。

鸳鸯集离县城虽然只有六七十里地，但对兰芝来说，要回家却比登天还难。她想起了罗敷，罗敷早已搬到县城，出嫁前就曾准备嫁过来之后去找她，但新婚时的甜蜜，丈夫走后的辛苦，使她几乎忘了这件事。如今，孤独的她身边好像只有这一个人可以说几句心里话，她想去找罗敷，但眼下每日里坐在织机前，什么时候才能踏出这个院子呢？

在日复一日的辛苦劳作中，兰芝终于等回了仲卿。

仲卿回到家中，先到上房向母亲问了安，梅梅站在一旁拉着仲卿的胳膊，憨憨地笑着说："哥，我想你了！"

"快去给你哥哥烧饭去！"

梅梅答应了一声，跑了出去。仲卿心下奇怪，进门不仅没见兰芝，怎么连烧饭也是让梅梅而不

never dreamed that behind the facade of happy married life there could lie such torment. She thought back to the carefree days of her maidenhood: She would roam happily with her friends in the fields, and at home she would read books and play her music. She also used to weave, but nobody forced her to, she mused ruefully. Her thoughts then strayed to Zhongqing. But Zhongqing was far, far away. She thought of her mother. She wanted to fly to her arms, and sob her heart out. She even missed that boorish brother of hers.

Her hometown was only sixty or seventy *li* away, but for Lanzhi it would have been easier to fly to the sky than to make a journey there. She was then reminded of her old friend Luofu. Luofu was not far away, having moved to the county seat with her family. Lanzhi had intended to visit her after she married Zhongqing, but the happiness of her honeymoon and the way she had felt so distraught after Zhongqing left to resume his post had driven all thoughts of Luofu out of her head. Now, in her loneliness, Lanzhi realized that there was only Luofu to whom she could turn to speak out the words which were in her heart. It tortured her to think that there was no way she could manage to get away from that accursed loom and out of the house to go and visit Luofu.

But as day followed dreary day, and finally, Zhongqing arrived on the doorstep. The first thing he did was to rush to pay his respects as a dutiful son to his mother. Meimei was present when he entered Lady Jiao's room, and in delight she grabbed him by the arm. "I've missed you so much!" she cried in her own guileless way, beaming all over her face.

"Off with you, and prepare lunch for your brother," said Lady Jiao. Meimei scampered away to the kitchen without more ado.

Zhongqing was puzzled. He hadn't seen any sign of Lanzhi

是让兰芝去呢？

"母亲，兰芝呢？"仲卿怯怯地问母亲。

焦母脸上的喜悦随着这句问话而烟消云散，嗔怪地说：

"怎么，还没问为娘无恙，倒先打听起媳妇来。真是娶了媳妇忘了娘。"

"母亲！"仲卿赔了个笑，"您想到哪儿去了，我只是说一进门娘和妹子都见过了，只是没见到兰芝，随便问一句罢了。"

他不再打听兰芝的事，与母亲拉了些闲话，焦母这才告诉他："到织房去看看她吧。"仲卿向母亲作了一揖，便返身朝织房走去。

"兰芝！"

兰芝一抬头，有些不敢相信自己的眼睛，一时百感交集，竟趴在织机上哭了起来。

"兰芝，我回来了！你这是怎么啦？"

仲卿以为他的出现会给兰芝带来欣喜，没料到兰芝会是这个样子。

"兰芝，兰芝。"

哭了一阵，兰芝心中的委屈发泄了一些，觉得好受了点儿，这才又抬起头来。她原本想丈夫回家后好好向他倾诉一番，但是哭过之后，她又改变了主意，面对心爱的人，她不想用烦心的事来占据这短暂相聚的时光。

since he arrived home, and why was Meimei sent to prepare his lunch and not his wife?

"Where's Lanzhi, Mother?" he ventured to ask.

The look of pleasure which had adorned Lady Jiao's visage upon seeing her son again vanished in an instant at this modest inquiry. "What do you mean by asking about your wife before you have had the common courtesy to ask about your mother's well-being?" she snapped. "Oh, I see. Now that you have a wife you don't need your old mother any more."

"Oh, mother!" cried Zhongqing, assuming an obsequious smile. "What a thing to say! It's just that I've only seen you and Meimei since I came home. I just wondered where Lanzhi was, that's all." He was careful not to mention Lanzhi again, but busied himself with small talk to keep his mother amused.

After a while, Lady Jiao said, in an off-hand manner: "Oh, by the way, you will probably find Lanzhi in the weaving shed." Delighted, the young man took his leave of his mother as soon as he decently could, and made a beeline for the weaving shed.

Lanzhi looked round at the sound of someone eagerly calling out her name. She could hardly believe her eyes when she saw her beloved husband appear in the doorway of her place of virtual imprisonment. In an instant, her mind teemed with a thousand emotions. Her head whirled, and she collapsed onto the loom in front of her, and began to weep.

"Lanzhi, I'm back ... why, what's the matter?" the young man cried, in consternation.

Lanzhi's first impulse upon getting a grip on herself and wiping away her tears was to pour out all her griefs to her husband. But on second thoughts, she found herself unwilling to spoil the precious short moments of his homecoming with distressful

"没什么，我只是想你，高兴得不知说什么好，所以才哭。"兰芝已经平静下来。

"那好，我们去吃饭吧。"

俗话说，久别胜新婚，这一夜的云情雨意自不必说。

第二天，因为仲卿在家，焦母破例没让兰芝进织房。可在婆婆的眼皮底下，兰芝总觉得浑身不自在。她向仲卿提议出去走走，还说她自从来到焦家，就没有出过大门。仲卿不大相信，但也没仔细追问，就答应了。

兰芝家在乡下，从未逛过城，她看到街上的一切都感到新奇而陌生。这种感觉使她心中的委屈与不快减轻了许多。

"兰芝！兰芝！"

刘兰芝突然听到有人在喊自己的名字，顺着声音望去，一个熟悉的面孔映入眼帘。

"是……是罗敷！"兰芝没想到竟在这里见到罗敷，她正不知到何处寻找，罗敷却在此时从天而降。

兰芝兴奋地拉着罗敷的手，不住地摇晃着，而罗敷的目光却转向了兰芝的身旁，兰芝连忙对罗敷说：

"这是我丈夫焦仲卿。"

matters. "It's nothing," she hurriedly assured Zhongqing, and assuming an air of perfect calmness. "I'm all right. I was so happy to see you that I couldn't find the right words to say to you. So I melted into tears, you see. That's all."

"Good, good," smiled Zhongqing. "Well, why don't we go and have lunch together?"

As the saying goes, "Parting only increases the ardor of newlyweds." And so there is no need to describe how passionate this first night of their reunion was for Lanzhi and Zhongqing. The next morning, as her son was at home, Lady Jiao made an exception to her rule, and did not banish Lanzhi to the weaving shed. However, as the girl felt herself ill at ease under her mother-in-law's eye, she quickly suggested to Zhongqing that they go outside for a stroll, remarking by the way that she had not left the courtyard since she had moved to her new home. Her husband thought this odd, but did not pursue the subject, and readily agreed to take the air with her.

Lanzhi had never been in a city before, having been raised in the countryside. And so, she was fascinated by all she saw in the bustling streets of the county seat. For a while, she forgot her cares, and her mood lightened.

All of a sudden, she heard someone calling her name. Turning in the direction of the voice, she found herself gazing at a familiar face. "It's.... It's Luofu!" she gasped in astonishment. It was as if her old friend had fallen from the sky.

Lanzhi grabbed Luofu by the hands, and shook them excitedly. Then, noticing that Luofu's eyes had strayed to Zhongqing beside her, she quickly introduced her new husband.

"What? You're married already?" Luofu seemed unable to

"怎么，你嫁给他了？"罗敷说不上心中是何滋味。

"这是我小时的伙伴罗敷。"兰芝对仲卿说。

焦仲卿微微一怔：

"我们好像见过面的。"

"是啊，是啊，在鸳鸯集的古桥边。"罗敷脱口而出，其实罗敷也和兰芝一样，自那次见过焦仲卿之后，也对他久久不能忘怀。眼见得兰芝嫁给了他，她心里还真有些嫉妒。

两姐妹此时虽各有心事，但都对邂逅相逢感到很高兴，三个人站在街心聊了一会儿，兰芝怕时间长了婆婆不高兴，就把自己的住处告诉罗敷，约她去串门，然后依依而别。

这一夜对罗敷来说真是不同寻常的一夜，她虽是个心大量宽的人，可是今晚她却怎么也睡不着了。

她回忆起一年多以前在鸳鸯集古桥边自己表演的那滑稽的一幕，但当她在记忆中搜寻焦仲卿的音容笑貌时，却总显得那么依稀模糊。她当时只觉得那个被自己指为相好的少年风致翩然，这足以使她久久难忘了。

今天又面对面地见到了焦仲卿，那张白皙的面孔，神采奕奕的眼睛，真让人为之失魂。罗敷感

contain her surprise.

Lanzhi then introduced Zhongqing to her childhood friend.

Zhongqing stared at Luofu, as if in a daze. "I think we have met somewhere before," he said, hesitantly.

"We have indeed," replied Luofu, with great animation. "By the old bridge in Yuanyang." In fact, Luofu had been as infatuated by the handsome young stranger as Lanzhi had, and no more successful at banishing him from her thoughts ever since. Suddenly seeing him here as Lanzhi's husband roused in Luofu no small pang of jealousy.

Nevertheless, the two girls were overjoyed at their chance meeting, and lingered gossiping in the street for a long time, while Zhongqing stood patiently by. Finally, it occurred to Lanzhi that her mother-in-law would not be pleased if she stayed out too long, and so she hastily described to Luofu where she was living, and extracted a promise from her to visit as soon as possible. They then reluctantly took their leave of each other.

That night was like no other for Luofu. Normally a happy-go-lucky girl, she found it impossible to sleep. She kept thinking back to how she had opened the curtain on a drama by her giddy antics, one year ago, by the old bridge in Yuanyang. And as the same memory kept coming back, so did the vision of the young man's handsome countenance and dulcet voice, although faintly. She felt that she would never forget how she had pointed, quite by accident, to such a comely youth as her lover. And today, coming face to face with him, she had nearly swooned with ecstasy. Luofu felt an inexplicable sensation of discomfort, as though some writhing worm were tickling her heart. At the same time, the remembrance of his finely chiseled features and somber manner made

到心里像有条虫子爬来爬去,痒痒的,说不上是什么滋味。她想到焦仲卿那略带忧郁的神情时,又像是饮了醇酒一样有些醉意。"唉!"她轻轻地叹了口气,开始埋怨上天:为什么自己点中的鸳鸯,却偏偏错配了兰芝呢?她又埋怨那个该死的媒婆说破天,为什么不为自己做成这门亲事呢?"焦仲卿,焦仲卿!"想着想着,她不觉失声叫出来,"有你这么个冤家埋在我心底,以后我还能嫁给谁呢?"

焦仲卿这次回家只住了两天,就匆匆返回了。兰芝为了好好享受这短暂的相聚,并没有把自己的辛苦向丈夫诉说。婆婆这两日也没显露出什么。仲卿虽然感到家中气氛有些不大对劲,但夫妇二人单独相守时,还是像新婚时一样。

焦仲卿前脚出门,刘兰芝后脚就进了织房,尽管依旧劳累不堪,但她的心情还是好多了。仲卿那每一个眼神,每一次抚摸,每一个亲吻,每一句话语,此时仍使她激动不已。正在这时,一个人推门进来。

"罗敷!"兰芝稍感意外,"你怎么来了?"

"想你呗。前两天我就想来,可你那夫君在家,我不想当个棒槌。"罗敷说这话有点言不由衷。

"快坐吧。"兰芝说着,却没起身,手中还在忙

her feel dizzy, but in a pleasant sort of way, as if she had imbibed mellow wine. She moaned, and started to throw the blame on Heaven for plunging her into the depths of despair that only hope-less love can bring to a young girl. Why had Heaven snatched this supreme prize from her and handed it to her friend Lanzhi? She then turned her resentment on the matchmaker: Why hadn't she arranged such a wonderful marriage for her? Poor Luofu cried aloud Jiao Zhongqing's name several times, ending with the wail, "You are my true love. We were destined for each other.... How can I ever marry anyone else?"

As her husband only had two days of home leave, Lanzhi did not want to spoil the brief spell of happiness they were al-lowed together by telling him of the problems she was having with her mother-in-law. At the same time, Lady Jiao herself had given no hint of her resentment of Lanzhi. So, although he had some inkling that all was not as it should be, Jiao Zhongqing spent the two days with Lanzhi as happily as he had on their honeymoon.

When her husband departed to return to the prefectural capital, Lanzhi resumed her weaving. Despite the fact that the work was just as fatiguing as before, her heart felt lighter. Every glance, every caress, every kiss and every word from Zhongqing had given her a thrill.

Just as she was reminiscing fondly about those two heav-enly days, there came a brisk knock at the door, and somebody entered. "Luofu!" Lanzhi almost screamed with delight. "What brings you here so unexpectedly?" "Thinking of you brought me here," Luofu said, not quite truthfully. "I would have come to see you earlier, but, what with your husband here, I didn't want to

着。

罗敷自己搬了个木墩靠近兰芝坐下，话题自然又转到焦仲卿，她问兰芝出嫁的感受，兰芝想了想，苦涩地一笑，说：

"天知地知我自知。"

"这话从何说起？"罗敷听出兰芝像是并不快乐，不解地问："焦仲卿不好吗？"

兰芝摇摇头，说：

"仲卿人很好，只是婆婆有些刻薄。"她把自己到焦家后的一切都详细地讲给了罗敷。

罗敷听罢却不以为然，说道："你呀，身在福中不知福。我若是嫁了焦仲卿这样的人，就是天天用油锅煎，也是心甘情愿的。"

听了这话，兰芝倒觉得有几分道理，想想与仲卿在一起时的幸福，辛苦点倒也值得。好吧，那就忍吧，婆婆总归是要老去的，有仲卿陪伴终身，也真该无怨无悔了。

"兰芝。"罗敷冲着兰芝诡谲地一笑，说："你知道吗，我可是恨死你了！"

"恨我？为什么？"

"还记得那年在桥边的情景吗？当时可是我把他指为相好的，没想到上天把他错配给你，我怎能不恨你呢？"

兰芝最了解罗敷口无遮拦的性格，虽然这个

intrude." "Sit down," Lanzhi urged her, while she herself did not pause in her work.

Luofu pulled up a stool near to her friend, and the two began to chat. It was not long before Luofu asked Lanzhi how she felt about married life. "Heaven knows, Earth knows, and I know," said Lanzhi, cryptically.

"What do you mean by that?" asked Luofu, puzzled. She sensed that Lanzhi was not happy about something. "What's the matter? Doesn't Zhongqing treat you properly?"

Lanzhi shook her head dismissively. "Zhongqing's a wonderful person," she assured her friend, "the problem is his mean mother." She then went on to relate all that had happened to her since she moved into the Jiao household.

Luofu, however, was not entirely sympathetic. "You don't know how lucky you are," she sniffed. "If I were married to Zhongqing, you could boil me in oil every day and I would still count myself blessed."

"She's right, I suppose," mused Lanzhi to herself. She then remembered how happy she and Zhongqing were when they were together, and decided that the little bit of inconvenience caused by her mother-in-law was worth putting up with. "Let her go on nagging me," she thought, "why should I care so long as I have Zhongqing to comfort me for the rest of my life?"

"Lanzhi." Her reverie was interrupted by Luofu, who said, with a sly smile: "You know, I really hate you." "Hate me? Why?" "Do you remember last year, by the bridge? I pointed out my lover, little suspecting that Heaven would be so perverse as to give him to you. Why shouldn't I hate you?"

Lanzhi knew quite well that Luofu was a flighty girl who didn't hesitate to come out with the most preposterous statements.

玩笑开得有些过火，但她心里却觉得格外熨帖，她庆幸上天这个"错配"，更感到这幸福的弥足珍贵。

"你要是不知珍爱，我可要把他抢过来喽！"罗敷越发放肆了。

兰芝捶了她一下，说：

"总是没正经！"停了一会儿，又把话题扯到罗敷身上：

"你是不是也待嫁了？"

"我呀！"罗敷无奈地翻翻眼皮，"我可没你那么有福气，这辈子算是嫁不出去了。"

"怎么会呢？像你这样的美人，提亲的人不踩破门槛才怪呢！"

"这话倒是不错，提亲的人是不少，可我不像你那么温顺，还没见男人长什么模样就嫁给他。幸亏你家仲卿长得好，若是嫁个癞蛤蟆怎么办？我是一定要嫁一个自己喜欢的人才行。"

"那你就一个也没看上？"

这句话正扎在罗敷的痛处，她脸上顽皮的笑一下子收敛起来。年轻女孩，哪个不巴望嫁一位如意郎君？罗敷心中的苦正来自兰芝，确切地说，是来自焦仲卿。自从那次桥头邂逅，罗敷同样把焦仲卿当成了样板，立誓要嫁给这样的男子为妻。每次有人登门提亲，她都要想方设法见男方一面。在她

Nevertheless, she couldn't help feeling that this time she had gone a little too far. At the same time, Luofu's teasing made her bless Heaven for its willful choice in bestowing so much happiness on her. "If you don't appreciate what a divine man you've got, I'll come and snatch him away from you," the little minx warned Lanzhi. The latter gave her a playful punch. "You can't be serious for one minute, can you?" Lanzhi charged. Then, after a pause, she changed the subject. "Luofu, aren't you going to get married any time soon?"

"Who? Me?" Luofu opened her eyes wide in mock astonishment. "I'm not as lucky as you," she said, with a shake of her head. "No, I'm going to remain an old maid for the rest of my life."

"What nonsense you talk!" protested Lanzhi. "A beautiful girl like you must have suitors battering the door down."

"Well, to tell you the truth, I have had some offers. But I don't fancy marrying any of the young men. Things haven't gone as smoothly for me as for you. Your family made you the perfect match, but what if they had chosen for you some fellow who was as ugly as a toad? I'll only marry someone I like, and that's that."

"Isn't there any young man you like?"

This inquiry from Lanzhi touched Luofu on a tender spot, and she had to suppress a mischievous grin. The fact is that as soon as she had first seen Zhongqing by the bridge, she had vowed that she would only marry a man like him. Ever since then, she had measured all the youths who came to ask for her hand in marriage by the impossible standard of perfection represented by Zhongqing. Needless to say, they all failed the test miserably. What's more, Luofu was such a strong-willed girl that her parents had long since given up any hope of trying to persuade her to marry a young man of their choice. However, it is not quite fair to

看来，没有一个能及得上焦仲卿三分。这罗敷是个很倔强的姑娘，她说不愿意，父母也拗她不得。要说没有一个能及得上焦仲卿，这话也不全对，因为前些日子说破天曾到秦家来为县令公子王瑞琪提亲。

罗敷的父母满口应承下来，还带着罗敷亲自到县太爷府上去了一趟。酒席间，罗敷与王公子见了一面，那王公子清眉秀目间还带着一种男子汉的刚气，罗敷一见便动了心。无奈几天之后，王县令家捎来口信，说王公子另有所爱，罗敷刚刚燃起的爱情就这样被浇灭了。

秦郎中夫妇弄不清县令家为何相不中女儿，再三追问说破天，说破天才吞吞吐吐地说了几句"性情不合"、"八字相克"之类的话，秦家还是悟不出真正的缘由。

大概是罗敷和兰芝分别太久，说起话来没完没了。这罗敷又是待字闺中，无人管束，所以久久不肯离去。她见兰芝有些疲倦，便说："我来帮你干一会儿吧。"

罗敷的手艺虽比不上兰芝，但也不算差。就这样边干边说，不觉又过了一个时辰。

罗敷来找兰芝，焦母本不太高兴，只是出于礼貌不好拒之门外。可这女子待了许久不出来，她怕耽误了兰芝的活计，便来到织房察看。此时罗敷正

say that no other young man could hold a candle to Zhongqing in Luofu's eyes. For, only a few days previously, the old match-maker we met earlier as "Talk Even Heaven into Anything" had called at County Magistrate Wang's mansion and proposed a match with Luofu for his son Ruiqi.

Luofu's parents had been highly pleased at the prospect of such a high connection, and had taken their daughter along with them to introduce her to the prospective groom. Although she had had only a glimpse of the young man, Luofu had been favor-ably impressed with his manly looks and genteel deportment. In a word, she had been smitten. Imagine her chagrin, then, when news was brought to her not long afterward that Wang Ruiqi was in love with another girl. Luofu's parents could not understand why nothing came of the introduction of the two young people. Interrogation of the go-between only brought mumbled excuses about their "characters" or "star signs" being incompatible, and the old couple were left in the dark.

Luofu and Lanzhi had a lot to talk about, after having been separated for so long. Besides, Luofu was not the typical meek sort of unmarried girl who dared not leave the house; she went wherever she chose, and stayed out as long as she liked. She was astute enough to see that Lanzhi was tired, as the latter never stopped weaving all through their long conversation, and offered to help, planting herself on the bench next to Lanzhi with-out waiting for an invitation.

Though not as skillful as her friend, Luofu was still a dab hand at the loom, and time flew past as the two girls worked and talked. Meanwhile, Lady Jiao, who had not been pleased when Luofu popped in to see Lanzhi, fearing that she might distract her daughter-in-law from her work, but could hardly bar the door to

织在兴头上，走梭如飞。焦母看到活儿没耽误，心中的不快减了几分。兰芝见婆婆进来，有点儿慌张，刚要开口，却被快嘴的罗敷抢了先：

"伯母，你看我织得好不好？"

焦母摸摸布，点点头：

"不错，不错。"

"那我以后常来帮你织布，好不好？"

"好哇。"焦母随口答道。

"伯母，您老人家身体真好啊。"罗敷没话找话地说。

"好什么，年纪大了，哪儿都有毛病。"

"我爹爹是个郎中，您哪儿不舒服，包在我身上。"

"哎，哎。"焦母听罗敷嘴巴甜甜的，长得又俏，倒有几分喜欢她了。

罗敷的嘴一会儿也不闲着，她又唠唠叨叨地向焦母讲述了自己的家世，讲了她父亲是如何从鸳鸯集到县城来行医的。

不知不觉，太阳已经偏西了。

"哎呀，我该回家了。伯母，赶明儿我再来陪您说话。"

罗敷风风火火地走了，焦母由于心情转好，破例没有给兰芝白眼，面带微笑地回到自己房中。

her, was wondering what business on earth could be keeping
her with Lanzhi all this time, came sneaking into the weaving
shed. She was grudgingly pleased to see that the two girls were
hard at work.

On seeing her mother-in-law, Lanzhi felt a twinge of alarm,
but before she could blurt out some excuse to pacify her, she
was forestalled by the glib-tongued Luofu: "Oh, Madame Jiao,"
"what do you think of my weaving?" Lady Jiao felt the cloth,
nodded, and said, "Not bad, I suppose." "I'll come more often in
future to help you with the weaving, shall I?" "If you like."

At this point, Luofu found herself at a loss how to carry on
the conversation with the taciturn old woman. Then, for want of
anything better to say, she asked, "Madame Jiao, how is your
health these days?"

"No better than can be expected at my time of life," came
the gruff reply. "Aches and pains all over."

"Oh, well, my father's a doctor," Luofu chirped. "Just let me
know what's wrong with you, and I'll have him take care of it."

"Is that so?" Lady Jiao brightened visibly on hearing this,
and Luofu, knowing full well how to pursue an advantage, prattled
on about how her family had come to move from Yuanyang and
settle down in the prefectural capital. She went into great detail
as to her father's medical skills.

Suddenly aware how late the hour was, Luofu said, "Oh, I
must be running along home. Madame Jiao, I'll come back
tomorrow, if I may, and we can continue our conversation."

The visitor had made such a good impression on the old
woman that after she left Lady Jiao forgot to give Lanzhi her usual
scolding, but left the weaving shed without a murmur and even
with the ghost of a smile.

春来暑往，刘兰芝已经嫁过来一年多了。这一年多对兰芝来说实在不易，她每天都要从早到晚地织布。前些天她得了一场病，病后的身体虽很虚弱，但婆婆没等她痊愈，就催她赶快上机织布。还是梅梅心疼她，不时地给她煮碗面汤，有时还放上一个鸡蛋。有一次梅梅进织房，见嫂嫂实在疲惫，便说：

"嫂嫂，你歇一会儿，我来替你织。"

兰芝一直觉得梅梅这孩子很善良，在自己寂寞单调、无休无止的纺织生活中，若不是这个小姑不时地来调节一下，她几乎要崩溃了。她让梅梅坐在织机前，看着她稍嫌笨拙的动作，不知怎么，脑子里又浮现出仲卿的身影。

"嫂嫂，嫂嫂！"

"哦！"兰芝如梦初醒，怔了一下，"梅梅，怎么啦？"

"嫂嫂，你看我织得好不好？"

兰芝看了看梅梅织出的两寸布，松松散散，不甚平整，说道：

"梅梅，你拉板的手劲不够，太松了。"

"那怎么办？"梅梅有些手足无措。

兰芝想，就这么一点点，也不致有大妨碍，于是安慰她说：

"没关系，梅梅，还是我来吧"

Spring went, and summer came around. Lanzhi had been married one full year now. It had not been an easy year for the girl, what with having to sit at the loom weaving from dawn to dusk. She had barely recovered from an illness a few days previously, when her mother-in-law had forced her back to work. The kind-hearted Meimei, however, did her best to look after Lanzhi, making nourishing soup and noodles for her, and occasionally managing to slip her an egg. One day, Meimei noticed that her sister-in-law was looking even more weary than usual, and said, "Why don't you rest for a while, and let me take over the loom for you?"

Lanzhi appreciated Meimei's care for her; indeed, she sometimes thought, if it were not for Meimei, she would have collapsed in total exhaustion long before. She let Meimei take her place at the loom. At first, she watched the youngster's clumsy attempts closely, and guided her hands, but after a while her thoughts strayed to Zhongqing. She didn't know how long she remained sunk in these pleasant distractions, but she was suddenly brought back to reality by Meimei's excited clamoring: "Lanzhi, Lanzhi! What do you think of my weaving?" The girl had left the loom, and was tugging at Lanzhi's sleeve.

Lanzhi looked at the two feet of cloth that Meimei had woven, and saw, to her horror, that it was hopelessly loose and lumpy.

"Meimei, you haven't been pulling the bar hard enough," she said. "The weave should be a lot tighter."

"Well, what can I do about it now?" pleaded the abashed Meimei.

"Don't worry, I'll fix it," said Lanzhi, soothingly.

But before she had a chance to rectify Meimei's poor workmanship, Lady Jiao barged in. She went straight up to the

也是无巧不成书，恰在这时，焦母走了进来，她习惯地摸了摸机上的布，突然瞪起眼睛问道：

"今天怎么织成这样？"

梅梅吓得不敢说话。兰芝看到婆婆脸色变得难看，又不想说是梅梅织的，连忙向婆婆陪罪。

"你呀！"焦母余怒未息，"不但织得越来越慢，还越发跟我捣起鬼来了。你吃着焦家的饭，就这样给焦家当媳妇吗？"

"这实在是儿媳的错……"

"说声错就完了？你看该怎么办？"焦母恨恨地哼了一声，扭身出去了。

兰芝忍不住哽咽起来。她真后悔不该嫁人，当姑娘的日子里，何尝有人这样难为她？她停下织机，擦了把眼泪。梅梅怯生生地拉着她的胳膊说：

"嫂嫂，全是我的错。"

"咱们都没有错。"

晚上她没有回房，她要把这匹布赶出来，梭子在她的手里来回穿飞，她心里的积怨也在渐渐升腾。虽然自己仍旧痴心爱着仲卿，然而仲卿却护持不了自己，这种爱付出的代价太大了。

离开焦家！像一道闪电，离开焦家的念头划过了兰芝的脑海。

loom and, with a practiced hand, felt the cloth on it. Then she whirled round in a fury. "What on earth do you think you're playing at?" she shrieked at Lanzhi.

Lanzhi's first instinct was to cover up for Meimei, now speechless with fear. But Lady Jiao brushed aside her stammered excuses.

"As if it wasn't bad enough you working slower and slower every day, you're now starting to provoke me deliberately! Is this how you repay your old mother-in-law for all she's done for you?"

"I'm sorry...."

"Just being sorry isn't good enough. What are you going to do about it? — That's what I want to know!" With that, Lady Jiao spun on her heel, and flounced out of the weaving shed.

Lanzhi was overcome by a fit of sobbing. For the first time, she began to regret having got married. As a girl at home, she had never had to put up with ill-treatment.

As she wiped her tears away she heard Meimei say, "Lanzhi, it was all my fault."

"No, no, it wasn't," Lanzhi hastened to reassure her. "It wasn't the fault of either of us."

As night fell, Lanzhi remained in the weaving shed instead of going back to her room, putting right the mess that Meimei had made of the cloth. As she worked furiously, she could feel the pent-up resentment within her rising to boiling point. Despite her devotion to her beloved Zhongqing, the young man seemed to be able to do nothing to protect her from humiliation at the hands of his mother. Did he deserve her love, she wondered.

She would leave the Jiao household! Yes, that's what she would do. The thought came to her like a flash of lightning.

焦仲卿又回到家中,向母亲问了安,便来到自己房里,还没坐定,门"吱呀"一声被推开了,无言的刘兰芝出现在门口。

"兰芝,这段日子还好吗?"

兰芝静静地站着,好大功夫没有回答,屋里死一般寂静。仲卿觉得这不像是夫妻别后的重逢,让人十分窒闷。突然,兰芝奔到床前,一头扑到床上,呜呜地哭起来。

房里异样的气氛,兰芝异样的表情,使仲卿压抑了重逢应有的激动。兰芝的泪水一直在流淌着。

"兰芝,你在家里受委屈了?"

兰芝终于止住哭泣,望着仲卿,问道:

"你这次回来,还要走吗?"

仲卿瞅着兰芝那双绝望的眼睛,说:"在郡里当差,岂能说不去就不去?"

"不能多待几天吗?"

"这……"

焦仲卿最怕兰芝问他这句话,因为他这次回来,是要打点一下行装,马上要随魏别驾出远门到中原去,郡里接到朝廷圣命,要太守在十日内,筹集百石粮米,火速押往北方的河内郡,以供军需。此行要经过不少郡县,且途中多有盗贼出没,万一不幸遭遇兵匪,莫说粮食,就是身家性命能否保住,都难以预料。他不愿意把实情告诉兰芝,怕她

The next time Jiao Zhongqing came home, he first paid his respects to his mother, and then went to the room that he and his wife shared. It was empty. As the young man stood wondering where Lanzhi was, the door was flung open behind him, and there she stood.

Zhongqing gave a cry of relief: "Oh, Lanzhi! How have you been since I've been away?"

The girl did not reply for a long time, but just stood mute. The room was as quiet as the grave. Zhongqing was stupefied. Something was amiss. This was not at all like a young wife welcome for her husband after a separation. Suddenly Lanzhi threw herself on the bed, and started to wail.

This left the young man completely dumbfounded. "Lanzhi, what's the matter? Has something gone wrong while I've been away?" He croaked.

When Lanzhi finally managed to stop crying and find her voice, she asked, "Will you go away again?"

Zhongqing, startled by her woebegone expression, stammered, "Well, yes, of course. I'm only on leave from my job at the prefectural capital. Naturally, I'll have to back there."

"Can't you stay longer than you did last time?"

This was what Zhongqing had been dreading to hear. The fact was that he had only been allowed to return home this time to pack some things he would need for travelling on an assignment to the Central Plains. His office had received an imperial order to escort a large amount of grain to the Yellow River area for use by the army. It was to be a long and perilous journey, and the road lay though areas infested with bandits and rebels. There was a good chance that he would lose not only the grain but his life as well. Naturally, he was most reluctant to reveal this to

担惊受怕。此次回来，太守命他两日内必须返回，不得有误。

焦仲卿把妻子搂进怀中，宽慰她说：

"兰芝，咱们的日子才开始呀，往后我天天与你厮守着，到那时，你可不许厌烦我。"

兰芝闭上眼睛，半晌，突然问道：

"你说，咱们天天厮守的日子还要多久？"

"这怎么好说呢？总会有这么一天吧。"

兰芝再也忍不住了，坐起来，对仲卿说：

"仲卿，要么明天我就跟你到郡里去，你我长相厮守；要么你索性把我休回娘家，我实在不想在你家待下去了！"

"怎么能说这样的话？"焦仲卿惊愕地看着兰芝那张憔悴的脸，他听得出，兰芝这话绝不是在跟他撒娇，她是认真讲出来的。

兰芝含着泪，把这一年多里所受的委屈向仲卿倾吐了一番，对于母亲的严厉，仲卿是了解的，但他没想到自己不在家的这些日子里，母亲竟然对兰芝如此尖刻。

他思忖了一会儿，决定明日向母亲求情，缓和一下婆媳关系。

"兰芝，你是个贤淑女子，你知道我对你是十分敬重的。母亲嘛，毕竟是老人，我们让她一步，忍上几年，总有好日子过的。"

Lanzhi. But he could not afford to delay longer than the two days allowed to him by his superior.

He pulled Lanzhi to him, and murmured soothingly: "My dear, our life together has just begun. It won't be too long before we will be together all the time. Until then, you mustn't pester me with questions."

His wife closed her eyes for a while, and then said, "How long will it be before we can be together all the time?"

"Oh, I don't know," replied Zhongqing, somewhat irritated. "But the day will come, I can assure you."

Then, as if she had suddenly made up her mind about something, Lanzhi sat bolt upright, and said, "Zhongqing, either you take me back with you to the prefectural capital tomorrow, or you send me back to my parents. I refuse to stay in this house any longer."

"What on earth are you talking about?" Zhongqing was stunned. Gaping at Lanzhi's pale, drawn face, he knew that she had spoken in deadly earnest.

By way of explanation, Lanzhi, fighting her tears, told him of all that had happened while he had been away, holding nothing back. Zhongqing was well aware of how stern by nature his mother was, but he had never imagined that she could have been so cruel to Lanzhi. He thought over what Lanzhi told him, and decided that on the next day he would have a heart-to-heart talk with his mother and try to smooth relations between her and his heartbroken wife. But first, he had to calm Lanzhi down and talk her out of her ultimatum.

"Lanzhi," he said in his most coaxing tones, "you are a loyal and dutiful woman, and you know that I hold you in the highest esteem. "But, you see, my mother is getting on in years, and we

"仲卿，小辈人礼让老辈人，这道理我再明白不过了，可是你们焦家的媳妇是太难当了。我还是要你回答我方才的话，要么明天我随你到郡里，要么我就回娘家，你看做何选择？"

仲卿欠了欠身说：

"你说的这两种办法我都无法选择。你知道，上天把你赐给了我，我能眼睁睁地让你离开我吗？至于你说要随我到郡里去，一是母亲不会应允，二是我本人也做不到。"

"为什么做不到？"兰芝打断了仲卿的话。

"这，这……"焦仲卿显得十分为难。兰芝觉察出丈夫像是有什么事瞒着她，追问道：

"仲卿，你我既为夫妻，还有什么话不能敞开心扉讲出来呢？"

焦仲卿迟疑了片刻，说道：

"那我就实话对你讲吧。"他把即将远行中原的艰危以及十万火急的时限原原本本地对兰芝讲了一遍，而后无奈地叹道：

"人生在世，不全是吉祥如意，有时也必须去做自己绝不愿做的事啊。此事我本不想对你讲，怕你担心，可你逼得我不得不说。如果你我二人有缘，我就会平安归来，如果我从此一去不返，那你再回娘家不迟。"

兰芝听罢，那颗僵硬的心一下子变软了，她

will just have to put up with her cranky ways for a few years. Then it will be our turn to enjoy the happiness together we deserve."

"My dear, I know perfectly well that young people must defer to their elders. But it is impossible for me to live in the Jiao household as the daughter-in-law any longer. I must insist on your giving me a reply to what I said to you just now: Are you going to take me with you tomorrow or are you going to send me back to my parents' home?"

Zhongqing drew himself up to his full height, and said, stuffily: "This is a choice impossible for me to make. You were bestowed upon me by Heaven itself. How could I just stand by and watch you leave me? As for accompanying me back to the prefectural capital, first of all, my mother would never allow it, and, secondly, ... er ... er ... I can't," he ended lamely.

"What do you mean, you can't?" Lanzhi interjected, a hint of suspicion in her voice.

"Well, it's like this....You see...." Zhongqing was clearly in a quandary, and Lanzhi was not about to let him pull the wool over her eyes.

"Zhongqing, we are husband and wife. How can you have any secrets from me?" she pleaded.

After dithering for a while longer, Zhongqing finally said, "All right, I'll tell you the truth." He thereupon told Lanzhi all about his mission, honestly explaining the dangers involved. At length, he sighed, and said, "Life is not plain sailing, and we can't have things our own way all the time. Believe me, I didn't want to tell you all this, for fear that you might worry. But you left me no alternative. Look at it this way: If we are destined to be together, I will return safe and sound; if I do not come back, then our love was never meant to be, and you should return to your parents'

理解了仲卿的无奈，在外为吏已是身不由己，如果自己在家里再不体谅他，那他的日子岂不比自己更加难过？想到这里，她换了一副口气，说道：

"仲卿，千万别以为我是真的想离开你，为了你，我能继续忍耐，你放心好了。"

"我的好妻子！"仲卿一下子把兰芝搂紧，开始如饥似渴地吻她，而此时已是四更天了。

第二天，兰芝没有起那么早，两人走出房门时，太阳已经爬上了树梢。兰芝顾不上仔细梳洗，便直奔织房而去。望着她瘦瘦的身影，焦仲卿心疼地走进母亲的房中。

仲卿还没把话说完，便被焦母打断了：

"儿啊，你一点也没看清为娘的心思，不是为娘心狠，更不是为娘逼着她起早睡晚，娘把她娶进家门，实指望你不在的时候，她能知冷知热地哄我高兴。可是这女人嘴巴太死，除了叫声娘，就没别的话跟我讲。没事就在屋里弹那破箜篌，我听见就心烦！一让她织布，她就一天到晚扎在织房里，其实就是为了躲着我，偶尔见了我，倒像我欠了她多少银子似的。再说，进门一两年了，也不见她有身孕，这样的媳妇，为娘能喜欢吗？"

"我倒没觉得她对人冷淡呢。"

home straightaway."

Hearing this, Lanzhi's heart melted, along with her steely determination to force her husband's hand. She understood the weight of duty which lay on Zhongqing's shoulders as a civil servant. If she didn't try to ease the burden for him by putting up with conditions at home, she realised, he would suffer just as much as she was suffering. Lanzhi sighed in resignation.

"My dear, please don't think that I would ever think of leaving you," she begged Zhongqing. "Just for your sake, I will put up with anything. Please put your mind at rest."

"Oh, my darling!" Zhongqing sobbed, hugging Lanzhi even tighter to his breast and kissing her hungrily.

The following day, the two of them rose late. After a cursory toilet, Lanzhi rushed to the weaving shed. Meanwhile, haunted by his wife's emaciated countenance, Zhongqing went to have a talk with his mother.

Hardly had he got a word out when Lady Jiao cut him short. "You don't understand the situation at all, young man," she sneered, dismissively. "I'm not harsh in my treatment of her. You must understand that. I don't force her to get up early and go to bed late. When I consented to her joining our family I was hoping that she could be of some comfort and assistance to me when you were away on your official duties. But she's a real sourpuss that one! Surly? Hah! Not a civil word do I get out of her. When she's go nothing better to do, she's sitting in her bedroom twanging that *konghou* of hers, and driving me to distraction with the racket. When I ask her to do a little bit of weaving, she skulks in the weaving shed all day, just to avoid me." The old woman paused, as if to put out of her mind some crushing grievance. But

"你当然觉不出，因为她对你可不冷淡！"焦母对兰芝积怨委实不浅，话里显然带着刺儿。仲卿不敢再言，只好陪着笑说："母亲，待我晚上也劝劝她，您老不要生气才是。"

then, as if to admit defeat in the struggle, burst out with, "On the rare occasions when our paths cross, she treats me as if I owed her money or something! And another thing." — Lady Jiao was in full gallop by this time — "She's been here over a year now, and there's not the slightest sign of pregnancy. How do you expect me to put up with a so-called daughter-in-law like that?"

"I didn't realize that she had been so cruel to you, Mother," wailed the abject Zhongqing.

"Well, no, of course you didn't," huffed the old woman. "That's because she's as nice as pie to you, isn't she?"

The pent-up spite Lady Jiao poured into these words shook her son rigid. He stammered, "Please don't be angry, Mother. I'll talk to her this evening, and then I'm sure everything will be all right."

◎第四章

母子反目生婚变

　　焦仲卿回到郡衙，急匆匆地来到别驾府。别驾姓魏，是个很爽直的北方人。说起这次押粮的差事，还要从他与许太守的关系讲起。

　　许太守是个很会攀附夤缘的人，他原本出身单寒，然而自小聪明，善解人意。年轻时曾随父亲到一位做官的远亲家去拜访，见到那深宅大院，朱门绣户，他心里怦然一动，想着自己何时也能飞黄腾达，过上这种日子。也是凑巧，正当他父子出门时，这位远亲的女儿带着个丫头回家，但见这女子年纪虽轻，却丰乳肥臀，相貌也丑陋无比，比身后的小丫头差远了。从长辈的话里，他了解到这位女子年已十八，尚未婚嫁。他当时心中暗笑：这么丑的姑娘，谁敢与她同床共寝？然而回到家后，他忽然转了念头：像我这样的人，要想荣华富贵，攀附豪门岂不是一条捷径？攀附豪门，莫过于婚姻来得最快。于是他把自己欲娶丑女为妻的想法告诉了父母。未过一年，他真的娶了这位远亲的女儿为妻。从此之后，他真可谓青云直上。岳丈先是帮他举了个孝廉，随后便在郡中为吏。后来岳丈入朝为

Chapter Four

A Mother-Son Quarrel Breaks Up a Marriage

To explain the background of Zhongqing's latest mission, it is first necessary to describe the relationship between Mounted Escort Wei of Lujiang and Jiao Zhongqing's superior, and the military governor of the region Commander Xu.

Commander Xu had been born into an impoverished family. From his childhood he had shown himself to be intelligent, but there was a scheming and manipulative side to his nature. While still quite young, he had accompanied his father on a visit to a distant relative who held an official post. The sight of the imposing mansion this relative lived in and it sumptuous furnishings had stirred an inordinate ambition in the young Xu's heart that some day he too would live in this fashion. One day, while his father was elsewhere, Xu happened to catch sight of his relative's daughter. The girl was fat and ugly, so much so that her drab maid looked a positive beauty beside her. Xu had heard from others that the girl was already 18 years old and unmarried, and it occurred to him that if he married her — for surely no one else would — he would find a shortcut to position and fortune. As soon as he had the opportunity, he put this proposition to his parents, who were delighted at the idea of their son rising in the world by this by no means unorthodox channel, and before a year was out the young people were wed. From that time forth, with the help of his father-in-law's influence and his own cunning, Xu rise through the ranks of officialdom was meteoric. When his

官，他更是一路高升。年方四十，已经坐到了庐江
太守的宝座上。

　　许太守与夫人独生一子，此儿的血统颇似舅
家，自幼肥硕，渐渐长大成人，那蠢笨之态，更非
同龄人可比。若只是身材像他母亲倒也无妨，可惜
此儿智力也颇低下，父母为教此儿，专门请了一位
饱学先生，谁知一年下来，也没认下几个字。太守
大人见孺子不可教，也就不再作无用之功，只想为
他订门亲事，有个孙子，聊作膝下之欢。魏别驾家
中恰有一女，虽然说不上天姿国色，模样倒也齐
整。此女年龄与许公子相若，于是许太守遣人为儿
子说媒。魏别驾原本看不起许太守的为人，又亲睹
其子那副尊容，当然舍不得把女儿嫁给他。为此，
许太守心里非常不快。恰好朝廷传旨要押粮赴中
原，于是许太守便把这件本该由主簿管的"美差"
交给了魏别驾。别驾在汉朝虽然也算是个不小的
官儿，但只是太守之副，要听命于太守。魏别驾心
知肚明，这趟差全是因为拒婚而遭的报复。

　　在众多的属吏中，魏别驾对焦仲卿独有所爱。
他原本想把女儿许配给焦仲卿，不想还没来得及
提亲，仲卿已经婚娶，于是魏别驾便不再考虑此
事，但对焦仲卿的信赖却依然如旧。他认为焦仲卿
处事平和，与物无违，办事牢靠，凡事交给他办，
便十分放心。因而此次中原之行，他挑选焦仲卿随

father-in-law eventually acquired a position at court, Xu was made military governor of Lujiang.

Commander Xu had only one child, a son who took after his mother, inasmuch as he was obese and dull-witted. He was always well behind other boys his age at learning, and even the best tutors were scarcely able to cudgel any knowledge into his head. Commander Xu despaired of his son ever amounting to anything, and fixed his hopes on getting the boy married off somehow, and having a grandson to dote on. Now Mounted Escort Wei had a daughter of about the same age as the commander's son. She could not be described as a raving beauty, but she was neat and attractive enough, and Commander Xu decided that she would make a suitable daughter-in-law. The prefect, however, held the commander in contempt, and loathed his dolt of a son, and sent Xu's go-between packing without even hearing the man out. Pricked by this slight, the commander seized his chance for revenge when an order came from the imperial court for an escort to convey grain from Lujiang Prefecture to the Central Plains. He foisted off this dangerous mission, which by rights was his own responsibility onto Mounted Escort Wei, who was nominally under his authority. The prefect, of course, was well aware that this was retaliation for his refusal to marry his daughter to the commander's son, but he was powerless to refuse.

Of all his colleagues and subordinates, Mounted Escort Wei was fondest of Jiao Zhongqing. He had wanted to betroth his daughter to young Jiao, but, as we have seen, his go-between had arrived to late, for Zhongqing was already married. Nevertheless, Wei continued to hold Zhongqing in high esteem, impressed by the lad's diligence reliability and competence. So it seemed the most sensible thing to do to entrust Zhongqing with

行，也是情理之中的事。

　　兰芝送走仲卿回到家中，没敢到婆婆房中，便赶紧溜入织房。轧轧的机声陪她度过了这个长长的夏日，直到明月正中，她才回到一灯如豆的空房。夏日的夜晚原本闷热难熬，而兰芝望着这空寂的房间，心中却不时腾起一股凉意。为了仲卿，她决定继续那无休无止的繁重劳作，直到等他平安归来。

　　日复一日，她的身体越来越疲惫，然而这种疲惫还好忍受，最令她不能忍受的，正是那不事劳作的漫漫长夜。这一天，兰芝破例在黄昏时便离开了织房，因为她近来已经达到一日两匹的极限，她不怕婆婆的察看。回到房中，她摘下挂在墙上的箜篌，箜篌上沾满了尘土。她把尘土仔细地擦去，缓缓地拨响了琴弦。

　　夏末的黄昏，蛙声鼓噪，蝉鸣聒耳，一曲《孔雀东南飞》飘出帘栊，呜呜咽咽，如泣如诉，压过了蛙声，压过了蝉鸣，在空中盘旋。一曲未终，焦母猛地推门进来，没好气地嚷道："大热的天你不好生歇着，还要弹这破琴来烦我，放下！"

　　兰芝早就想到会有这样的结果，她不想再委屈自己，因为无论她如何起早贪黑，累死累活，不多言，不多语，总也讨不到婆婆的欢心。她平静地说："母亲，你自管歇息，媳妇不过弹弹箜篌，也

this important job of escorting the grain.

After she had seen her husband off again, Lanzhi avoided her mother-in-law's room, and stayed all day in the weaving shed. It was only when the moon was high in the sky that she returned to her gloomy bedroom. The summer nights were stuffy, and Lanzhi found them difficult to pass — indeed they wearied her more than the laborious days — but she had made up her mind to endure any hardship, fixing her mind on the day Zhongqing should return

One day, she left off her work at dusk, earlier than usual. She did not fear a scolding from Lady Jiao, as she had finished a record two whole bolts of cloth that day. Back in her room, she took down her *konghou*, carefully wiped away the dust that had accumulated on it during many months of misuse, and began to play it softly.

The plaintive notes of "The Peacock flies Southeast" drifted out through the window into the night, like sobbings of anguish, hushing the clamor of the cicadas and frogs. But before the tune finished, Lady Jiao burst into the room, bawling, "Nobody can get a minute's peace with you making that racket! Stop twanging that thing at once!"

Lanzhi was not surprised by this interruption, for she had long realized that no matter how she tried she could never please the old woman. She replied, with perfect composure: "Mother-in-law, why don't you go and rest? I'm not playing loudly. I don't know why you have to keep flying into a temper."

Lady Jiao was dumbfounded. She had been used to having the whip hand over her daughter-in-law, and the last thing she had expected was that this meek and timorous girl would answer

没做什么对不起焦家的错事，您老何至于生这么大的气？"

"……"焦母一向霸道，更习惯了兰芝的低眉敛气，万万没想到兰芝也会顶嘴，一时不知说什么好，愣在那里。

兰芝第一次在婆婆面前说了一句顺气的话，心里陡然泛起一阵满足和欣快，她在等着婆婆下一步的反应，看她究竟能把自己怎样。

焦母虽然气急败坏，但不愿失去自己的威严："我看你这么有闲心，还是不累。去，织布去！"

"我今天已经织了两匹，不去了！"兰芝声音不高，却是一字一板，针锋相对。

"没了规矩了！梅梅，来！把她拖到织房去，今晚不让她睡！我倒要看看乾坤能不能倒着转！"

"怎么啦？这是怎么啦？"梅梅一副哭腔，显然是被吓坏了。她怯怯地向嫂嫂房里走来。

兰芝冷冷地笑了一声，从容地站起身，把筻筷挂回墙上，走回床前，放下幔帐，坐在帐前。

梅梅来到兰芝面前，央求说："嫂嫂，看在我的面上，你先回织房吧。嫂嫂，我陪着你！"说罢，呜呜地哭了起来。

兰芝把梅梅轻轻地拉到床边，给她擦擦眼泪：

"梅梅，不哭，没有你的事。"

"嫂嫂，我求你。"

back.

Lanzhi, on the other hand, felt a surge of elation at having
spoken her mind for the first time to the old termagant. Smugly,
she waited to see what Lady Jiao would do next.

Despite this temporary setback, the old woman struggled to
reassert her authority.

"What do you think you're doing, lazing around here like
this?" she barked. "You can't possibly be tired already. Get back
to your loom!"

"I've already woven two whole rolls," replied Lanzhi, calmly
but pointedly. "I'm not going to do any more weaving today."

"We'll see about that, you impertinent creature," shot back
Lady Jiao. "Meimei, come here!" she yelled over her shoulder.
"Take her back to the weaving shed, and make sure she works
all night. The world's not going to be turned upside down in my
house — not if I can help it! "

Meimei crept in, wailing in alarm. "What's the matter? What's
happened?" she cried.

Lanzhi gave a mirthless laugh, stood up in a leisurely fashion,
hung her *konghou* back on the wall, and went to sit on the bed.

Meimei approached her, and pleaded, "Lanzhi, for my sake,
please come with me to the weaving shed." She sobbed pite-
ously as she said this.

Lanzhi drew her gently to her, and made her sit beside her
on the bed. Wiping the girl's tears away, she urged her: "Meimei,
please don't cry. This has nothing to do with you."

"Oh, please, I beg you," Meimei appealed again.

"No!" Lanzhi said, in a tone so firm that the other two could
hardly believe their ears. "No more weaving for me tonight. I know
perfectly well that I'm the daughter-in-law, and I can assure you

"不！"兰芝的倔强此时显现出来，"嫂嫂今晚不再织布。不过你放心，嫂嫂是焦家的媳妇，不会不干活儿光吃饭的。可今天，说什么我也不去了。"

面对兰芝的强硬，焦母自觉丢了面子，可一时又毫无办法，嘴里不停地骂着走了。

从此之后，兰芝与婆婆像是成了陌路之人。焦母何曾受过这样的顶撞，在屋里闷了两日，兰芝也不来认错，虽然天天还去织房，却不像以前那样悄悄地溜进去，也不再低着头了。

已是第三天了，没吃早饭的刘兰芝正默默地投着梭子，突然听到院里传来婆婆声嘶力竭的叫喊：

"我叫你弹！我叫你再弹！"

"叭"的一声。兰芝仿佛意识到什么，急忙奔出来，一眼望见院中的石凳前，她那张珍存了十几年的箜篌已经碎成了几截。她不顾一切地扑在箜篌上，止不住抽泣起来。好大一会儿，她才缓缓起身，眼里充满了怒火，盯着焦母，半晌也没有眨一眨眼。

中秋已过，焦仲卿终于又回到家中。他此次中原之行虽然历尽艰难，也还算有惊无险。许太守是个很会做表面文章的人，对焦仲卿揄扬之外，还破

that I have not the slightest intention of not earning my keep around here. But I've done enough weaving for one day, and I'm not doing any more, and that's final!"

This little speech convinced Lady Jiao that she had lost the confrontation. Seething with rage and muttering dark curses, she stormed out of the room.

From that time on, Lanzhi and her mother-in-law made a great show of ignoring each other's existence. Lady Jiao shut herself away in her room, fuming with anger at this unexpected defiance, for two days, waiting for Lanzhi to come and apologize. She waited in vain. Lanzhi, for her part, went to the weaving shed every day as usual. But unlike before, she didn't slink there with lowered head.

On the third day, Lanzhi was at the loom weaving away even before she had had breakfast when out of the blue she heard her mother-in-law shrieking in the courtyard: "I'll teach you to go strumming this thing! So you think you're going to try creating this hideous row again, do you?"

There followed an ear-splitting cracking sound. Lanzhi leapt to her feet, with an awesome realization of what was happening. She raced out of the weaving shed, and saw, scattered all over the courtyard, pieces of her beloved *konghou*, which she had cherished for ten years. It had apparently been smashed on a stone bench nearby. In a paroxysm of anguish, she threw herself on the fragments of the instrument. Finally, she rose, and fixed her blazing eyes on her mother-in-law.

Just after the Mid-Autumn Festival had passed, Jiao Zhongqing returned from his mission to the Central Plains. The

例给他放了两旬长假。焦仲卿非常高兴，可以有这样长的时间与爱妻从容相聚了，他哪里会想到家中已成一团乱麻。

他快马加鞭奔回了家，推开院门，喊了一声："母亲，我回来了！"

听到是仲卿的声音，焦母迎了上去，一边给儿子掸着身上的尘土，一边念叨着：

"累了吧，快去歇着，我去给你烧茶。"

仲卿笑吟吟地说道："母亲，您先到屋里坐，让兰芝去烧茶。"

"还是我去吧，你媳妇我可不敢使唤。"

焦仲卿听母亲话里有话，一时不知怎么应对。母亲转身离开，他一眼望见兰芝呆呆地扶着织房的门框，便向她走去。

焦母并不知道儿子去中原的事，也就没觉得仲卿这次回家与往日有什么不同。

兰芝这些日子却饱受煎熬，每天晚上都要向上天祈祷，希望丈夫不要发生什么意外。如今果然盼到丈夫平安归来，她那一颗悬着的心才算放下。她不理会婆婆的冷言冷语，只要仲卿在，就是幸福的。

"一路上还好吧？"兰芝问道。

"好，好，虽然辛苦，好在没遇到什么危险，真是上苍降福了。"

journey had been fraught with danger, but the young man fortunately managed to complete it unscathed. Commander Xu, being a man who loved ostentatious gestures, lavished praise upon Zhongqing for his successful completion of the escort, and gave him an unprecedented 20 days' vacation. The young man was delighted at the prospect of being able to spend so long with his beloved. Little did he suspect that he would find an ominous situation at home.

As soon as he could get away, he rode like the wind, never stopping until he reached his mother's house. Pushing open the courtyard gate, he called out, "Mother, I'm home!"

Lady Jiao hurried out to greet him, brushing the dust from his clothing and saying at the same time: "You must be tired after your journey, son. Why don't you sit down and rest, while I make you some tea?"

Zhongqing smiled, somewhat confused. "But mother," he protested, "you should rest too. Let Lanzhi make the tea."

"Oh, no. I'd better do it," the old woman replied. "I don't dare to order my daughter-in-law around these days."

Zhongqing gaped in astonishment as his mother went off to make the tea. At that moment, he spied Lanzhi leaning against the door frame of the weaving shed. He went up to her.

Lady Jiao was unaware of her son's perilous journey to the Central Plains, and she thought that his home visit this time would be just as brief as before. In the meantime, Lanzhi had been smoldering with pent-up anger and praying fervently to Heaven that her husband would return safe and sound. Seeing him appear before her very eyes, all her resentment melted from her heart, all the unkind words her mother-in-law had spoken to her were forgotten in a flash, and she was filled with happiness.

焦仲卿此时只想好好看看兰芝，发现兰芝又憔悴了许多。

"兰芝，这阵子身体有什么不舒服吗？"

"还好。"兰芝没有马上把自己与婆婆之间的争吵告诉仲卿，因为她不想让丈夫一进门就感到不愉快。

"仲卿，茶好了，来饮茶吧。"

仲卿答应了一声，拉着兰芝的手说："走，咱们饮茶去。"

没想到兰芝却说："你去吧。"回身又进了织房。仲卿心中纳闷，走进上房，对母亲说：

"我这么久没回家，就叫兰芝一同过来说说话吧。"

"她呀，她才不会来跟我说话呢！"

"母亲，兰芝是不是让您老人家生气了？"

"她都快把为娘气死了！"焦母像受了天大的委屈，竟从怀中掏出一方帕子，开始擦拭眼泪。

仲卿上次回来便已知道母亲与兰芝不甚相合，但没想到会闹到如此地步。他心里开始发慌："母亲，兰芝有什么不对，你可以说她，可别把身子气坏了。"

"说她？我敢吗！"

见母亲如此伤心，仲卿没敢追问原因，但只看

"How was your trip?" she asked.

"All right," Zhongqing replied, nonchalantly. "There were some rough spots, but no real danger, thanks be to God."

He was preoccupied with gazing at Lanzhi, and disturbed to find her pale and wan.

"Have you been feeling all right while I've been away?" he inquired.

"Well, yes, I suppose so." Lanzhi was loath to break the news of her quarrel with Lady Jiao to Zhongqing and upset him before he had had time to rest after his long journey.

Just then, the old woman called out, "Zhongqing, tea's ready!"

The young man responded, and then, taking his wife by the hand, said, "Lanzhi, let's go and have a cup of tea together."

To his great surprise, Lanzhi replied with a curt, "You go," and, turning on her heel, entered the weaving shed. Downcast, Zhongqing went into the living room, where he complained to his mother: "After all this time away, I was hoping to have a long talk with Lanzhi."

"Her?" snorted the old woman. "She won't come and talk while I'm here."

"Mother, has Lanzhi done something to annoy you?"

"She's just about to vex me into my grave, that's all," was the savage reply, following which Lady Jiao took a handkerchief out, and dabbed her eyes with it.

Zhongqing had already sensed on his previous visit home that his mother and his wife did not get on too well together. But he had never suspected that they would fall out like this. It was with a rising sense of panic that he asked, "But mother, if she does something wrong you can speak to her about it. You mustn't upset yourself needlessly."

眼前的情景，就知道婆媳的矛盾不易调和。他记得兰芝说过想离开家的事，便试探着问母亲：

"兰芝的脾气是有点倔，要不行，我在郡城赁间房，免得她老待在家里惹您不快。"

"啊？"焦母听罢，叫了一声，"你怎么能想出这样的鬼主意来？这不明明是娶了媳妇不要娘吗？"

"哪有这个意思？"仲卿连忙辩解道，"我是看您老总不高兴，心疼您老人家呀！"

"胡说！心疼我，怎么不说把我接到郡城去？"焦母更生气了，又开始哭天抹泪："你爹爹下世早，我实指望你能步步升迁，娶个好媳妇帮我操持，把日子过得像个样儿，也好对得起你那九泉之下的爹爹啊！"

"母亲，升迁哪有那么容易，你不大把地送银两，谁来提拔你？像咱们这般家道中落，哪有那么多的银子！赶上这么个兵慌马乱的年头，能在郡里当个差，凑凑合合维持生计，就算是谢天谢地了。媳妇有些不是，毕竟是小辈人，您老多耽待些，我看兰芝整日里纺线织布，也算是个会过日子的女人。"

"你总是护着她来气我！"焦母也憋了很长时间没人诉说，如今尽管与儿子话不投机，到底是自己的亲生骨肉，说起话来不必顾忌。"她刚进门

"Me? Speak to her? I wouldn't dare!"

Seeing his mother in this state of distress, Zhongqing felt that he'd better not question the old woman any further as to the reason for the estrangement. He had a foreboding that it was not going to be easy to restore harmony in the house, especially when he remembered how, the last time he was at home, Lanzhi had mentioned that she wanted to leave and go back to her family. He decided to try to soothe the old woman's ruffled feelings by saying, "Oh mother, you know that Lanzhi has a stubborn streak in her. I'll tell you what I'll do: I'll rent a place in Lujiang and take her there to live with me. That will stop her getting on your nerves all the time."

"What sort of ridiculous talk is that?" yelled Lady Jiao. "I suppose you mean that now you've got a wife you don't need your old mother any more. Is that it?"

"Oh, mother! Really! How can you say such a thing?" Zhongqing was shocked at this allegation. "I was just concerned about your health and happiness, that's all."

"What rubbish!" snarled his mother. "If you were really concerned about me you would invite me to come and live with you in Lujiang." Then, in mounting fury, she wailed, "After your father's untimely death, I fervently hoped you would rise in the world, step by step, and marry a nice girl, so that we could live a respectable life, and I could face your father in the next world."

"Mother, it's not that easy to 'rise in the world,' as you put it," Zhongqing reminded her, in a calm but bitter tone. "You need a tidy sum of money to do that, and in our family's circumstances that's out of the question. Getting an official position, even as a lowly clerk like I am, which allows us to keep body and soul together, was a Heaven-sent blessing in these troubled times.

时还算拘谨，可最近越来越不像样，不但懒惰许多，还跟我大吵大闹，为娘实在是咽不下这口气啊！"

上次回来兰芝说受不了，这次回来娘又说咽不下，仲卿真感到左右为难。在他看来，兰芝文静寡言，勤于纺绩，对自己体贴入微，已经是个很懂事的媳妇了，他真不知道母亲想要的是什么样的人。他站起身来想走。

"哪儿去？"焦母厉声地问。

"去劝劝兰芝。"仲卿闷闷地答道。

"她是个听劝的人吗？坐下，听为娘说。"

仲卿无奈，只好垂着头重新坐定。桌上的茶已经凉了，他虽然干渴，现在也没心思喝了。

"仲卿，娘养你这么大不容易……"

"这我知道的。"仲卿打断了母亲，因为这句话他听过不知多少遍了。"母亲，我也太不容易了，您跟兰芝这样水火不容，让儿子怎样才是？您就不为儿子想想吗？"

"我怎么不为你想？为娘早已为你想好了！"焦母一句话把仲卿堵了回去。

这使他感到有些愕然，不觉抬起头来望着母亲，问道：

"娘，你为我想好了什么？"

"为娘要你把刘兰芝休了，再为你寻头好亲

As for Lanzhi, you must remember, Mother, that she is very young and inexperienced. You should make allowances for her. Anyway, she seems to spend all day in the weaving shed, so she must be making her contribution to the household income."

"You're always taking her side just to vex me," grumbled Lady Jiao. Then, suddenly she poured out all her pent-up hatred of Lanzhi on the head of her hapless son:

"When she first entered this house she was Oh-so-nice-and charming, wasn't she? But that didn't last long, did it? She's been getting lazier and lazier, and — not only that — she's constantly picking fights with me, and that insolent tongue of hers, I tell you, is driving me to distraction. I can't put up with it a moment longer, and that's that!"

Zhongqing remembered that the last time he had returned home, it had been Lanzhi who had given him an ultimatum. Now his mother was doing the same thing. He felt that he was in a desperate quandary. At the same time, he couldn't understand how his mother could have become so antagonistic to Lanzhi, who seemed to him to be refined, quiet, hard-working and devoted to her husband. The young man stood up.

"Where do you think you are going?" demanded Lady Jiao.

"To reason with Lanzhi," Zhongqing replied, miserably.

"Reason?" hooted his mother. "With her? Don't be ridiculous! Sit down; I haven't finished."

Zhongqing slumped back in his seat. The tea on the table had long since grown cold. Despite his weariness and thirst, Zhongqing had not even thought of touching it.

His mother launched into another tirade. "Zhongqing, I had a hard time bringing you up...."

"Yes, yes, Mother, I know," her son interrupted. He had, in

事。"

"啊?"焦仲卿大吃一惊,他万万没想到母亲会说出这种话来,有些不相信自己的耳朵,"您说什么?"

"休了刘兰芝!"

焦母言辞坚决,不容置辩,看来这想法在她脑子里已经不是三日五日了。

"这不行!"焦仲卿脑子里嗡嗡了好一阵,才清醒过来。他深爱兰芝,她的文静,她的才华,她的热情,都是别的女子难得具备的。母亲整日里把她关在织房里,已经把她变成了一个织妇,这本已经够残酷的了,如今还要将她休弃,焦仲卿怎么也不能接受。

"怎么不行?"焦母气呼呼地反问,"你年纪轻轻见过什么世面,一个刘兰芝就把你迷住了?你怎么就不问问娘要为你再娶一个什么样的好媳妇?"

"我不相信还有比兰芝更好的女人。谁我也不要,我就要兰芝!"

"好啊,怪不得那女人那么大胆跟我作对,原来是你在后边给她撑腰!我,我不活了!"焦母突然站起来,冲到仲卿面前,揪住仲卿的前襟,瞪着眼睛问道:

"你说,我还是不是你娘!"

fact, received this piece of information many times before, and didn't want to hear it again. "But it's not easy for me either, what with you and Lanzhi fighting like cats and dogs. What on earth do you expect me to do. Have you ever thought about me?"

"Thought about you?" screeched Lady Jiao. "Well, I should think I have! As your mother, I've never been allowed to think of anything else, have I?" This little exaggeration took Zhongqing somewhat aback. With misgivings, he asked, "Well, mother, what do you want me to do?"

"Get rid of Lanzhi," was the unhesitating reply. "Then I'll find a better wife for you."

"What?" Zhongqing squeaked, hardly able to believe his ears.

"Get rid of her, I said." The old woman's uncompromising tone left no doubt that she had been mulling this course of action for some time.

Zhongqing felt his head reeling. "But that's impossible," he croaked. Then the true picture emerged in his mind. He loved Lanzhi for her refined and warm character, qualities in which she was far superior to any other woman. His mother must be jealous of her; that's why she shut her up in the weaving shed all day, to make a miserable drudge of her. Now she wanted to drive her away. It was insufferable.

"What do you mean 'impossible'?" Lady Jiao countered. "What can you know about the world at your age? She's got you wrapped around her little finger. Besides, you haven't even asked me what kind of wife I have in mind for you, have you?"

"I don't believe there can be another woman to compare with Lanzhi," Zhongqing was adamant. "I don't want another woman. I only want Lanzhi."

"I see. No wonder she's been so brazen in her dealings with

焦仲卿从来没见过母亲如此大怒，吓得说话也不利索了：

"母亲，母亲……你这是怎么了？"

"你如果还认我是你娘，那就要听为娘的话，我一天也不想再见刘兰芝那副哭丧脸了！"

"那也得容我先跟她说说呀！"

院子里，织机的撞击声和秋蝉的鸣叫声混合为一，显得沉闷而肃杀。焦仲卿欲行又止地蹭到织房门口，他不知如何面对兰芝。

这时，梅梅从外面回来了，见到哥哥，高兴得又蹦又跳：

"哥，我说我今天早上怎么左眼皮直跳，原来是你回来了！"

"哎。"仲卿心不在焉地答了一声。

他一向待小妹很好，他们兄妹早年丧父，相依为命，他从来对妹妹都是爱护有加。

梅梅也早就习惯了在哥哥面前撒娇耍赖，她对哥哥又敬又爱，在她看来，哥哥是天底下最可依赖的人。自从哥哥出门，嫂嫂进家，她虽不能常和哥哥在一起，但她对这个新嫂嫂也很满意，嫂嫂就是哥哥的化身，所以每当母亲与嫂嫂发生冲突时，她总是不自觉地护着嫂嫂。她还从未见过哥哥对她如此冷淡。

"梅梅，你先去帮娘做饭吧。"

me." Lady Jiao assumed an air of aggrieved resignation. "You've been secretly backing her to deliberately annoy me. That's it, isn't it? Oh, I can't go on living like this!"

Zhongqing had never seen his mother as angry as this, and stammered in his dismay: "But, Mother ... what, what has got into you?"

"If you still regard me as your mother, you will do as I say. And I'm telling you that I never want to see that little sourpuss's face again. And that's final!"

"Well, let me go and talk to her," Zhongqing pleaded.

Out in the courtyard, the air was filled with a dull and mournful chorus consisting of the steady clacking sound of the shuttle and the rising and falling chattering of the cicadas. Zhongqing hesitated at the door to the weaving shed, wondering how he was going to break the news of his mother's tantrums to Lanzhi.

At that moment, Meimei come out of the weaving shed, and, seeing Zhongqing there, came beaming and bouncing toward him.

"Brother, you're back!" she cried. "I've been looking out for you all morning."

Zhongqing and Meimei had been very close ever since their father died. He had always taken special care of her, and the girl had never hesitated to show her fondness for her elder brother. Meimei both loved and respected Zhongqing, and felt that he was the one person in the whole world she could rely on. When he married and went away to take up his official post, Meimei had transferred her affection for him temporarily to Lanzhi, and felt that her loyalty lay with her sister-in-law in clashes between Lanzhi and Lady Jiao. So when Zhongqing replied to her warm welcome with a curt grunt, she was flabbergasted.

看到哥哥这样，梅梅也不敢再多嘴，赶紧溜进了厨房。

焦仲卿走进织房，呆呆地看着兰芝织布，半晌，才说："兰芝，你太辛苦了。"

兰芝没有抬头，眼泪却淌了下来。

晚饭后，焦仲卿与刘兰芝双双回到自己的房里。

仲卿一直不说话，兰芝觉得奇怪，先开口道："仲卿，把你这一路上的事讲给我听听，好吗？"她太想听仲卿说话了。

"嗨！也没什么，无非是风餐露宿、提心吊胆八个字而已。"仲卿苦笑了一声。

"我知道。"兰芝轻声地说，把身体挨近仲卿，像从前一样地依偎在他怀中，她渴望仲卿抚摸她的头，她的脸，她的胸。可是，他却没有。

兰芝静静地听着仲卿的心跳。她没有听到婆婆和丈夫的交谈，自然理解不了仲卿此刻的心绪，可怜的兰芝还在等待着与仲卿离开这个令她窒息的家，自由自在地比翼双飞呢！

仲卿终于开口了：

"兰芝，弹一曲箜篌吧。"

兰芝从仲卿怀中坐起来，惆怅地说：

"仲卿，你再也不会听到我弹箜篌了。"

Without any pretence at ceremony, Zhongqing then said, "Meimei, go and help mother with the dinner."

Not daring to ask her brother any questions, the girl slunk off to the kitchen.

Zhonqing entered the weaving shed, and stood for a long time watching his wife at work. When he finally addressed her, she turned and looked at him with tear-filled eyes.

After dinner, Zhongqing and Lanzhi retired to their bedroom. The young man was silent for so long that Lanzhi was finally forced to speak. More to break the embarrassing silence than anything else, she asked him to tell her about his trip to the Central Plains.

With a sardonic smile, Zhongqing said, "Oh, there's nothing much to tell. Just eating and sleeping in the wilds. A lot of worry and fretting. That's all."

Lanzhi moved closer, and snuggled up against her husband, as they been used to doing. She was eager for him to stroke her hair, her face, her breasts. But Zhongqing made no such move.

Lanzhi could feel Zhongqing's heart beating wildly. She was puzzled, for she knew nothing of the altercation that morning between the mother and son. She was longing for Zhongqing to take her away from that suffocating household, so that they could spread their wings and soar together!

After what seemed like ages, Zhongqing spoke again.

"Lanzhi, play a tune on the *konghou* for me."

She sat up, and said, in a heartbroken voice: "Zhongqing, you'll never hear me play the *konghou* again."

"What?"

"Your mother smashed my *konghou*."

"为什么？"

"箜篌被你娘摔碎了！"

"为什么？这是为什么？"焦仲卿的情绪一下子激动起来，在房间了踱着，"这究竟是为什么！"

身处两难之中的焦仲卿在兰芝面前始终说不出母亲要把她休回家的话，他宁可认为母亲只是一时的气话而已。在母亲面前，又极力劝慰，说兰芝已经知错愿改，今后不会无端惹母亲生气。好在他这一次在家住的时间长，有他在中间调和，婆媳倒也表面上相安了数日。看看两旬长假转眼将满，第二天仲卿便要回郡，晚上，焦母把仲卿叫到自己房里，说：

"看在你的面子上，为娘再忍耐些，若是这女人再敢在我面前放肆，我可绝不再留情面！"

"是是。"焦仲卿但求安稳，不管娘的话多么难听，他也只有忍耐。

再说焦母既已有了休媳的心思，对兰芝越来越看不上眼，尽管兰芝日日陪着小心，还是免不了马勺碰锅沿。

这一日又是春暖花开的季节，兰芝很想念自己的母亲，也很想念鸳鸯集的山山水水，她已经劳累太久，忍耐太久，所以向焦母请求回娘家去待几天。焦母一听，心里便有九分不快，她没说答应也

"What on earth for? Why did she do that?" Zhongqing was horrified at what he heard. He leapt to his feet, and paced in a torment of agitation around the room. "But, why?" he kept crying.

Zhongqing kept from Lanzhi the news that his mother wanted him to discard her. He then proceeded to pacify the old woman, now that he had a fairly long leave of absence, and managed to bring about, if not a reconciliation then certainly a truce, between her and Lanzhi.

On the evening before Zhongqing was to return to his post, his mother summoned him to her room, and said, "I warn you that if that slip of a girl dares to step out of line with me again while you're away, she'll regret the day she was born."

"Everything will be all right, Mother," the young man hastened to assure her. "You know that I've spoken to her, and she understands that she must be careful of her behavior in future."

Lady Jiao, however, was still intent on driving Lanzhi from the house, and after Zhongqing left, she let her feelings of enmity for the girl become more and more obvious. No matter how deferential and unassuming Lanzhi was careful to be, it seemed that everything she did grated on the old woman's nerves. One balmy spring day, just as the flowers were beginning to bloom, Lanzhi found herself thinking of her mother, and the hills and waters of her native Yuanyang. The constant toil and nervous tension she had undergone in her mother-in-law's house were beginning to take their toll, and she longed for the familiar warmth of her old home. When she timidly asked Lady Jiao if she could take a few days off to visit her mother, the spiteful old woman said neither yes nor no. She simply snarled, "Have you finished that cloth you were supposed to be making?"

没说不答应，只是问兰芝：

"这批线织完了吗？"

"织完了。"兰芝生怕婆婆嫌她怠慢，所以近些天，每天都织到夜深，昨天更是织到鸡鸣。她感到自己已经无可挑剔了，才敢向婆婆提及此事。

焦母卧在床上，眼皮耷拉着，不冷不热地说："外姓人倒底是指望不上。"

"娘。"兰芝隐忍着，好言说道："媳妇自从进了焦家，一直没回过家，只是惦记着母亲的身体，才敢向您张这一回口。"

小姑梅梅端着面汤走进来，恰好听见她们的话，宽解母亲说："娘，家里有我呢，就让嫂嫂回娘家看看吧。"

"我还不至于没人伺候。"焦母怒气未消，"你这位嫂嫂就算身在咱家，不还是我女儿为我端茶煮饭吗？我何尝指望她来？不过是看出她那颗冷冰冰的心罢了。"

"娘，嫂嫂不是整日里织布吗，人家也没闲着。"

"顶嘴！"焦母指桑骂槐地说："真是把你惯坏了！老老实实地在家待着，哪儿也不许去！"

兰芝听出这话是说给她的，心里委屈到极点，她决定不再与婆婆理论，扭身回到自己房中，粗粗地打点了一番，便出了焦家，径自往鸳鸯集去了。

这下可把焦母气了个半死，她真想追出去狠

Lanzhi, anticipating that Lady Jiao would blame her for thinking of a holiday before even completing her work, had been working late into the night to finish her latest task, and the previous night had worked until cockcrow. So she was sure that the old woman could not possibly find any fault with her.

Lady Jiao lay back on her bed, and looked at her daughter-in-law from under drooping eyelids.

"You can never rely on outsiders," was her puzzling comment.

"It is only because I am worried about my mother's health that I have been so bold as to ask you to excuse me for a few days, that's all," Lanzhi said in a deferential tone.

Just then, Meimei entered, with a bowl of soup. She had been eavesdropping, and had heard the above exchange. "Mother, I'm here to look after you," she said eagerly. "Why not let Lanzhi go and visit her old home for a few days?"

"I'm not short of someone to wait on me," the old woman retorted. "It's having a daughter-in-law who thinks of nothing but her old home and is as frigid as ice when it comes to doing her duty by her old mother-in-law that distresses me."

"But, Mother, you force Lanzhi to spend all day weaving," protested Meimei. "She has no time to pay proper attention to you."

"Shut your mouth!" bawled Lady Jiao. Although she faced Meimei, it was obvious that her barbs were aimed at Lanzhi. "She's not going anywhere. Her place is right here!"

This vicious outburst made Lanzhi's mind up for her. Knowing that it was useless to try to argue with the old woman, she strode out of the room, hastily threw some things she would need for her journey together, and marched out of the Jiao house in the direction of Yuanyang.

狠地抽打兰芝一顿，可惜腰疼，难于行走，她扶住院门破口大骂。

梅梅怎么也劝不住，急得直哭。恰在这时，梅梅看见罗敷从远处经过，像是捞了根救命的稻草一般：

"罗敷姐姐，快来劝劝俺娘吧。"

"呦，伯母，您这是跟谁生气呀？"

"嫂嫂回娘家了，我娘不高兴了。"

焦母一见到罗敷，像是遇见了知己，索性一把鼻涕一把泪地数落起兰芝的不敬不孝，说到后来，竟有些咬牙切齿：

"这回我一定要休了她，让刘家脸面丢尽！"

罗敷偷眼窥见焦母铁青的脸，猜想她一定是早有此心了。不过她还是好言相劝：

"伯母，您别生气，兰芝就是有些不是，您老尽可以教训她。若要休她回去，难道让仲卿哥哥孤身一人过日子吗？"

"我早为仲卿选好新人了。"焦母听罢罗敷的话，像是受了刺激，冲口把心里话抖了出来。

罗敷是个聪明透顶的姑娘，她早就感觉出焦母对自己的亲热非同一般，她猜想这个新人可能就是自己。此时她心里不知是种什么滋味，从小兰芝就跟自己相好，怎么能鸠占鹊巢，将她的丈夫据为己有？如果这样，日后如何面对兰芝？可是反

When she saw this, Lady Jiao flew into a towering rage. Her first instinct was to rush after the girl, and give her a good thrashing, but her chronic backache prevented her from doing so. So she hobbled to the courtyard gate, and stood there leaning on it and screeching at the top of her voice. In vain did the distraught Meimei try to calm her. Glancing around in desperation, Meimei saw Luofu approaching in the distance, and, like a drowning man clutching at a straw, called out to her: "Luofu, come here quickly! Help me with my mother. She's upset."

Luofu hurried up to them, and asked what the matter was.

"Lanzhi's run away, and it's given my mother quite a turn."

As if a bosom friend had appeared on the spot, Lady Jiao poured her heart out to Luofu. To the accompaniment of a storm of weeping, Luofu heard all about the perfidy of that ungrateful daughter-in-law. Finally, Lady Jiao ground her teeth ominously, and hissed, "I'll get rid of the little hussy for good this time. That Liu family's going to lose all the face it's got. You just see if it doesn't!"

Stealing a glance at the old woman's livid face, Luofu guessed that she had had such a scheme up her sleeve for a long time already. She addressed Lady Jiao soothingly: "Madame, you mustn't get yourself so worked up. Lanzhi has her shortcomings, I know, but you should be able to straighten her out. If you expel her from the house, how will Zhongqing be able to manage all alone?"

"I've already chosen a new wife for him," Lady Jiao retorted, stung at Luofu's mild rebuke.

Luofu was an astute girl, and she had long been aware that Lady Jiao liked her. So it was not difficult for her to guess that the "new wife" the old woman had in mind was herself. The thought

过来一想，自己也没做错什么事，造成这种后果的是兰芝自己。上天或许原本就是错配了姻缘，兰芝或许原本就不该拥有仲卿。想到这里，她心中坦然了许多。

刘兰芝赌气出了家门，一直朝鸳鸯集走。县城离鸳鸯集那么远，她走一天也未必能走到。可她顾不了那么多，就是累死，她也不愿再回焦家。

大约走了十来里路，她远远看到前面有个骑马的人很像仲卿，于是加快脚步迎了上去。二人越走越近，焦仲卿见迎面走来的竟是兰芝，觉得诧异，他翻身下马，匆匆地赶到兰芝面前，问道："你这是往哪儿去呀？"

刘兰芝也绝没想到能在路上遇见焦仲卿，她真想抱住丈夫大哭一场，可她还是抑制住了激动的情绪。

焦仲卿此次回来并不是定期的休假，而是到居巢县王县令那里为太守送一件重要文书。她从兰芝满腹委屈的诉说中知道：母亲与兰芝的关系已经难以维系下去。他劝兰芝随他暂回家中，并信誓旦旦地告诉兰芝，既然婆媳势同水火，他决心说服母亲允许他在郡城赁房居住，把兰芝接到城里去。

焦仲卿与刘兰芝回到家时，罗敷已经离开焦

troubled her at first, for she remembered how she and Lanzhi
had been close friends since childhood. How could she play the
"cuckoo in the nest" by snatching her husband away? How could
she ever face her best friend again if she did that? On the other
hand, she reasoned, prompted by a little voice somewhere in-
side her, it wasn't her fault that this marriage was rocky. Oh no,
surely Lanzhi only had herself to blame, didn't she? Perhaps
Heaven never intended Lanzhi and Zhongqing to be soul mates
in the first place? Luofu found this last surmise surprisingly
comforting.

Yuanyang was more than a day's journey away, but Lanzhi,
fuelled by pent-up fury, was determined that even if the alterna-
tive was to die of fatigue on the road she would never return to
that hateful Jiao household.

She had gone about ten *li* or so when in the distance she
spied a rider. With a gasp of delight, she recognized Zhongqing
coming toward her. The young man spurred his horse, and as he
drew near, leapt from its back and dashed to his wife.

"Lanzhi, where are you going?" he cried.

Lanzhi's first impulse was to throw herself in Zhongqing's
arms, and cry her heart out. But with a superhuman effort she
suppressed her feelings for the time being.

Zhongqing's return this time was not on leave of absence;
he was conveying an important document to Prefect Wang, who
was acting as the commander of Juchao County. He had all along
feared that it would be difficult for Lanzhi and his mother to main-
tain cordial relations, but he persuaded Lanzhi to return home
with him, promising her that if she would only put up with the
situation for a little while he would try to talk his mother into allow-

家。焦母见兰芝又回到家中，也顾不得儿子的脸面，便大吼起来：

"叫她滚，叫她滚！"

"母亲，"仲卿连忙相劝，"我这就带她走，我在郡城赁间房，不让她在家惹您生气。"

"什么？你好大的胆子！"焦母从座上立起身来，"我要她滚出焦家，是要休了她。你是我儿子，你不能走，你怎么敢跟我说这种不忠不孝的混账话？"

刘兰芝悄悄回到自己房中，她这是第一次听到婆婆要休自己的话。这一回她彻底明白了：她与仲卿的无限恩爱，很快会化为乌有了。这本该是她心里最难过的一刻，可是不知为什么，此时的她突然感到一种如释重负的轻松。她静静地坐在床边，就是新婚初夜坐的那个地方。婆婆还在叫嚷，仲卿还在劝阻，加上梅梅的哭声，整个院里乱糟糟的。但这些嘈杂似乎离兰芝越来越远，对于她来说，这些已经无足轻重了。

兰芝一天也没吃饭了，日晡之时，梅梅很懂事地把饭菜给嫂嫂端进来，央求说："嫂嫂，你多少吃一点吧！"

"好妹妹，嫂嫂不饿，你端回去吧。"

"嫂嫂。"梅梅又抽泣起来。

焦仲卿拖着疲惫的脚步跨进这曾经给他无限

ing him to take Lanzhi to live with him in Lujiang.

Luofu had already left when Zhongqing and Lanzhi reached home. As soon as Lady Jiao saw her daughter-in-law, despite the presence of her son, she began to bawl: "Get rid of her! Get rid of her!"

"Mother," Zhongqing hastily interceded, "I've come to take her away, so that she's no longer in your way. I'm going to rent a house in Lujiang, where the two of us can live together."

"What? You've got a nerve!" the old woman yelled, springing from her chair. "I want her out of this house this minute. Do you hear? Send her back to her old home, where she belongs. You are my son; how can you abandon me? What sort of disgraceful, unnatural talk have you come here with?"

Hearing this, Lanzhi finally realized that her mother-in-law wanted Zhongqing to divorce her. She crept back to her old room. So the wonderful love that she and Zhongqing had enjoyed had come to nothing in the end. That was the most hurtful thing she could imagine. And yet, somehow she felt lighter at heart for the knowledge. She sat in silence in the same place she had sat on her wedding night. She could hear Lady Jiao still ranting and raving, and Zhongqing trying in vain to calm her down. On top of it all, she could hear Meimei crying. The courtyard was in an uproar, but it was as though the row had nothing to do with her.

It became late afternoon, and Lanzhi had had nothing to eat all day. The thoughtful Meimei appeared with a tray of food, and urged her sister-in-law to eat. But Lanzhi said she was not hungry. At this, Meimei began to cry again.

At that moment, Zhongqing entered with dragging footsteps, the room where he had once found so much comfort. He found Lanzhi sitting quietly, staring at the bare wall where her beloved

温情的新房，兰芝还静静地坐在床边，面朝着墙，那面曾经挂着箜篌，如今却空荡荡的墙。

焦仲卿颓唐地坐在椅子上，一只胳膊无力地搭在桌面，另一只手撑住自己的额头。

"仲卿，"兰芝的语气显得镇静而平和，"有些女儿家的话我还没有来得及跟你说，因为我想把它埋在心里更久些，让它像陈年的老酒。可是，现在我特别想对你说。"

"兰芝，想说你就说吧。"

"你知道，自从咱们在鸳鸯集邂逅一面，我就认定你一定就是我的夫君，你的影子在我心里像扎住了根，挥之不去，这种痛苦折磨了我一年多，上天才真的把你交给了我，这绝不是巧合，这是命中注定。可是后来，我渐渐地明白了，其实你并不真的属于我，我知道迟早会有这么一天，上天还会把你从我身边收回去，这也是命。仲卿，你不用为难。我们都服从命运吧，因为任何人都不可能与命运抗争。"

"兰芝，我舍不得你！"仲卿听罢，语调哽咽了，心中无限酸楚。他想起两人相处不多的日子里，兰芝那一颦一笑，举手投足，都与他梦想中的女子一模一样。他这一辈子不追名，不逐利，惟想有一个琴瑟相和的女子相伴终身。无奈世间的事就是如此不尽人意，他始终不明白为什么珠联璧

konghou had once hung.

Zhongqing slumped exhausted into a chair. He sat there, one arm stretched lifelessly across a table, and the other propping up his weary head.

"Zhongqing," Lanzhi said in a low monotone. "There is something that has been on my mind for a long time. It is a matter that has been fermenting inside me like old wine, and now, I feel, is the time to reveal it to you."

"What is it? Say what you have to say."

"You know that ever since we met by chance in Yuanyang I have been convinced that you were destined to be my husband. Your image has been implanted in my heart. All the sufferings that I have undergone in the past year or so I endured them because I thought that Heaven had given you to me. I accepted our union as decreed by fate. But as time went by I began to realize the truth — that in fact you were not destined for me. And so, I knew that sooner or later Heaven would take you away from me. Zhongqing, don't be sad. We must all follow our destinies, because no one can defy fate."

"Lanzhi, I can't give you up!" Zhongqing uttered a choking cry. He felt desolate, as memories of their short time together came flooding back; how every look, every gesture of Lanzhi had been those of the ideal woman of his dreams. Fame and fortune meant nothing to the young man. All he desired was a soul mate. It tortured him to realize that in this world he could not have his heart's desire, and it baffled him how the woman who was the perfect match for him could become so hateful in his mother's eyes.

"I don't want to give you up, either," said Lanzhi, "but there's no help for it. We cannot oppose a parent's wish. But if you truly

合的神仙鸳侣，在母亲眼里就成为宿世不解的冤家对头！

"我也舍不得你。"兰芝静静地说，"可是这没有用，父母之命谁能违拗，如果你心里有我，那就来世再做夫妻吧。"

焦仲卿心中更凄凉了，突然，他抬起身，匆匆地走出房门，又来到母亲房中。

"母亲，孩儿求你了，千万不要把兰芝休了！"

"休得再说，这种不懂事的女子，我绝不能留她！"母亲的话斩钉截铁，毫无商量的余地。无论仲卿如何央求，甚至跪在母亲面前，也无济于事，焦母终究没有退让一步。

"仲卿，别这么没情没绪的，男子汉休妻是件光彩的事，丢人的是刘家，你难过什么？你怎么就不问问为娘为你选的新人是谁？"焦母全然不理会儿子此时的感受，只管说着，"就是秦郎中家的罗敷。这孩子又漂亮，又勤快，嘴又甜，一见她我就高兴。"

焦仲卿头脑里一片空白。

"母亲你不要说了，兰芝辛辛苦苦地在咱们家过了两年，你说休就把她休了？母亲不要再逼迫孩儿了，我不会再娶。"

"那焦家的香火怎么往下传？"

"香火？"焦仲卿苦笑了一声，"我的心都冷透

love me, we will be together as man and wife in the next life."

These words chilled Zhongqing's heart even further. Suddenly, he jumped to his feet, and rushed out, in the direction of his mother's room.

"Mother," he wailed, "I beg you not to drive Lanzhi away."

"My mind's made up," the old woman said obstinately. "I can't put up with that uncouth hussy. She's not staying here!" No matter how her son cajoled and pleaded, on his knees too, Lady Jiao did not budge one inch from her position that Lanzhi must go.

"Zhongqing, don't be so squeamish," she said contemptuously. "Turning such a wife out of doors is the right and proper thing to do. Besides, she's a Liu, isn't she? Well, then. Where's the difficulty? And another thing: Why haven't you asked me which girl I've picked to be your new wife?" Lady Jiao was completely oblivious to her son's feelings on this matter, simply rattling on and on. "Well, I'll tell you anyway. She's Doctor Qin's daughter Luofu. She's pretty, hard-working and nicely spoken. I liked her the very minute I set eyes on her."

The young man's mind went completely blank with astonishment when he heard this. When he recovered his wits somewhat, he stammered, "Mother, how can you talk like that? Think of all that Lanzhi's suffered here for the past two years. You can't throw her out just like that. No, please don't press me any longer. I declare that I will not re-marry."

"Then, who will there be to sacrifice to the ancestors of the Jiao family after you're gone?"

"Sacrifice to the ancestors?" Zhongqing gave a mirthless guffaw. "I couldn't care less about the ancestors."

"Well, even if you don't, I do!" said the old woman, shocked

了，哪里还顾得上什么香火！"

"你不顾我要顾！"焦母又生起气来，"焦家就你这么一根独苗，我岂能任凭你一意孤行！刘兰芝是个不下蛋的鸡，这一点我早就看出来了，你还拿她当宝贝，傻瓜！"

"母亲，你不能这么说！这一两年，我与兰芝守在一起总共才几日？我说要把她接到郡城，你老又不允，日日逼着她纺线织布……"

"照你这么说，倒全成了我的不是了！"

"若是休了兰芝，我终身不娶！"焦仲卿平生第一次向母亲怒吼。

"好大胆！"焦母火冒三丈，"娘还做不了你的主？休不休刘兰芝得听我的，娶不娶罗敷，也由不得你！"

焦仲卿突然觉得灯影中的母亲渐渐变成了一头面目狰狞的猛兽，张开大口，像要吞噬自己。

at this impiety. "You are the last of the line. You have a duty to do, and I'll see to it that you do it! Liu Lanzhi is barren. I realized that a long time ago, but you are still doting on her, aren't you? You're a fool. That's what you are."

"Mother, please don't talk like that. In the past two years since we've been married, Lanzhi and I have only had a few days to be together. I wanted to take her to live with me in the prefectural capital, but you refused to allow it. Instead, you kept her here weaving all day."

"Oh, so I suppose it's all my fault, isn't it?"

"I'm telling you, Mother, if you send Lanzhi away, I'll never marry anyone else." It was the first time in his life that Zhongqing had addressed his mother in such a frigidly angry tone.

The old woman flew into a towering rage. "How dare you?" she screamed. "I am your mother, and you will do as I say. If I say that you will divorce Liu Lanzhi, you will divorce Liu Lanzhi. And if I tell you to marry Qin Luofu, that's precisely what you will do!"

It seemed to Zhongqing that in the flickering light given out by the oil lamp his mother's face resembled that of some snarling beast, its jaws extended wide to tear and rend him.

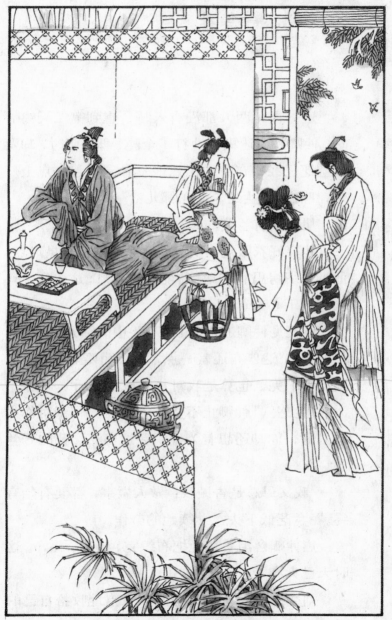

◎第五章
兰芝含悲辞焦母

　　这一夜，两人都没有入睡，直到第二天鸡啼时，仲卿才迷迷糊糊地打了个盹，再睁眼时，却发现兰芝已经不在身边了。他一骨碌爬起来点上灯烛，叫道："兰芝，你在哪儿？"

　　屋里没有兰芝的身影。

　　他穿好衣服走出房门，天上还闪着繁星点点。他听到织房里有响动，窗前还亮着灯，这才吁了口气，放下心来。

　　兰芝见仲卿进来，没停下手中的活儿，只抬头对他说："这匹布还差一点，我天明要上路，走之前把它织完，也算是我对焦家挽定最后一个结。"

　　"兰芝！"仲卿止不住热泪盈眶，"母亲对你如此刻薄，你却还想着为她织完这匹布，我的好兰芝！"

　　"我父母总是告诫我：做人做事，都要有始有终。"兰芝低下头，继续她的劳作。

　　焦仲卿含泪看着她把布织完，卸下，叠好。这时天已大亮了。

　　刘兰芝回到房中，开始一点点地收拾自己的

Chapter Five

Lanzhi Bids a Grim Farewell to Lady Jiao

That night, there was no sleep for either Zhongqing or Lanzhi. At cockcrow, the young man stirred, bleary-eyed from a doze, to find that his wife was no longer beside him. He fumbled to light the lamp, and called out, "Lanzhi, where are you?"

There was no sign of her anywhere in the room.

Hastily dressing, Zhongqing hurried outside. Stars were still twinkling in the sky, but already the sound of the loom could be heard from the weaving shed, through the window of which a light gleamed. Zhongqing breathed a sigh of relief.

When Zhongqing entered the weaving shed, Lanzhi did not stop her work, but raising her head, said to him: "I have to finish this piece of cloth before I set out at first light. Then, I will have fulfilled my duty to your mother."

The young man could not stop the tears flooding his eyes. "Lanzhi, your devotion to my mother despite the harsh way she has treated you is sublime!" he croaked.

"My parents admonished me to be strict and proper in my conduct always," Lanzhi replied. Then she lowered her head, and continued with her work.

Tearfully, Zhongqing watched her finish the piece of cloth, unload it from the loom, and put it on a pile of other bolts of fabric.

By this time, day had dawned.

Lanzhi returned to their room, and began to get her luggage ready. Zhongqing, slumped in a chair, watched her through glazed

箱笼。焦仲卿像是瘫了一样颓坐在椅子上，先是哽咽，渐渐地哭出声来。这一次兰芝没有来劝他，因为这哭声是爱的另一种表达方式，她愿意听他痛痛快快地哭。

兰芝把箱笼里面的东西一件件地拿出来。

"仲卿，你过来。"兰芝轻声地呼唤。

仲卿缓步来到兰芝面前，用饱含泪水的眼睛望着她。

"仲卿啊，我知道你是个重情义，轻财货的仁人君子，我的这些陪嫁，你还没有来得及细看。如今我要走了，你总该过过目了。"兰芝说着，打开一个包袱，拿出一顶红罗帐，四角垂挂着棱形的檀香囊。

"这香囊是我自己绣的，看，漂亮不漂亮？"

仲卿攥住一只香囊，贴在自己胸前，对兰芝说：

"我们把它挂起来吧，日后我睡在这里，就像看见了你。其他东西，你先带回家去好好保存着，待我们重新团聚时，再……"

"不用了，你若是再娶，新夫人未必看得上眼。到那时，若是新夫人嫌弃，你就把这顶帐子连同其他物件都施舍给穷人吧。"兰芝把箱中的东西一件件地交待完，才像是了却了心事般吁了一口气。

焦仲卿双手捂住脸，过了好大功夫，才说：

eyes. Before long, he started to sob, and then abandoned himself to a storm of weeping. But, for the first time, his wife did not hasten over to comfort him; she wanted to hear the sound of him weeping.

One by one, Lanzhi started to bring out the things she was going to take with her.

"Zhongqing, come here," she summoned him, as if unconcerned with his anguish.

The other approached her, heavy-footed and heavy-eyed.

"My dear, I know that you are a gentleman rich in principles and poor in goods. I don't think you have had a chance to examine the things I brought with me as a dowry. Now that I'm about to leave you, you might as well cast your eyes over this." As she spoke, she unfolded a cloth wrapper, and took out a length of red gauze. From each of the four corners there hung pyramid-shaped sachet smelling of sandalwood.

"Pretty, isn't it?" Lanzhi asked.

Zhongqing took one of the sachets, and pressed it to his breast. "I want to hang it up here, and then when I go to sleep, I will sleep dreaming of you," he said. "Take all the other things back home with you, and keep them safe. Then, when we are together once more.... Once more...."

"What is the use?" Lanzhi said with a scowl. "When you remarry, your new bride won't want to look at this. In that case, you can give it — and all the rest of my dowry — to the poor as charity." So saying, she handed over to him the rest of her dowry, bit by bit, and then, as if a great load had been lifted from her mind, she sighed.

Zhongqing remained silent for a long while, hiding his face in his hands. Then he said, "Lanzhi, your words make me feel as

"兰芝,你不要这样说,我的心都快要碎了!我已经跟母亲说过,除了你,我谁也不会再娶。魏别驾不久就要调任豫章太守,我若是能随行,就把你接到豫章,山高水远,天各一方,到那时母亲也奈何我们不得了。"

兰芝苦笑了一声。

"别难过了,我要梳洗了,你去给我打盆清水来,好吗?"

洗过脸,兰芝打开妆匣,把铜镜插在座上,精心地往脸上施了层淡淡的粉,又用胭脂膏把嘴唇细细地涂了涂。然后拿起梳子,慢慢地梳理着满头乌云,挽了一个高髻。她看见仲卿在注视着自己,低声问了一句:"仲卿,我美吗?"

焦仲卿没有回答,伸手拿起笔:"兰芝,我也来学一学前朝的张敞,为你画画眉吧。"

兰芝莞尔一笑。

梳洗完毕,兰芝又拿出一件精美的绣襦。

"这是什么图案?"仲卿虽然心中悲伤,但还是认真地端详着,他看到上面绣着疏疏落落的蓝色花卉,问道。

"这是孔雀兰。在我们相遇的地方,开满了这种兰花。我当时绣它的时候,本想作为一个纪念,永远珍藏。没想到真的嫁了你。"她把绣襦在胸前比量了一下,望着屋顶,不无惆怅地说:"这件衣

though my heart is about to shatter. I have already told my mother that I will have no one but you for my wife. Mounted Escort Wei will soon be transferred to Yuzhang, as prefect. If I can go with him, I want to take you too. It is a place far from here. My mother will never find us there."

But Lanzhi's only response was a bitter laugh.

"Oh, don't trouble yourself," she said. "Listen, I have to get washed and changed, so will you be good enough to fetch a basin of clean water?"

After completing her ablutions, Lanzhi opened her jewel box, took out a bronze mirror, and set it up on a stand. Then she proceeded to powder her face lightly, and dab her lips with rouge. Then she took a brush, and slowly arranged her hair into a jet-black cloud around her head. She turned to Zhongqing, who was still staring, mesmerized, at her. "Am I beautiful?" she asked.

Instead of answering, Zhongqing picked up a brush. "Lanzhi, shall I paint your eyebrows?"

Lanzhi smiled.

She finished her toilet, and then held up a superbly made brocaded blouse.

"What is that pattern on it?" Zhongqing asked, attracted to the design and forgetting his heartbreak for the moment. Inspecting the blouse closely, he found it decorated with a scattering of blue flowers.

"Those flowers are peacock orchids," Lanzhi explained. "They were blooming all over in that place where we first met. I sewed them as a remembrance which I could treasure always. I never thought that I would end up actually marrying you."

She held up the blouse, to measure it against herself. Then, gazing at the ceiling, she sighed, "It took me a whole year to

服是我花了整整一年的功夫精心绣成的，如果我能穿着它与你同行在街上，满街的人都来看咱们，你一个翩翩君子，我一个锦绣玉人，旁人该是多么羡慕！唉，可惜呀，因为忙着织布，你又不常在家，竟然没有一次上身的机会。今天，我要把它穿回去。"

妆扮完了的刘兰芝像换了一个人，身上的绣襦特别合体，把那一束纤腰衬托得袅娜多姿，下身穿了一条淡蓝色的长裙，更显出她那修长的身材。脸上的粉黛虽然施得很淡，但唇如朱丹，眼若点漆，一笑之间，皓齿晶莹，真如仙女一般。在仲卿眼里，新婚时的妻子也没有如此美丽动人，他不禁心如刀割。

兰芝款移莲步，来到婆婆房中。焦母斜靠在床头，旁边的机凳上，小姑梅梅默默无语地噙着眼泪，正在给母亲捶腿。

兰芝向焦母施了一礼，说：

"婆母受媳妇最后一拜。媳妇从小长在乡间，不甚懂得贵人家的规矩，多承婆母照顾，媳妇会把婆母的情义牢记在心，永世不忘。媳妇如今一去，永无还日，再想孝敬婆婆也没有机会了。还望婆母养好身体，少些烦恼，福寿双全，也算是媳妇的一点祝愿吧！"

梅梅哭出声来，她走到兰芝身边，仰起泪脸

complete embroidering this garment. Oh, if only I could wear it walking down the street with you, how the people would all stare at the elegant young scholar and his graceful lady! How they would envy us! What a pity that I was so busy weaving and you were so seldom at home that we never had such a chance. But I'm going to wear this today, as I leave this place."

When she had finished dressing and putting on makeup, Lanzhi looked like a different person. The embroidered blouse fitted her perfectly, accentuating her narrow waist. Below it extended a light-blue skirt, hugging her slim figure. Through the light dusting of powder on her face gleamed her black, lustrous eyes and ruby-red lips. When she smiled, there was a dazzling flash of pearly-white teeth. To Zhongqing, Lanzhi was even more beautiful than she had been on their wedding night. And he felt as though a sharp knife was turning in his heart.

Lanzhi paced on her little lotus feet to her mother-in-law's room. There, she found the old woman sprawled on the bed. Beside her, seated on a low stool, Meimei, with a tearful countenance, was massaging her mother's legs.

Lanzhi bowed to Lady Jiao, and said, "Mother-in-law, I have come to take my final leave of you. Being a child born in a rustic hamlet, I am unused to the ways of genteel households. I will never forget the care you have shown for me. I am leaving for good, and I regret that I will no more have the opportunity of showing my devotion to you. I sincerely hope that you will look after your health, and not allow yourself to worry. My twin hopes for you are long life and happiness."

At this, Meimei burst into tears, and rushed to Lanzhi's side. Looking up at her sister-in-law with a tears-stained face, she said, plaintively: "Are you really leaving us?"

问：

"嫂嫂，你真的要走？"

"梅梅，好妹妹，还记得刚来的时候吗？那时你可没有这么高，也没有这么秀气呀。"兰芝把小姑搂在怀里，任凭她的泪水打湿自己的绣襦。

"梅梅，我走了以后，你还会有新嫂嫂的。我们姐妹相处了这么久，嫂嫂有什么不周到的地方，你会原谅嫂嫂的，是吧？"

梅梅哭得更伤心了。

"叫你哥哥去雇车。"焦母不耐烦，打断了她们的话。

"哥哥已经去了。"

兰芝重新回到自己的房中，她此行要带走的只有一个包袱，只是几件换洗的衣物而已。她望着曾与仲卿共枕同眠的雕花木床，摸一摸床边刚刚卸下的那顶稍显陈旧的幔帐，这一切都给她留下过美好的回忆。她又望望墙上那曾经挂着箜篌的地方，如今空荡荡的，什么也没有了。"古人常说琴瑟和谐，"她怔怔地想着，"破琴绝弦，这本身就不是一个好兆头，这或许就是母亲常说的命。"

焦仲卿雇好车回来，兰芝拎起了包袱。

"兰芝，你还有什么话要对我说吗？"

"仲卿，我这次回家，肯定烦闷无比，若是那

"Meimei you've grown so tall and poised since I first moved here. You're quite a young lady." And she hugged the girl to her, allowing her tears to wet the front of her precious blouse.

"After I leave," Lanzhi said, softly, "you will have a new sister-in-law. I hope you will forgive me for anything I failed to do for you in the time we lived together."

But Meimei only cried more heartbreakingly than ever to hear this.

"Tell your brother to go and hire a carriage," Lady Jiao's harsh voice interrupted this tender scene.

"He has already gone to hire one," Meimei sobbed.

Lanzhi returned to her room. She was only going to take one bundle of clothes with her on her journey. As she picked it up and prepared to leave, she took one last look at the carved wooden bed where she had shared a pillow with Zhongqing. She stroked the bed curtain, and a host of bitter-sweet memories came flooding back. But then she looked at the wall where her *konghou* had hung. It was bare and drab. She remembered with sadness the ancient saying about a man and wife being as fit for each other as a zither and lute. "But my zither is smashed and its strings are broken," she thought to herself. "I must have been born ill-fated. Or perhaps this was what my mother often warned me my lot would be."

When Zhongqing returned with the carriage, he asked his wife: "Lanzhi, have you anything else to say to me?"

"If I only had my *konghou*, I could perhaps console myself a little during the lonely days that lie ahead. But, alas, it lies here in pieces in the Jiao household. I have only one request to make of you, and that is that you buy me another *konghou* at some convenient time. Then I can play it, and think of you."

张箜篌还在，我还可以借它来消愁解闷，可惜它已碎在焦家。我只求你一件事，日后若得方便，替我再买一张箜篌，我弹起它，就像面对着你，行吗？"

"别说一件，就是千件万件，我也会答应你！"仲卿接过兰芝的包袱，一眼瞥见桌子上的公文，吓出一身冷汗，这公文本该昨天就送到县衙，没想到家事突变，使他险些忘掉了公干。他把兰芝扶上车，对车夫说：

"到城外大路口停下来等我，我随后就到。"

车轮吱吱呀呀地滚动起来，梅梅站在大门口，突然大哭起来，还没哭几声，便被母亲狠狠地拉进院里，"嘭"地一声，大门被关上了。

焦仲卿急急忙忙到县衙了却了公务，便飞身上马，直奔城外。出了城门，就看见兰芝的车子在前面等着，他加了一鞭，飞快地朝前赶去。

上路了，兰芝在车中不时掀开帘子凝视着骑在马上的仲卿，只见他低垂着头，表情木然。车轮轧轧，马蹄嗯嗯，伴着这对棒打的鸳鸯越走越远。

眼看着接近了鸳鸯集，刘兰芝让车子拐了个弯，停在古桥边。她缓缓地下了车向前走去，又走到当初与罗敷、艳艳一起玩耍的地方。

焦仲卿也牵着马走过来，他知道此刻兰芝的

"Well, of course I will," cried the young man. As he took the bundle from Lanzhi's hand, his eye was caught by an official-looking message on the table. He broke into a cold sweat: It must have come from the county magistracy the previous day, and he had been so absorbed in his family troubles that he had almost overlooked it completely.

Zhongqing hastily helped Lanzhi into the carriage, and ordered the driver to wait for him just beyond the city wall.

As the carriage rumbled away, Meimei, weeping uncontrollably, watched it go from the gateway. But she did not even have time to see it disappear into the distance, before Lady Jiao dragged her roughly back inside, and slammed the gate shut.

In the meantime, Zhongqing dashed to the magistracy, completed the official business that awaited him at top speed, and then rode like the wind to the city gate. When he spied the carriage halted on the road ahead, he lashed his horse into a full gallop.

On the way out of the city, Lanzhi had kept raising the blind and gazing backwards out of the carriage window, eager to catch sight of Zhongqing, and now she saw him, his head lowered and a grim expression on his face. They traveled on together, toward Yuanyang. All that could be heard was the rumbling of the cart wheels and the clip-clop of the horses' hooves.

When they reached Yuanyang, Lanzhi directed the carriage driver to halt near the old bridge. She alighted, and sauntered to the spot where she had been playing with Luofu and Yanyan on that fateful day. Zhongqing dismounted, and followed her, leading his horse. He was quite aware of what was going through his wife's mind at this moment.

"Lanzhi," he said, "You must not worry. Nothing can shake my determination in this matter. I am as unmovable as a rock.

心情。

"兰芝，你切不必多想，我的心如磐石之坚，不会动摇。你只管耐心地等我数日。"

"仲卿，婚姻大事非同儿戏，我是个得了休书的人，你若是不移旧情，那你母亲将如何待你？"

"母亲不过是一时负气，待我们到了豫章，沉上一段时间，她的气消一消，也就只能依从我了。"仲卿这话显然经过了深思熟虑。

兰芝略一沉吟，说道：

"可我如今回到家中，颜面全无，我的母亲和兄长能容我吗？我担心她们会很快把我嫁出去，这些你想过吗？"

焦仲卿微微一怔，说心里话，他辗转一夜，只想着如何对付母亲，却没想到兰芝回家后的处境。可魏别驾究竟何时调任，又不是他焦仲卿左右得了的。既使魏别驾调任，他能否随行，也还不得而知。

"兰芝，我相信上天终会成全有情眷属。只要你守住自身，我焦仲卿今生今世绝不负你！"

兰芝被仲卿的真情感动了，她是相信仲卿的，君子之言，一诺千金。况且婚后这几年情深意笃，兰芝当然心中有数。

"仲卿，兰芝今生遇见你，已是死而无憾了。你

Please make up your mind to wait for me patiently — just for a few days." Lanzhi replied, "My dear, marriage is not a child's game. I am a woman who has been expelled from my husband's house. If you still cling to your old affection for me, how do you think your mother will treat you?"

"Oh, my mother tends to fly off the handle from time to time. But after you and I have been at Yuzhang for a while, she'll calm down and get over her bad temper." It was clear that he had spent some time cobbling this argument together.

Lanzhi hesitated while she mulled over his words. Then she said, "But you don't realize that I am returning home in disgrace. What will my mother and brother say? I'm afraid that they will try to get me married off to somebody else in a hurry, before the scandal spreads. Have you thought about that?"

Zhongqing gave a start of alarm. The truth was that he had been too busy worrying about how to handle his own mother to think of anything else. It had quite slipped his mind that Lanzhi's mother and brother would have their own grievance about the way the girl had been abused. Moreover, he did not know when Mounted Escort Wei would be making his journey to his new post at Yuzhang, or even if he would be allowed to accompany him. Zhongqing made another attempt to reassure Lanzhi.

"My darling, I firmly believe that marriages really are made in Heaven. We are destined for each other. Preserve your purity, and you can rest assured that I will never forsake you in this life."

Lanzhi was moved by his sincerity. Wasn't there an old saying that a gentleman-scholar's word was worth a thousand pieces of gold? Besides, she had been married to Zhongqing long enough to be thoroughly convinced of his ardent love for her.

"My dear, now that I have found you in this life, I would die

既然有此誓言，我自然会守身如玉。你有磐石之心，我有蒲苇之意。磐石最坚固，蒲苇最柔韧。兰芝有死而已，上苍为证！"

"好，我们一言为定。"

二人深情地对视了许久，恋恋而别。仲卿骑上马，头也不敢回，一路扬镳，如逃而去。

兰芝母亲见兰芝回来，初时还以为是回家探望，及至兰芝说明原委，母亲才大吃一惊：

"兰芝啊，你可给为娘丢尽脸面了！我从小教你纺线织布，裁剪缝纫，教你弹琴识字，知书达礼，又给你找个好人家，实指望你能做个好媳妇。如今却被人家休了。天啊，我这是造了什么孽呀！"她不由得捶胸顿足地大哭起来。

"娘，女儿对不起您老人家。"兰芝低下头羞惭地说，"可是母亲也该相信女儿，不是女儿不侍奉丈夫，不孝敬婆婆，实在是做焦家的媳妇太难，你不知道女儿都累成什么样子了。"

"苦命的孩子！"兰芝母亲捶着床，"往后你可怎么办呀？"

"娘，"兰芝也开始啜泣，"您不要为我担心，听天由命吧。"

不大会儿，哥哥继宗回来了，进门后见到兰芝，显出几分高兴，问了句：

without regret. Because you have given me your pledge, I will keep myself pure for you. You compare yourself to a rock. Well, I compare myself to a cattail reed. A rock may be hard, but a cattail reed is tough and pliant. Even if I should die, Heaven will be the witness to my fidelity." "Good," said Zhongqing, relieved. "We are bound by a mutual vow then."

He and his wife gazed at each other with deep emotion for a long time, in silence. Finally, with the utmost reluctance, they moved apart. Zhongqing mounted his horse, and, nor daring to look back, galloped away furiously, as if fleeing from something.

Lanzhi's mother's first reaction upon seeing her daughter again was delight, thinking that this was a surprise visit. Her joy soon turned to horror, when Lanzhi told her the real reason.

"What disgrace you've brought upon this family!" she cried. "Ever since you were little, I taught you everything that a wife should know: I showed you how to weave and do needlework; I taught you how to play the zither and how to read; I instilled a perfect sense of decorum into you. I even arranged a fine marriage for you, in the full confidence that you would make a perfect bride. And now, what? You've been turned out of your husband's house like a stray cat! Oh, Heaven above! What terrible sin have I committed that I should have to endure this calamity?" She followed up this plaint with a beating of the breast, a stamping of the feet and a storm of tears.

"Mother, I'm so terribly sorry," cried Lanzhi, hanging her head in mortification. "But you've got to believe me; I was never remiss in my wifely duties, or less than perfectly respectful to my mother-in-law. It was just that my life in that Jiao household was intolerable. You don't know how I suffered."

"妹子回来了，待几日？"

一句话问得兰芝不知如何应答，只好含糊其辞地敷衍了一声：

"哥哥累了吧，歇息歇息。"

继宗很兴奋，说：

"我正要去郡里找妹夫。前几天，我有个朋友到郡上去办事，打听到妹夫与魏别驾关系甚好，我想能不能让妹夫替我说句话，让我也到郡里当个小差？"

"他只是一介小吏，哪有这么大面子。"兰芝推托道。

刘继宗不死心，反倒来了兴致，"哎，你可别小看了焦仲卿，魏别驾既然很器重他，像我这样的区区小事，赏个面子也就办了，有什么难处？"

兰芝母亲听得不耐烦，没好气地说：

"别说焦仲卿是个小吏，就是太守，也帮不上你的忙了！"

"什么意思？"

"你妹妹被焦家休了。"母亲又气又恨地说。

继宗"啊"了一声，一双眼直盯在兰芝脸上，"这，这，嗨！做官的没他娘一个好人。焦仲卿算个什么东西，也想摆官架势休妻纳妾。"

"哥哥，此事全不怪仲卿。"兰芝本想给哥哥解释几句，但继宗却没好气地说：

孔/雀/东/南/飞/

"You wretched girl!" shouted her mother, this time pummeling the bed in rage. "What do you think you're going to do now?"

Lanzhi choked back her own tears. "Mother, please don't worry. Heaven will take care of everything."

Before long, Lanzhi's elder brother Jizong came home. As soon as he saw Lanzhi, he beamed with glee, and asked her how long she intended to stay. Lanzhi evaded this embarrassing question by saying, "Jizong, you must be tired. Please go and rest."

But the lad seemed to be too excited about something to take any notice of this, and burbled, "You know, I was just about to go and visit your husband. A few days ago, a friend of mine came back from a business trip to Lujiang, and he said that he'd heard that your husband was a favorite of Mounted Escort Wei. So I immediately thought that he might put in a good word for me, so that I can get an official post there too."

"Oh, my husband is only a minor clerk," Lanzhi stammered, in painful confusion. "He has no influence at all."

Jizong, however, was not at all put off by this. "Come now, Lanzhi," he coaxed, "you are being far too modest about Jiao Zhongqing. I know that Mounted Escort Wei thinks highly of him. He will have no trouble doing a little favor like this for me."

At this point, his mother lost all patience. "Whether Jiao Zhongqing is a minor clerk or the boss of the whole office makes no difference!" she snarled. "He can't help you now."

"What do you mean?" the young man cried, in dismay.

"Your sister's been kicked out of the Jiao household. That's what I mean."

Jizong whirled round on Lanzhi, and glared at her with eyes as big as saucers. "Oh, I see," he sneered. "As soon as he becomes a petty official, the first thing he does is ditch his wife."

"怎么，不怪焦仲卿怪谁？难道是怪我不成？"

"谁说怪你了？"母亲打断儿子的话，"妹子刚回来，你这个当哥哥的该宽慰她几句才是，怎么倒自家吵嚷起来？不懂事的孩子！"说着，泪水又汪在眼眶里了。

俗话说，好事不出门，恶事传千里。焦家休妻的事，没过两三天，就传遍了居巢县。人们大都是说长论短，闲言碎语，无非是茶余饭后磨牙而已。真正关心此事的，只有两个人，那就是秦罗敷和王瑞琪。

兰芝离开焦家，罗敷早就料到了，只是没想到这么快。然而事情毕竟已成现实，她钟情数载的焦仲卿如今又是孑然一身了，这使他心里充满了喜悦，同时也充满了恐惧。喜悦的是，凭着她对焦母的观察，焦母再选的新人，非她莫属。她其实并不喜欢这个老太太，在她看来，是兰芝太懦弱，又太固执，换了自己，准能把老太太哄得开心，就算哄不好，她也能把老太婆制得服服贴贴，不敢欺负自己。她恐惧的倒是焦仲卿，她知道焦仲卿对刘兰芝的感情并没有断绝，对自己也从未表示过任何关注。对罗敷来说，对付焦母并不难，赢得焦仲卿的心却没那么容易。然而兰芝既已离开了焦仲卿，毕

"This was not Zhongqing's fault," Lanzhi said, mildly, and was just about to explain what had happened when her brother roughly interrupted her: "Not his fault, eh? Well whose fault was it? Mine I suppose!"

"Nobody's blaming you," his mother cried, impatiently. "I thought you might show some sympathy for your sister, instead of kicking up a fuss. You have no sense of decency." And the tears started to flow once more.

As the saying goes, good news scarcely gets outside the house, while bad news zooms off a thousand miles in an instant. Within three days, the whole of Juchao County knew that Liu Lanzhi had been sent home by her mother-in-law. Two people had a particular interest in the gossip — Qin Luofu and Wang Ruiqi.

Luofu had known that it was only a matter of time before Lanzhi would be expelled from the Jiao household, but she hadn't expected it to happen so quickly. She was delighted that her secret love Zhongqing was single again, and at the same time afraid. She was happy because she had carefully observed Lady Jiao, and was sure that when she came to choose another wife for her son she would choose her. Although she did not like the old woman, Luofu was sure that she could stand up to her cranky ways and eventually they would get on well together. Lanzhi was too timid, Luofu often thought; she let the old crone walk all over her. What she was afraid of was that Zhongqing might still be in love with Lanzhi. He had never taken any particular notice of Luofu. Dealing with his mother would be no problem, she decided, but it would not be so easy to win Zhongqing's heart. Nevertheless, now that Lanzhi had gone, Luofu was determined not to miss this Heaven-sent opportunity.

竟是天赐良机，机不可失。

罗敷立即把焦家休妻的事跟父母说了，当然，她还是个未出嫁的姑娘，不好贸然在父母面前袒露内心。

罗敷母亲也听说了此事，不无惋惜地说：

"多好的女孩呀，也不知犯了什么错，落到这步田地。"

"兰芝姐自是好性儿，他丈夫焦仲卿更是个好后生，又前程远大，真可惜了。"罗敷有意夸赞焦仲卿。"要是换了我，就算婆婆厉害，我也不吃她那一套。"停了停，她诡谲地凑到母亲耳边，低声地问：

"娘，你说当婆婆的对儿媳都是黑心吗？"

"那也不一定，全看缘份呢，不是有句老话说：酒逢知己千杯少，话不投机半句多吗？"母亲对人际之间倒是看得很透。

"娘说得对。其实兰芝姐家我也常去，那个焦婆婆对我总是有说有笑，不像个歹毒的人。"说到这里，罗敷终于憋不住了，索性单刀直入地向母亲摊牌：

"娘，要是焦家向咱家提亲，你们愿意吗？"

罗敷的父亲推门进来，恰好听见了女儿的话，很认真地说：

"有什么不愿意，女大当嫁嘛。再说那焦仲卿

She wanted to discuss the news of Lanzhi's dismissal with her parents. But, being an unmarried girl, it was not considered a fit subject for her to broach. Fortunately, Luofu's mother brought it up first, by saying, "I don't know what that nice young girl did to deserve this calamity."

Luofu, taking her cue from her mother's compassionate tone, sighed, "Yes, she is really a good-hearted girl. And her husband, Jiao Zhongqing, is such a fine young scholar, with a splendid career in front of him. What a shame!" She then added, after a short pause: "But if I had been in Lanzhi's place I would certainly not have put up with Lady Jiao's bullying as long as she did." She then slunk up to her mother, and whispered in her ear: "Mother, do you think mothers-in-law are always nasty to their daughters-in-law?"

"Oh, that's not at all the case," was the indignant reply. "It all depends on fate. There's an old saying: 'A thousand cups of wine are not enough when treating a bosom friend, but half a disagreeable word is too much.'" Luofu's mother prided herself on her knowledge of human nature, and Luofu was anxious right then to flatter her: "You are absolutely right, Mother. I have visited the Jiao household many times, and Lady Jiao has always a smile and never a cross word for me. She doesn't seem to me like a vindictive person at all." At this point, Luofu couldn't keep her secret hope to herself any longer, and came right out with what she had been wanting to ask all along: "Mother, if Lady Jiao wanted me to be her son's new wife, what would you say?"

Just then, Luofu's father entered the room. He had heard this last sentence, and without hesitation he said, "We would say yes, of course. For one thing, it's high time you got married; for another, although that fellow Jiao Zhongqing hasn't achieved fame

现在虽然还不是达官显贵，可到底是在郡里当差，听说咱们县太爷见了他也还要敬几分呢！"

秦郎中最看重的就是家世和身份，上次说破天大包大揽地要把罗敷说给王公子，他高兴得几夜睡不好。后来没说成，他老大的遗憾，骂罗敷有眼无珠，不识敬重。直到后来得知是县令家公子没相中罗敷，他才不再说什么。方才女儿这话不管是真是假，只要他焦家肯提这门亲，自己一定会答应下来的。

再说王瑞琪，在他眼里，浓妆艳抹的女子是最让他难以忍受的庸俗之辈。别看他未涉沧桑，却时常感叹人生如白驹过隙，荣华富贵也不过是过眼烟云，惟有找到一个知音女子相伴终生，才不枉了男儿一世。自从见过刘兰芝之后，那一点娴雅之态，便使他再也无法忘记。可惜天意难违，迟了一步，使他无缘与兰芝琴瑟相谐。因为他心中有了兰芝，因此说媒的人屡屡碰壁，连父母也对他无可奈何。对于瑞琪来说，兰芝被遣是件天大的喜事，使他终于有了希望。他已经等得太久了，等得太苦了。

王县令这几天恰好公干外出，这王瑞琪竟等不及父亲回来，便急急地求母亲作主，到鸳鸯集刘家提亲。王夫人有些为难，这到底关乎儿子的终身

and fortune yet, I've heard that the county magistrate thinks quite highly of him."

Doctor Qin was a person who put great store by social status. When a match had been in the offing for his daughter and Wang Ruiqi, the son of the county prefect, he had been too excited to sleep for several nights. Then, when the negotiations had come to naught he blamed his daughter for having ideas above her station and turning the young man down. When he found out that it was young Wang himself who had spurned the offer, he did not have the grace to apologize to the girl. Now he was only too pleased to give his consent to a marriage alliance with the Jiaos.

As for Wang Ruiqi, he had long been tired of fashionable girls with their thick makeup and gaudy attire. In addition, although he was still too young to have had much experience of the ups and downs of this world, he could not help feeling that life was passing him by. Being the scion of a wealthy family, fame and riches had no attraction for him. The fact was that he felt that only if he found a soul mate would his life be worth living. And Lanzhi, he was sure, was that person. He had been so smitten at his first sight of her that he had been unable to get her out of his thoughts ever since. But, alas, he had been fated to lose his true love by one tardy step. Matchmakers came and matchmakers went, but Wang Ruiqi could think of no one but Lanzhi. So when he learned that Lanzhi had been sent away at her mother-in-law's insistence he was overjoyed at the prospect that suddenly lay open before him, when he had been wallowing in the depths of despair.

It happened at this time that his father was away on business for a few days. Unable to contain himself until the prefect returned, Ruiqi badgered his mother to approach Lanzhi's parents.

大事，她一个人怎么能担这么大的干系。可瑞琪却像着了魔一样，似乎耽搁一天，兰芝就又会被别人抢走。无奈之下，她叫来家仆，吩咐道：

"快去把说破天喊来！"

"慢着！"瑞琪觉得自己与刘兰芝都不是凡俗中人，叫这样龌龊的媒婆撮合神仙眷侣太煞风景，他自作主张地吩咐仆人：

"把何主簿请来，说王瑞琪有要事求他。"

家仆答应一声，一溜烟地跑了出去。不大功夫，气喘吁吁地转回来禀报公子：

"何主簿，何主簿他随老爷一道到邻县去了，此刻不在县里。"

"怎么这么不巧！"瑞琪急得直跺脚，可也实在是无法可想。

王夫人知道瑞琪的脾气，也不再劝他，扭头对愣在厅中的仆人说：

"快去给公子倒茶，去去心火。"

But his mother balked at the suggestion. After all, this was a matter which would have a most weighty bearing on the whole course of her son's future life, and she was reluctant to take the responsibility for the consequences on her own shoulders. But Ruiqi pestered her relentlessly, whining that delay by even so much as a single day could see Lanzhi snatched away by some other man. Finally, with a sigh of resignation, she summoned a servant.

"Fetch Talk Even Heaven into Anything, the matchmaker," she ordered.

"Oh, no! Just a moment!" Ruiqi cried. He was outraged at the thought that a special couple like himself and Lanzhi should have their blessed union arranged by a mercenary old crone like Talk Even Heaven into Anything. He turned to the servant, and said, "Tell Secretary He that Wang Ruiqi wishes to have a word with him."

The man scuttled off on his errand. But before long, he returned panting to report that Secretary He was unavailable, as he had gone with the prefect on a trip to a nearby county.

Ruiqi howled, and stamped his foot in vexation. His mother, knowing full well the lad's ungovernable temper, did not even try to calm him down, but ordered the servant to pour him some tea, hoping that that might have a soothing effect on his tantrums.

◎第六章
瑞琪山坳遭劫难

　　王县令与何主簿一行第二天就回到了县里，瑞琪却像是等了一年那样漫长。县令进了家，刚刚换下官服，还没来得及进餐，瑞琪便急不可耐地催着母亲快与父亲商议此事。王夫人跟县令说了没几句话，抽空出来，嗔怪瑞琪道：

　　"你这孩子这么不懂事，总该让爹爹歇息歇息，到晚上我细细地与他商量，事才可行。像你这样唐突，万一老爷说不行，你怎么办？"

　　瑞琪是个任性惯了的人，他绝不相信父亲会逆着他的意愿，赌气地说："爹爹要是不同意，我今天就撞死在这儿！"

　　"好好，我进去说。"王夫人无可奈何地瞪了瑞琪一眼，转身进门去。

　　王县令正呷着茶，见夫人回来，随口问了一句：

　　"这几天我没在家，家里有什么事吗？"

　　"要说有事，也没什么事；要说没事，还真有件大事。"王夫人笑吟吟地坐在县令身旁。

　　"此话怎讲？"

Chapter Six
Waylaid by Robbers

The following day, Magistrate Wang and Secretary He returned. The magistrate had hardly changed his clothes, and still had not had time for a bite to eat, before Ruiqi, consumed with impatience, was trying get his mother to talk to the old man about his desire to marry Lanzhi. He received an angry rebuke.

"You stupid little oaf," his mother snapped. "You won't even give your poor father a chance to catch his breath after such a tiring journey. I'll have a heart-to-heart talk with him this evening; that'll be soon enough. If you annoy him now, he'll definitely say no. Then what will you do?"

Ruiqi was a spoilt brat, used to having his own way. He couldn't imagine his father refusing him anything. So he said, petulantly: "If Dad doesn't agree right now, then I'll dash myself to pieces right here. So there!"

"All right. All right," said his mother hastily, knowing how ungovernable her son was, and fearing a scene. "I'll go and talk to him now." Glaring at her unruly offspring, she turned on her heel, and left the room.

Magistrate Wang was sipping tea when his wife entered. He looked up, and casually inquired about the household affairs in his absence. Taking a seat beside him, and assuming an ingratiating smile, his wife said, "Well, I wouldn't normally bother you with the usual trivial details. However, something rather impor-

"老爷，那年中秋你和瑞琪见过的那个弹箜篌的刘兰芝，还记得吗？前几天让焦家休回娘家去了。"王夫人慢慢地把话头往自家事情上引。

"嗨！"王县令笑得差点把茶喷出来，"这事跟咱家有什么关系！"他咬着留在口里的茶根，似乎记起了什么，换了种口气说："那个女子看上去很聪慧，婆家为什么要休她？"

"清官难断家务事，这种事谁能说得清楚！"王夫人说，"街上的人议论此事，都说那个女子很文静，是焦家老太太刁蛮，没日没夜地逼着人家纺线织布，还时时寻人家的不是。要是这样的女孩在咱们家里做媳妇，我这个婆婆断断不会难为她的。"

"听你这么说，是刘兰芝受委屈了？"王县令仍是心不在焉，因为他并没有意识到夫人话里有话。"你呀，看样子没有当婆婆的命啊！"他想起了前些日子秦家带过来的罗敷姑娘，那相貌几乎无可挑剔，可惜儿子看不上，自己也无可奈何。

王夫人像有些不服气，说："你怎么知道我没有当婆婆的命？要是把刘兰芝娶进门，我不就成了婆婆了吗？"

王县令还以为夫人在说笑话，随口道："就算刘兰芝是个再好的女子，也没法再进咱们家的门。"

tant has, in fact, cropped up."

"Oh? What?"

"Do you remember that girl called Lanzhi whom you and Ruiqi heard playing the *konghou* at the Mid-Autumn Festival once?" his wife started her narrative, being careful to approach the subject in a roundabout way. "Well, a few days ago her mother-in-law — Lady Jiao — sent her back to her parents."

"Hah!" The prefect's involuntary reaction nearly caused him to spurt a mouthful of tea. "Well, what has that got to do with us?" he asked. Then, chewing thoughtfully on some tea leaves, he said, in an altered tone: "I seem to recall that she was a very bright girl. Why did the old woman kick her out?"

"Ah, my dear, you are so wrapped up in your official duties that you wouldn't know about these things," said his spouse, archly. "But the whole town knows that that vindictive Lady Jiao resented Lanzhi, who is a very refined and gentle girl. The old woman kept her at the loom day and night. And she was always finding fault with her. I tell you, if a girl like that were my daughter-in-law I certainly wouldn't ill-treat her."

"Do you mean that it wasn't Lanzhi's fault that she was sent away?" The prefect still hadn't caught his wife's drift. "Anyway, it doesn't look as if you'll ever be anybody's mother-in-law." He was thinking about how his son had turned up his nose at that nice-looking girl Qin Luofu only a few days previously, when she was introduced to him.

"What makes you so sure that I'm destined never to become a mother-in-law?" his wife retorted. "I could become Liu Lanzhi's mother-in-law."

The prefect thought that this must be some kind of joke, and he scoffed, "Liu Lanzhi is a nice enough girl, I suppose. But she'll

"为什么？"

"这还用问吗？我堂堂的一县父母，怎么能把一个被人家休了的女子娶进门来呢？"

"要是瑞琪执意要娶呢？"

"你说什么？"王县令突然警觉起来，他又想起曾经让何主簿打听过刘兰芝，看来这小子一直没把她忘记，如今刘兰芝又成了孤身一人，想必瑞琪又重动了娶她的念头。王县令虽然对刘兰芝也有好感，但如今她已是个被人遗弃的女子，作为县太爷娶这么个儿媳，岂不是老脸无光？但他又深知瑞琪性情执拗，一时也不好硬驳回去。沉吟片刻，说道："此事缓议吧。"

瑞琪就在门外，父母的话他都听见了。父亲没有断然拒绝此事，这使他原来紧揪着的心稍稍松弛下来，最后听到父亲说此事"缓议"，神经又绷紧了，他控制不住自己，大步跨进房门，"扑通"一声跪在父亲面前：

"爹爹，孩儿对刘兰芝心仪已久，若是爹爹心疼我，求爹爹速速遣媒议亲，不要像上次那样耽搁了。"

王县令瞅着眼前这个痴心的儿子，心软下来，他手捻胡须久久沉吟，终于开了口：

"就依你吧。"

王夫人的脸上顿时堆起笑来，她好像比瑞琪

never marry into our family."

"Why ever not?"

"Well, it goes without saying, doesn't it? How could the most respectable household in the county admit a girl who's been thrown out of her first husband's home?"

"But, what if Ruiqi has set his heart on marrying her?"

"What?" cried the prefect, in astonishment. Then, he suddenly remembered the time he had sent his secretary to make inquiries about the girl. So, he thought, Ruiqi has been thinking about her ever since, and now that she is single once more his hope of marrying her has revived. He was acutely aware that for his son to marry a divorced woman, no matter how fine a person she was, would be a loss of face for a man in his position. At the same time, he was uncomfortably conscious of how pig-headed his son could be when he was intent on getting his own way. Magistrate Wang thought for a while, and finally sighed and said, "We'll discuss this matter later."

All this time, Ruiqi had been eavesdropping just outside the door. He was relieved that his father had not opposed the match outright, but at the same time he was dismayed to hear him postpone making a decision. Unable to contain his impatience, he rushed into the room and threw himself down on his knees in front of his parents.

"Father," he cried in an agonized voice, "I have long loved Liu Lanzhi. If you care for me at all, I beg you to arrange our marriage at once. Please don't delay like you did the last time."

The pathetic figure of the besotted lad softened his father's heart. At length, after stroking his beard in deep thought, the prefect announced, "Very well, have it your own way."

The smiles that wreathed his wife's face upon her hearing

更激动，又嗔又喜地说：

"傻小子，还不快谢谢爹爹！"

瑞琪也如梦初醒，恭恭敬敬地给王县令叩了个头，忙不迭地问：

"爹爹，遣谁做媒人？"

"那自然是何主簿。"

何主簿禁不住瑞琪连夜的软磨硬泡，第二天一早就放下所有的公事，来到鸳鸯集。他先找到里正胡坎，由他带着来到刘兰芝家。还没进门，胡坎便在院外高声喊起来：

"兰芝娘，兰芝娘！"

兰芝母亲边答应边出来开门。

"兰芝娘，你好福气呀！"胡坎看也不看兰芝母亲一眼，拥着何主簿径直往院里走。

兰芝娘无精打采地说："我家正晦气，哪有什么福气！"

"县里何主簿何大人亲自来看你啦，还不快烧茶？"胡坎仍旧大着嗓门说。

"兰芝呢？"

"兰芝在西厢房读书呢。"

胡坎看了何主簿一眼，带着逢迎的口气夸赞说：

"这女子就是与众不同，焦家真是有眼无珠，

seemed to show that she was almost as happy as Ruiqi, whom she pretended to scold: "Well, hurry up and thank your father, you foolish boy!"

As if abruptly awoken from a dream, Ruiqi kowtowed obsequiously to his father, but lost no time asking whom he intended to send as the go-between. "Secretary He, of course." Was the reply.

After a long evening spent enduring young Ruiqi's endearments and threats, Secretary He, putting aside his official tasks, set off at first light the following morning for Yuanyang. There, he sought out Hu Kan, the village head, who guided him to the Liu residence. They halted outside the courtyard gate, while Hu Kan called out to Lanzhi's mother, who bustled out to admit them.

"I've got good news for you, Madame," said Hu Kan, as he led Secretary He inside.

"Our family has suffered such a spell of ill luck recently, sir, that we dare not even think of good news," replied Lanzhi's mother.

"Well, how about a cup of tea for an exalted guest like this gentleman here?" demanded Hu Kan in his usual bluff manner. "He's the secretary of the county you know. By the way, where's Miss Lanzhi?"

"She's reading in her bedroom, sir," said her mother.

Hu Kan shot a sly glance at Secretary He, and proceeded to ooze flattery. "Your daughter, Madame, is an outstanding girl. That vulgar Jiao family obviously has no taste at all, having failed to recognize this, and driving the poor waif out so heartlessly.... Tragic! Most tragic!" At this point, he pulled himself up short, as if he had said something untoward. Slapping his own cheek, he muttered, "Oh, here I am, rattling on.... Forgive me please." Then,

这么好的媳妇让他给休了……"他自觉语失,啪地打了自己的脸一下,"瞧我这嘴,真是胡说八道。"算是给兰芝母亲道了歉,紧接着又说:"兰芝娘,何大人给兰芝提亲来啦!"

"有劳大人了。"兰芝母亲对何主簿表示了谢意。兰芝回家四五天了,她这个当娘的虽然心中烦乱,但毕竟是自己的亲生女儿,也不好多说什么。她只担心女儿被休名声不好,再嫁个像样的人家也不容易。如今何主簿亲自登门提亲,想必这人家不会差。想到这里,她心中倒有些欣慰。

兰芝母亲打发女儿去烧茶,然后把二人让进屋,敬了上座,何主簿便把此次来意说明,最后还特地强调了瑞琪对兰芝的久久仰慕之情,胡坎也不失时机地补上几句:

"王老爷家的三公子,那人品,那学问,莫说是百里挑一,就是一万个人里也不准能挑出一个来呢!"

"也是兰芝姑娘娴雅,打动了公子的心。"何主簿打断了胡坎的话,又对兰芝母亲说,"其实给三公子提亲的人成群结队,三公子一个也相不中。居巢县里有名的美人秦罗敷,论模样也算天姿国色了,三公子硬说她俗不可耐。嗨,男女之间的事儿,真是说不清!"

兰芝母亲听了何主簿一番话,心下早应允了。

businesslike: "The fact is, Madame, that Secretary He here has come with a proposal of marriage to your daughter. There now. What do you think of that?"

Lanzhi's mother could hardly believe her ears. She had been very much afraid that the disgrace of the repudiation of her daughter by the Jiaos would firmly close the door to any other marriage alliance with a respectable family. And now, after only a week or so, here was the offer of a most suitable match!

She hastened to send Lanzhi to make tea, while at the same time ushering the visitors into the best room. There, Secretary He formally explained the reason for his visit, taking care to impress upon Lanzhi's mother how his master's son had long been infatuated with Lanzhi, and how highly he respected and admired the girl. No sooner had he done this than Hu Kan chimed in with a paean of praise highlighting the superior qualities, especially the intellectual attainments, of Wang Ruiqi, the magistrate's third son.

"And Lanzhi, such an elegant and charming child," cooed the secretary, butting in, "has quite won my young master's heart. I need not tell you, Madame, that the young man has been besieged with offers of marriage. But not another girl will he so much as look upon. In fact, he even went so far as to call Qin Luofu — the belle of Juchao County and said to be one of the most beautiful young women in the country — 'too coarse for words'! Really, the ways of love are unfathomable indeed."

Listening to all this, Lanzhi's mother was eager for the match to come off. But, the bitter experience of Lanzhi's first marriage made her cautious about this new proposal. She simpered, but said nothing.

Disturbed by her lack of response, Hu Kan urged her:

但有了上次的教训,她不敢再贸然做主,只是陪着笑脸应酬着。胡坎见她不吐口,心中奇怪,催促道:

"你赶紧给个痛快话,何大人还要回去复命呢!"

恰好兰芝沏好茶送上来,兰芝母亲说了声:"烦二位在此稍坐用茶,待我与兰芝说一声。"说罢拉着兰芝来到西厢房。

进了屋,母女二人相对坐下,母亲轻声地说:"兰芝,没想到这么快就有媒人登门。"她把何主簿方才的话原原本本地讲了一遍。

兰芝听出母亲对这门亲事很满意,她也理解母亲此时的心情,可母亲哪里理解自己的心情?

"娘,有些话我还没来得及对您说。焦家把我休弃,全是婆母的意思,仲卿也是被逼无奈。临分别时,他对我发下誓言,一定要把我娶回去,生生世世不再分离。"

"傻孩子,焦仲卿如果能当得了他娘的家,你也不至于落到今天的下场呀!"

兰芝母亲深知婚姻大事绝不是焦仲卿一句誓言就管用的。

"娘,女儿不管焦仲卿的话是真是假,我只是不想再嫁。仲卿是个仁人君子,我们情深义笃,他

"Madame, I must ask you to give your consent without delay, so that Secretary He may depart to report on the success of his mission."

At this point, Lanzhi entered with tea. Her mother then said, "May I trouble you gentlemen to rest here a while and enjoy your tea, while I have a word with my daughter apart?" With that, she pulled Lanzhi back to her bedroom.

They sat facing each other, and Lanzhi's mother addressed the girl in coaxing tones:

"Listen, Lanzhi, I never thought that you would get a new offer of marriage so soon." And she went on to explain in detail all that Secretary He had said.

It was clear to Lanzhi that her mother was delighted with this proposal. She also understood how her mother's feelings had been heart by the misfortune that had come upon the family because of the failure of Lanzhi's first marriage. But how could her mother know what was in Lanzhi's own heart?

"Mother," she said, "there is something I have not had chance to explain to you yet. My expulsion was all Lady Jiao's doing. Zhongqing could not help it. Just before we parted, he swore a solemn oath to me that he would take me back, and that we would never be parted again as long as we lived."

"You feather-brained child!" her mother exploded in exasperation. "If that Zhongqing had had the gumption to be master in his own house, you would never have come to this sorry pass! Don't you understand?" She was well aware that "solemn oaths" sworn by Jiao Zhongqing would be of absolutely no avail whatsoever when it came to mending a broken marriage.

"At any rate, Mother, I don't care whether Zhongqing meant it or not; I definitely do not want to get married again." Lanzhi was

绝不会负我的。"

母亲劝了多时，可兰芝绝没有回头的意思，无奈之下，她也在想：若焦仲卿真是个痴情男儿，过一段时间再把女儿娶回去，倒也不失体面。于是她不再劝女儿，回到正房，颇带歉意地对何主簿说：

"回大人，小女生性固执，她说自己刚刚回家，心绪烦闷，不想立即就议婚事。请大人回县老爷和少爷，容我们一段时光，待小女创痛平复之后，再慢慢议及，不知可否？"

何主簿尚未开口，胡坎就先说话了：

"兰芝怎么如此不懂事体，县老爷的面子她也不给吗！"

"这倒不是的！"兰芝母亲连忙解释说，"小女只是刚刚遭人遗弃，几天来一直神思恍惚，若是对县令大人及公子再有得罪，那就更无颜面了。"

何主簿朝兰芝母亲摆摆手说：

"兰芝姑娘真是多虑，王大人的为人一县百姓都可以作证，不仅为官清廉，为人更是谦和。公子既对兰芝姑娘一往情深，更不会委屈了她。你不妨再去劝劝，让她放心。"

兰芝母亲不得已，只好对何主簿说出了实情。

何主簿听罢，沉吟片刻，好心地提醒道：

adamant on this point. "But I firmly believe that Zhongqing is an upright gentleman," she went on. "We have a deep and eternal love. He would never abandon me."

Eventually, Lanzhi's mother realized that she was wasting her breath trying to persuade her daughter to accept the proposal of marriage from Wang Ruiqi. Consoling herself with the thought that Jiao Zhongqing might be genuinely in love with Lanzhi, and might eventually take her back — in which case, the Liu family honor would be restored — she returned to the visitors, and, with an apologetic smile, said to Secretary He:

"Sir, I am afraid my daughter is of a stubborn nature. Besides, she has only just returned home, and she has not yet got over her recent upset. Nothing could be further from her mind at this moment than a hasty remarriage. Perhaps we should give her some time to recover her spirits, and then we can discuss this matter again. What do you say?"

Before the secretary could find his tongue, Hu Kan protested, "Has Miss Lanzhi no sense of propriety, Madame? Does she not realize what a loss of face that would be for the prefect?"

"Oh, sir, please don't say such a thing," Lanzhi's mother cried. "My daughter has only recently been thrust out of her husband's home, and for these past few days has been in the depths of despondency. She fears that in this frame of mind she might displease the prefect and the young master. And that would be an even bigger affront to them."

Secretary He waved a hand to dismiss such an objection. "I fear, Madame, that your daughter worries needlessly," he said. "Magistrate Wang, as everyone in the county can testify, is a man not only of integrity but also of a most amiable character. In addition, the young master has long harbored a deep affection

"这显然是焦仲卿一时感情用事。自古以来，婚姻大事都是父母之命。兰芝姑娘以再嫁为耻，不过是为焦仲卿这话所惑。依我看来，你做母亲的要劝女儿清醒些，切莫因别人一句甜言蜜语错过一世好姻缘。"

兰芝母亲觉得此话十分有理，但她最了解女儿的心性：她想定的事，不是一时半刻能劝过来的。于是又向何主簿陪笑说：

"何大人所言极是，请大人暂且回衙，容我慢慢劝她，一旦小女回心转意，便可立即完婚。"

再说王瑞琪在家里度日如年，好不容易等到何主簿回来，得到的却是这么个结果，心下当然不快。但他静下来一想，刘家并没有回绝此事，只是刘兰芝与焦仲卿旧情未断，倒也算是个有情有义的女子。想来想去，他觉得此事不宜空等，他要亲自登门，向兰芝表白自己的心迹。要让兰芝看到自己并不比焦仲卿差，这样的话，她就不会再抱着那没有结局的期待了。

第二天一早，王县令刚刚出门，瑞琪便吩咐家人备马，又把昨晚准备好的一个木箱捆到马上。一切收拾停当，他回到院里，对王夫人说：

"母亲，我今日要外出一趟。"

"到哪里去？"王夫人感到突然，边问边随着

for Miss Lanzhi; it is unthinkable that she could in any way offend him. You should go back and talk to her again. Tell her to put her mind at ease."

At this, Lanzhi's mother found that she had no alternative but to tell the visitors the real state of things. The secretary was silent for a while, mulling over her words. Then, he addressed Lanzhi's mother sternly: "It is clear that this impasse stems from a mere whim of Jiao Zhongqing's. Since ancient times it has been a precept that marriages are decided by the parents. Miss Lanzhi regards re-marriage as shameful only because Jiao Zhongqing put that silly notion in her head. It seems to me, Madame, that your duty lies in enlightening your daughter. You should certainly not allow the beguiling words of some outsider interfere with a most desirable marriage."

Lanzhi's mother found this argument reasonable enough, but she knew her daughter's temperament too well to have any hope of dissuading her from a course she had set her mind on pursuing. With a ghastly smile, she pleaded with Secretary He: "Sir, you are absolutely right. If you would be so good as to return to the county seat for a little while to give me an opportunity to talk this matter over further with my daughter, I am sure that I can make her change her mind, and the marriage can be arranged."

In the meantime, Wang Ruiqi was waiting impatiently at home. When Secretary He finally did return, and report the outcome of his mission, the boy's heart sank. However, containing his despair, he reasoned carefully that he had not been rejected outright, and that the only thing standing in the way of his happiness was Lanzhi's lingering affection for Zhongqing. This showed,

瑞琪往外走，见马上驮着一个箱子，又顺口问道："带箱子做什么？"

瑞琪拉过马，答道："母亲，我要亲自到刘兰芝家去一趟，让她真正了解我的诚心。这箱子里是我给她备的一份礼物。"

王夫人摇摇头，叹道："瑞琪，你真是鬼迷心窍了！还是等你爹爹回来商量过再作打算吧。"她摸摸马上的箱子，"这箱子里到底是什么？"

"母亲不必多问，这箱里非金非银，非锦非缎，但我敢说，刘兰芝会喜欢这份礼物，她会答应嫁给我。"瑞琪说罢，朝王夫人一挥手道："母亲请回吧，我上路了。"

"哎，你不等你爹回来吗？"

也是老天不作美，王公子带着家仆走了一个多时辰，路程还没有过半，天空突然阴了下来，看看马上就要下雨，两人又没带雨具，家仆说道：

"公子，咱们先回刚才路过的那个村里避避吧，等下过这阵雨再走。"

"胡说，怕什么！"王公子呵斥了一声，头也不回。

风越刮越猛，瑞琪的马发出声声嘶鸣，他狠狠地往马屁股上加了一鞭，那马长嘶一声，加快了脚步。

thought he, looking on the bright side, what a truly loving girl she was! Finally, he decided that it would be fatal to delay any longer, and he must go and make his proposal in person. He would throw himself at her feet. Then, when she saw that he was in no way inferior to that fellow Jiao Zhongqing, she would no longer wish to cling to her futile longing for him.

Early the following morning, as soon as his father had left the house, Ruiqi ordered his servants to saddle a horse for him. He fixed a wooden box he had prepared the previous evening to the horse, prepared himself for a journey, and went to say goodbye to his mother. He explained that he was going in person to woo Lanzhi, and the box contained a present for her.

His mother shook her head sadly, and sighed, "Ruiqi, this is preposterous. You should wait until your father returns, and talk it over with him first." She then fingered the box. "What's in it?" she asked.

"Don't ask too many questions, Mother," said the boy, with an artful smile. "It's not gold; it's not silver; it's not silks nor satins. But it's something that I'm sure Lanzhi will like. As soon as she sees it she'll agree to our marriage." Then he waved to his anxious mother, and took his leave.

The day was overcast, and Ruiqi and his manservant had been on the road for not much more than an hour, less than halfway on their journey, before storm clouds gathered, and it seemed that a heavy fall of rain was imminent. As the pair had set out without wet weather gear, the servant suggested turning back to a village they had just passed, to wait out the spell of rain.

"Nonsense," scoffed Ruiqi, anxious to press on, "a drop of rain won't hurt us."

突然间，从山坳里窜出几个穿着破烂黑衣的汉子，王公子大惊，倒吸了一口冷气，只见这几个人来到面前，手里都拿着木棍：

"下马说话！"

王公子意识到这伙人来者不善，一看便知是他乡流窜来的逃兵。假如是在县里，他根本不会把此辈放在眼里，可眼下是在路上，前后左右找不到援手之人，他的心扑通扑通地紧跳，又惊又怕，只得下马，壮着胆子问道：

"你们要干什么？"

"干什么？我们不想伤人，只想找口饭吃活下去！"其中一个身材高大的黑衣人举起手里的棍子敲着马上的木箱，"把里边的东西给我们留下，咱们大路朝天，各走一边。"

公子身后的家仆已经吓得浑身哆嗦，听到他们说"找口饭吃"，连忙解下身上背着的干粮袋走上前，说：

"这里就是吃，吃的。"

"滚！"黑衣人一边厉声喝斥，一边抡起棍子，把他打得"哎哟"叫了一声，翻倒在地。几个逃兵哈哈大笑，其中一个讥讽道：

"这个大傻瓜，难道我们就缺你这口干粮！"

逃兵们狂笑一阵，冲到公子马前准备搬箱子。王公子是个读书人，何尝见过这种阵式，他猛地扑

A strong wind arose, which got fiercer all the time. Ruiqi's horse found it heavy going, and whinnied in distress. The young man had to lash it mercilessly to keep it stumbling forward.

Suddenly, out from a defile in the mountains charged a group of ruffians dressed in shabby black clothes and wielding staves. Terrified, Ruiqi reined in his horse, as the gang blocked the road ahead of him.

"Get down from your horse!" one of them commanded. Ruiqi immediately recognized the strangers as fugitive soldiers from some other region. If he had been back in Juchao, he would have had nothing to worry about from such riffraff; but here on a lonely road, with no help in sight, it was a different matter. His heart thumped as he slid reluctantly from his horse's back. Putting on a brave face, he demanded, "Well, what is it you want?"

"What do we want?" echoed a hulking fellow. "We don't mean any harm, Young Master. Just a bite to eat to keep body and soul together, that's all." As he said this, he tapped Ruiqi's box with his club. "Just give us what's in this here box, and we'll go our separate ways."

Ruiqi's servant, meanwhile, had broken out in a cold sweat, and his teeth chattered. When he heard the words 'a bite to eat' he rushed forward, and deposited the bag of grain he had been carrying on his back at the leader of the gang's feet.

"Sir, there's plenty of food for you here!" he gasped.

"Get out of here!" roared the other, and fetched him a blow with his club that sent the poor servant spinning along the ground.

Some of the other villains hooted with laughter, and one jeered, "That numbskull thinks we're short of a handful of dried grain."

Cackling with glee, the bandits swarmed round the box. Ruiqi,

上去护着箱子，哀求道：

"列位，今天不凑巧，我身上没带多少银子，可这箱子里不是你们要的东西。"说完，在身上摸了几下，掏出一点散银，拱手道：

"列位莫要嫌少，权算我对列位的一点意思。"

为首的黑衣人接过公子手里的银子，不屑地说："呸，就这么一点点。"他把手一招，几个逃兵不由分说便把箱子夺过来，放在地上打开，几颗脑袋都凑到了箱子上去看，里面的东西果然让他们大失所望，原来只是一张箜篌。那个为首的十分气恼，嘴里边骂边把箜篌提起来，恨恨地说："这东西有屁用！"说着，把箜篌往路边的大石头上狠命一摔，箜篌发出"嗡"的一声响，应声而碎。

王公子没想到他们会把箜篌摔碎，此刻他内心的恐惧已经消失，剩下的只有一腔怒火。他直着眼睛扑过去，口里大叫："劫匪！劫匪！"猛然间，他的头顶被木棍狠狠地击了一下，眼前一黑，摇摇晃晃地倒在了地上。

不知过了多长时间，他才隐隐约约地听到家仆呼唤他的名字。他睁开眼，看见仆人伏在面前，急切地叫着：

"公子，公子，你可醒了，吓死我了！"

dismayed at such a turn of events quite alien to a person of his gentle upbringing, frantically tried to stop them rifling the box, at the same time pleading, "Gentlemen, unfortunately, you have come at an unfortunate time. I have not much silver on me today. As for the contents of this box, they are of no use to you, I assure you." At the same time, he fumbled for some spare pieces of silver he was carrying about him, and offered them to the gang. "I know this is not much, gentlemen, but please accept it as a token of my esteem," he stammered.

"You're right. It isn't much," growled the ringleader as he snatched the silver. Then, at a signal from him, the others took the box, laid it on the ground, and opened it. To the great disappointment of the robbers, the box contained nothing but a *konghou*! The leader, enraged, snatched up the instrument, and cursed. "What the Hell's the use of this thing?" he bawled, and dashed it to pieces against a roadside rock.

At the sight of this act of vandalism, all Ruiqi's fear was replaced by a fiery fury. Glaring at the leader of the ruffians, he roared, "You thieving scoundrel!" Hardly were the words out of his mouth when he received a sickening blow from a club on the back of the head. The world turned black, Ruiqi's knees buckled beneath him, and he collapsed on the ground.

He did not know how much time had passed when he dimly heard his name being called. He opened his eyes, to see his servant bending over him. "Oh, Master, you've come round at last!" the main said, relieved. "I've been worried to death about you."

With a great effort, Ruiqi managed to sit up. He wanted to stand up, but the aching in his head dissuaded him from making the attempt. He closed his eyes again, and asked, "Have the

瑞琪费力地挣扎着坐起身，他想站起来，可是头疼得厉害，只得又闭上眼睛：

"劫匪走了？"

"走了。"

"马呢？"

"被抢走了！"家仆哭丧着脸说，"公子的琴也被砸烂了。"

"唉，天绝我也！"瑞琪大叫了一声。

家仆跟着王县令十几年，眼看着公子从小长大，第一次见公子如此痛哭。他笨嘴拙舌，也不知该怎么劝公子，只是不停地说：

"保住性命就是万幸了！没丢了性命就是万幸！"

风渐渐地小了，远处传来一阵马蹄声，这声音越来越近，有个人影出现在路上。啊，是何主簿。

原来瑞琪走后，王夫人越想越觉得儿子亲自到刘家求婚十分不妥，忙派人到县衙禀报县令。王县令听后说了句："真是荒唐！"命何主簿立即去将瑞琪追回。

何主簿一路上正在思忖着到了刘家如何打圆场，没想到半路上便遇到了这位倒霉的公子，着实吃惊不小。他向家仆问明情况，然后扶公子上马。瑞琪骑在何主簿的马上，又回头看看那张被摔碎的箜篌，长叹一声道：

robbers gone?"

"Yes, sir."

"Where's the horse?"

"They stole it, I'm afraid, sir." The servant added, with a particularly mournful countenance: "And they smashed your *konghou*, too."

"It seems that Heaven has turned its face against me," moaned Ruiqi.

His servant, who had been with him for ten years, and watched him grow from a boy to a man, had never seen his master so distressed. He could find no suitable words to comfort the young man, but could only say, over and over again: "You are lucky to have escaped with your life, sir."

The wind had died down to a gentle breeze by this time, and wafted on it from afar came the sound of a horse's hooves. The sound grew louder, and suddenly the rider came into view. It was Secretary He.

After Ruiqi had left to go and see Lanzhi, his mother had worried that this might be a somewhat improper step to take, and had sent a man post-haste to report to her husband in his office. The prefect had been furious at his son — "reckless young fool" had been his exact words — and had dispatched his secretary to gallop after him and bring him back.

As he hastened along the road, Secretary He had been wondering, with some misgivings, how on earth he was going to smooth things over when he reached the Liu house in the wake of Ruiqi's impetuous mission. So he was astounded to come across the young scapegrace only halfway there. Learning what had happened from the servant, he helped Ruiqi onto his own horse. As he was being led back home, Ruiqi turned and gazed

"难道我与刘兰芝如此无缘？"

媒婆说破天风风火火地在县城大街上走，恰好碰见何主簿，何主簿不想理她，于是低着头装没看见，可说破天却不识相地凑了过来：

"呦，何大人，不认得我啦？"她挥着手里的一条小汗巾，在何主簿眼前晃了晃，"去年到县太爷家里给少爷提亲，还是您把我领进去的哪。"

"哦哦，"何主簿勉强应付，"记得，记得，您老这是到哪儿去呀？"

说破天煞有介事地拉住何主簿的衣袖，诡秘地说："咱们就不能说句话？"于是把何主簿拽到路边。

"老身今天可有大事要对主簿大人说呢！"说破天还在卖关子。

"婆婆有什么事快说，我还有公干呢。"何主簿心中很不耐烦。

"告诉你吧何大人，老身今天要去做桩媒。你知道县南焦家的媳妇刘兰芝让她婆婆休了，焦仲卿齐齐整整的一个人，又在郡里当差。哎，这焦仲卿可真是交了桃花运了，何大人你猜猜，这一回焦家托我说的是哪家女子？"

"哪家的？"何主簿敷衍着问了一句。

"就是曾经给三少爷说的那个秦罗敷哇！"说

sorrowfully on the fragments of the ruined lute, and sighed, "Is that the fate of my love for Lanzhi?"

The matchmaker Talk Even Heaven into Anything was stalking along the street, when she caught sight of Secretary He. The latter, lowered his head, pretending he hadn't noticed her, and tried to scurry by. But the old woman was not to be snubbed so easily. She went straight up to the secretary, and said, in mock surprise: "Oh, Mr Secretary, Sir! Don't you remember me?" Then, waving a handkerchief in his face, she prompted him: "Last year, I acted as a go-between for your master's son. It was you who introduced me, Sir."

Secretary He forced himself to reply. "Yes, yes, of course I remember you. Where are you off to in such a hurry?"

The old woman plucked the secretary by the sleeve, and intimated that she had something confidential to discuss with him. "Could I have a word with you, Sir?" she said in a furtive whisper, as she pulled him to the side of the road.

"It's a matter of great importance," she muttered mysteriously.

"If you have something to say, get it off your chest quickly," said the secretary, irritated. "I have official business to attend to."

"Well, Sir, the fact is that today I have a match to negotiate. You know that Lady Jiao in the south of the county kicked out her daughter-in-law, Lanzhi. Well, Lady Jiao's son, Jiao Zhongqing, is such a fine young man. He's a clerk in the prefectural office, you know. Well, I must say he's lucky in love, because just guess whom I've been asked to seek as a new wife for him!"

"Who?" the secretary asked, wondering what all this had to do with him.

"Qin Luofu — the one your master's third son had his eye

破天神采飞动，"何大人，我听说三少爷至今未娶，咱居巢县第一大美人就是秦罗敷，眼高着呢。何大人，老身可是一片好心，今日我去秦家一趟，这罗敷十有八九就成了焦家的媳妇了，我可真为三少爷后悔莫及呀！"

何主簿原想等她唠叨完就走，可是听完说破天这几句话，他心里倒真有些触动。王公子自从上次到鸳鸯集半路遇劫，心身俱伤，还在家里养病，他或许应该明白与刘兰芝今世未必有缘。据何主簿所知，县令夫妇对刘家并不满意，相比之下，倒是对罗敷姑娘更有好感。想到这里，何主簿认真地对说破天道：

"婆婆委实是一片好意，我先代公子谢了。这么着，你老先缓一缓，待我回了王大人，看此事该如何办，好不好？"

"好哇！"说破天道，"何大人，您可要快一点儿啊，老身多等一天，就是几两银子的进项呢！"

"哦，"何主簿明白了说破天的意思，连忙从怀中掏出几钱碎银递给她，说："就烦婆婆等一天，明天此时，你到县前说话。"

说破天看了看银子，笑得眼睛眯成了一条缝。

不过何主簿的银子还是打了水漂儿，王公子对焦家娶不娶罗敷的事根本不关心，他心里始终想着的是刘兰芝。只不过眼下伤得不轻，无法起

on!" screeched the old woman with glee. "Sir, I hear that the young master is still not married. Now, Qin Luofu is the most beautiful girl in Juchao County, and she has her sights set way up high. But, I have a tender heart, you know, Sir, and can assure you that if I go to the Qins today, Luofu will without a shadow of a doubt become the new daughter-in-law of the Jiaos, and that would be such a shame for poor young Master Wang!"

Secretary He had been intending to go on his way as soon as the matchmaker finished her blathering. But her final convoluted sentence gave him an idea. Wang Ruiqi was still recuperating from the injury he had received when he was waylaid by the robbers on his way to see Lanzhi in Yuanying. He was suffering in both body and mind, convinced that he was never destined to have Lanzhi for himself in this life. The secretary knew that the magistrate and his wife disapproved of the Lius, but had a high opinion of Luofu. At this point, he said to the go-between: "Madame, on behalf of the young master, let me thank you for your kind sentiments. Please be so good as to delay your business a while, until I have had a chance to consult my master on this matter."

"All right," Talk Even Heaven into Anything replied. "But please make haste, Sir. Time is money in my business."

"Oh, er, yes, of course." Secretary He took the hint, and drew out some pieces of silver from an inside pocket, and handed them to the old woman, who beamed with pleasure. "Please wait for one day, and we'll discuss this business further at this time tomorrow in front of the county office," he said.

But it turned out that the secretary had wasted his money. Wang Ruiqi had no objection whatsoever to Luofu's becoming the daughter-in-law of Lady Jiao; Secretary He did not know that

身，他已决定等到伤势好转，还要再到一趟鸳鸯集。

再说焦仲卿回到郡里，一直关心着魏别驾的调任。可每次问起此事来，魏别驾总是支支吾吾，闪烁其辞，这使焦仲卿心中越发没了底。他不知何时才能向兰芝有个交待，惶惶不可终日。

一天，焦仲卿正在官厅中与魏别驾交谈着，门吏忽然进来禀报：

"魏大人，居巢县王县令与何主簿前来求见。"

焦仲卿连忙起身告辞："魏大人有公事，小人暂且回避。"

"不必。"魏别驾有些神色茫然地说，"你们县里来的人，你听听也无妨。我今天还是庐江郡别驾，你是我的属下，谅他们也不至于介意吧。"说着，叫了声："请。"

王县令与何主簿走进厅来，恭恭敬敬地向魏别驾施了礼。魏别驾笑着朝二人挥挥手："看坐。怎么，等不及了？"

"不敢。"王县令又是一揖，"下官刚刚从许太守那里领命回来，太守大人吩咐小县来看望魏大人。小县久仰魏大人威名，巴不得魏大人早些光临鄙县，不知魏大人准备如何？"

魏别驾呵呵大笑道："许太守何必如此容不下

it was Lanzhi the young man had long had his eye on, and he was only waiting for his wound to heal before setting off for Yuanyang again.

When Zhongqing returned to his post at the prefectural office, the first thing he wanted to find out was when Mounted Escort Wei would be setting off for his new assignment. But, to his consternation, every time he brought the subject up, Wei gave an evasive answer. So, not knowing how long it would be before he could go and fetch Lanzhi, the poor swain was on tenterhooks all day long.

One day, as Zhongqing was discussing some matter with Mounted Escort Wei, the door attendant hurried in, and reported that Magistrate Wang of Juchao County and Secretary He wanted to see the prefect.

Zhongqing hurriedly excused himself, but Mounted Escort Wei detained him. "There's no need to run away," he said placidly. "I can't see any harm in your listening on a matter concerning your own county. As you're my assistant, I don't suppose our visitors will mind." Then he called out, "Please enter!"

Magistrate Wang and Secretary He came in, and bowed obsequiously to Mounted Escort Wei, who smiled and waved them to seats. "Gentlemen, I hope I haven't kept you waiting," he said.

"Oh, not at all, not at all," wheezed Magistrate Wang. "I have just come from making my report to Commander Xu, and he ordered me to call on you to pay my respects. I have long admired your respected name, Sir, and hoped you would deign to pay a call on our humble county."

The mounted escort chuckled. "The commander's a hasty man, it seems," he said. "I received my transfer orders not ten

魏某，魏某接到调任之命尚未一旬，就让王县令登门催促？"

"哪里哪里，魏大人千万不要这样想。"王县令倒像是出于本心，"小县绝不敢催促。"王县令与何主簿仍旧站在那里，没敢落座。

焦仲卿听得心中糊涂，初时还以为是魏别驾调任豫章的圣命已经下达，心中好一阵高兴，再往下听，便觉得不对劲了，别驾到豫章去，与居巢县有何关系？他莫名其妙地瞅着魏别驾，问道：

"魏大人，王县令是来送大人吗？"

"不，县令大人是来接我的。仲卿，本别驾几天以前就不再是庐江郡别驾，而是居巢县丞了。"

"啊！"焦仲卿像被兜头浇了一桶冷水。怪不得这几天魏别驾对调任之事总是吞吞吐吐，肯定是许太守私下里上了谗言，把魏别驾贬为居巢县丞了。焦仲卿这才理出了思路。唉，官场竟然是如此凶险。这个许太守，先是逼迫魏别驾出行中原，企图让他死于非命。幸而魏别驾命不该绝，平平安安地回来了，而且还受到朝廷的嘉奖。不知许太守背地里又捣了什么鬼，但仅看魏别驾今天遭贬的下场，谁个心中不明白？

王县令很识趣地向魏别驾告辞退出。焦仲卿难以相信魏别驾被贬为居巢县丞是真的，随后也走出官厅，追上王县令与何主簿，说道：

days ago, and already he has sent you, Sir, to hurry me on my way."

"Oh, no, not at all, I assure you, Sir," Wang protested, with mock sincerity. He and Secretary He were still on their feet, not yet daring to sit down.

Zhongqing was puzzled by this exchange. When he first heard that Mounted Escort Wei had been ordered by the emperor to take up a post at Yuzhang, he had been overjoyed. Now, he was not so sure. What had the move to Yuzhang to do with Juchao County? He looked blankly at the prefect, and asked, "Excuse me, Sir, but has Magistrate Wang come to escort you to Yuzhang?"

"No, Zhongqing," his superior replied. "I ceased to be the prefect of Lujiang some days ago. My new post is that of assistant to the magistrate of Juchao County."

Zhongqing felt as though a bucket of cold water had been thrown over him. No wonder Mounted Escort Wei had given evasive answers every time he had brought up the subject of the move to Yuzhang! The young man guessed that this demotion was the result of Commander Xu spreading slander about Mounted Escort Wei. Officialdom really was a dangerous arena, he thought to himself. Commander Xu had forced Mounted Escort Wei to make a perilous journey to the Central Plains, hoping that he would meet a violent death on the way. But when the prefect had not only returned safe and sound but with an imperial commendation too, Xu had set to work behind the scenes to encompass his enemy's downfall. It was plain to see Xu's hand in this career setback for Mounted Escort Wei.

Meanwhile, Magistrate Wang tactfully took his leave, whereupon Zhongqing also excused himself and hurried after him.

"王大人，何大人，借一步说话。"

两人停了下来，告诉焦仲卿此事确凿无疑，焦仲卿这才死了心，他怔怔地仰头望天，脚像被粘在地上一样，想挪一步都挪不动。

"仲卿兄弟，我还没来得及向你道喜呢！"何主簿说。

焦仲卿以为何主簿在讥刺他，但他与何主簿素无恩怨，况且自己想随魏别驾前往豫章的主意何主簿并不知道，也就无从讥刺。想到这里，焦仲卿倒疑惑起来，问道：

"不知仲卿何喜可贺？"

"你母亲已经给你定亲了，新人是咱居巢县的秦罗敷，此事难道不可贺？"

何主簿这话对焦仲卿来说，既让他感到意外，又不是特别意外。不意外是因为自己在家时，母亲就曾提到过罗敷的事，意外的是，母亲对自己的婚事竟然操办得如此之紧。一旦与罗敷定下，与兰芝的关系将如何处理？眼见得带领兰芝远走高飞的打算化为泡影，下一步该如何走，他心里一片茫然。

天色已晚，王县令与何主簿等住进了离郡衙不远的一家客舍，刚刚盥洗完准备休息，忽然有郡中吏人来到店里，说许太守唤何主簿速到府上说

Scarcely able to believe that Mounted Escort Wei had been assigned such a lowly position as that of assistant county magistrate, he asked the magistrate and Secretary He if it was true. When they assured him that it was, Zhongqing stood rooted to the spot, plunged into the depths of despair.

He was startled out of his gloomy reverie by the secretary's saying, "Master Zhongqing, I have not had the chance to congratulate you."

At first, Zhongqing thought that the other was mocking him. But then, harboring no grudge against the secretary and realizing that the man could not have known how much he had been looking forward to accompanying Mounted Escort Wei to Yuzhang, he simply said, "I beg your pardon. On what am I to be congratulated?"

"Your mother has arranged a match for you," Secretary He replied. "Your second wife will be Qin Luofu of our Juchao County. Surely that is a matter for congratulations."

This information surprised and didn't surprise Zhongqing at the same time. It didn't surprise him, because his mother had often spoken warmly of Luofu; what did surprise him was the swiftness with which his mother had moved to arrange another marriage for him. But what on earth would become of his relationship with Lanzhi once he was betrothed to Luofu? His plan to flee with Lanzhi to a far-off place seemed to be dissolving in front of his very eyes. He was at a complete loss what to do next.

As the evening shadows were gathering, Magistrate Wang and Secretary He put up for the night in a guesthouse not far from the prefectural office. They had washed, and were getting ready to retire to bed, when a prefectural official arrived

话。何主簿是个胆小怕事的人，自己只是个县里的小主簿，现在郡守大人传唤，他心中十分忐忑。对于太守此举，王县令也心中没底，但他毕竟比何主簿老练些，镇定自若地对何主簿说："无论何事，且去听听无妨。"

"我们没有开罪太守大人吧？"何主簿神情有些慌乱。

王县令眼珠转了两转，说："开罪太守大人，也轮不着治你的罪，你怕什么？"

"是是！"何主簿索性定住了神，管他呢，是吉是凶，听完再说。

unexpectedly, saying that Commander Xu wanted to see Secretary He immediately. Now the secretary was a timid man by nature, and such a peremptory summons from so exalted a personage as the commander put him all in a dither. Magistrate Wang too was somewhat perturbed by the message, but, being somewhat more experienced than the secretary, calmly advised the latter not to hesitate, but to go and see what the commander wanted, there being nothing, he was sure, to worry about.

"But perhaps we have offended the commander?" stammered Secretary He.

"If the commander is displeased about something, it can hardly be your fault, can it?" said Wang, with a sigh of exasperation.

"I suppose not," said the secretary, calming down a little.

As to whether good fortune or calamity awaited Secretary He, we shall discover in the course of time.

◎第七章
太守逼嫁鸳鸯集

　　且说何主簿被唤进太守家中，已是夜静时分，他惴惴不安地跟着吏人进了书房。太守一见何主簿，吩咐了一声："看坐。"

　　何主簿深深作了一揖，说：

　　"小的不敢。小的一向在县里奔走，不知太守大人唤小人何事？"

　　"没事不会请你的。"许太守把手中的茶壶放在桌上，眯着本来就不大的眼睛，慢条斯理地说。

　　"能为太守大人效力，小人不胜荣幸。"

　　"听说你挺会保媒呢，你这个县主簿可干得不赖啊！"

　　何主簿不知太守葫芦里卖的什么药，立刻双腿跪下。

　　"不，小人一向恪尽职守，保媒之事断断没有！"

　　"慌什么，我又没要惩处你，我这是在夸你能干。"许太守还是那副不紧不慢的口气，"听说你给王县令的三公子说了一趟媒，让女家回绝了，有这事吧？"

Chapter Seven
Commander Xu Forces Lanzhi to Wed His Son

It was late at night when Secretary He arrived in the presence of Commander Xu. The secretary, his knees knocking, was led by a servant into the commander's study, where he was sternly ordered to be seated.

The secretary made a low bow, and apologized for not being available earlier, as, he said, he had been running around town on official business. He then inquired the reason for this summons.

"It was not for nothing that I sent for you," drawled the commander, putting his teapot back on the table and narrowing his already slit-like eyes still further.

"I would consider it an honor if I were able to render any slight service to Your Lordship," purred the secretary.

"It has come to my notice that you are good at arranging matches," said the commander. "As the secretary of the county, you must have much influence in that direction, eh?"

At this, Secretary He, who could not yet fathom what was up the commander's sleeve, thought that, to be on the safe side, he'd better deny any dabbling in that field. This he did, vehemently, falling to his knees.

"There's no need to lie," Commander Xu assured him, "I'm not going to punish you. Just commending your ability, that's all." He continued, in tones neither hurried nor hesitant. "I have heard that you arranged a match for the third son of Magistrate Wang.

何主簿的心吊到了嗓子眼儿，看来许太守已经把自己到鸳鸯集为王公子求亲之事了解得清清楚楚了，还有什么可辩解的。是凶是吉，听天由命吧。

"老夫是任人唯贤，"许太守挪一挪肥胖的身躯道，"你既然懂得说媒之事，今天就委托你为老夫说一桩婚事。"

"不知大人要小的玉成何人？"何主簿听出了点儿门道，不像刚来时那样紧张了。

"不瞒你说，老夫有一犬子，年已二十，尚未婚娶。现在老夫要你再去一趟鸳鸯集，为犬子作成这门亲事。"

"这……"

"怎么，不行吗？"许太守见何主簿面有难色，声调里透出一种不容置辩的强硬。

"不不！太守大人误会了。"何主簿连忙否认，可他心中确实有所顾虑，除了怕得罪王县令外，他又风闻太守的儿子是个痴呆，那刘兰芝连风流倜傥的王公子都不肯嫁，怎么能答应嫁给太守的傻儿子呢？他不敢贸然答应此事。

"小人的意思是说太守大人的虎子应当娶一位显宦之女，才称得上门当户对，那刘家女儿是个乡村女子，又是被婆家休了的，怎么配进太守大人这深宅大院？"

The girl's family turned him down. Is that right?"

The secretary's heart jumped into his mouth. "He knows all about my trip to Yuanyang on that matchmaking errand for young Wang!" he thought, in a panic. He couldn't for the moment think how he could explain it away, and wondered whether he was in hot water or not. In despair, the secretary resigned himself to fate.

"Now, you see," said the commander, shifting his vast bulk to make himself more comfortable, "I am the sort of person who appoints people on their merits. And, since you have the gift of the gab when it comes to matchmaking, today I'm assigning you to arrange a match on my behalf."

"May I inquire for whom my paltry services are required?" said the secretary, much less nervous now that he was beginning to suspect where all this was leading.

"For my son," was the prompt reply. "He's already twenty years of age, and still unmarried. I want you to go back to Yuanyang, and arrange a match for him with a family there."

As the secretary simply stood there gaping, Xu barked, "What's the matter? You don't want to go, is that it?" The tone of his voice left no room for doubt as to the answer he expected.

"No, no, please do not misunderstand, " the secretary gabbled. However, his mind was filled with misgivings. Apart from the fact that he was afraid to offend Magistrate Wang, he had heard that the commander's son was a dolt of the first order. If Liu Lanzhi had spurned the dashing young Wang, how on earth could anyone expect her to accept an offer of marriage from Commander Xu's blockhead of a son? Obviously, he had to think of some delaying tactic.

"You see, sir, it's just that I was thinking that the esteemed young master should marry a girl from a high-ranking official's family. Only then would your two families be regarded as suitably

"不错，刘家女儿是个乡村女子，可我听说她祖上是在朝做官之人，你知道吗？至于说被婆家休了，老夫也略有耳闻，那只能说刘兰芝错嫁了人，她婆家有眼无珠。哼，可惜这是些民家琐事，不然的话，对这样的糊涂人，老夫定要治她的罪。"许太守倒拿出一副颇为不平的架势，"这些不是你操心的事，你只管到刘家去说，若是此事做成，老夫是不会薄待你的。"

何主簿还是不敢应承，喃喃地说："那刘兰芝是个倔女子，上次小人去鸳鸯集给王公子说媒，任凭小人磨破嘴皮，她也不答应。小人笨嘴拙舌，不会说话，望太守大人派个能言善辩之人，小人着实无能。"

"婚姻大事岂能由她自己做主？你去对她母亲说，她愿意嫁也得嫁，不愿意嫁也得嫁！"

何主簿明白了太守的意思，分明是要强娶刘兰芝，他也只有听命而已。

他怏怏地回到客舍，王县令正像热锅上的蚂蚁，焦急地等他回来，一见面，便迫不急待地问道：

"太守唤你何事？"

"唉！"何主簿长长地叹了口气，不敢正眼看王县令，他低着头，说道："王大人，此事说大则大，说小则小。事情也不关王大人，只可怜瑞琪公

matched. That Liu girl is the daughter of a lowly country squire. Moreover, she has already been expelled from her first husband's house. I hardly think it proper for a young woman like that to be accepted into your own prestigious mansion, Your Lordship."

"Yes, she may be a country girl now, but I have heard that she is descended from a court official in the olden times," objected the commander. "Didn't you know that? As for her divorce, that only shows that the marriage was a mistake in the first place — and that her mother-in-law didn't appreciate Liu Lanzhi's fine qualities, that's all." He snorted, "Hmm! Unfortunately, that was a private matter; otherwise I would have prosecuted that muddle-headed old woman." As he said this, Commander Xu looked as though Lady Jiao had offended him personally. "Anyway," he went on, "you don't have to bother your head about that. All you have to do is go to the Lius and ask for Lanzhi's hand in marriage for my son. Pull this off, and you won't find me ungrateful, I assure you."

Secretary He still dithered. "But, Your Lordship," he pleaded, "that Liu Lanzhi is as stubborn as a rock. That time I went to Yuanyang, I talked myself hoarse to persuade her to accept Magistrate Wang's son. But she wouldn't budge an inch. I simply don't have the gift of the gab, Indeed, you would be far better off sending someone who has a better way with words than I do."

"Do you mean to tell me that she's going to decide an important matter like marriage all by herself?" the commander sneered. "What you do first of all is go and see her mother, you dunderhead! She's the one with the final say."

It was then that the secretary realized that Commander Xu's intention was to force Lanzhi to marry his son. So, there was nothing for him to do but comply with the commander's order.

Downcast, Secretary He trudged back to his lodgings, where

子，不知他是否能忍受得了。"

王县令慢慢听何主簿说完，心里像是堵了一块石头，他虽然并不十分赞成瑞琪娶刘兰芝，但他也明白刘兰芝在儿子心中的分量，如果刘兰芝被太守家娶过去，不等于要了儿子的命嘛！可如今太守要强娶刘兰芝，自己也无计可施。

何主簿也知道王公子是个情种，可是如果为了刘兰芝而与太守相抗，恐怕事情就更难收拾了。更难办的是自己，他不知自己为太守去刘家提亲，王县令会怎么想。也不知他不去为太守提亲，会落得什么下场。官场难啊，官场难！

魏别驾准备离任了，焦仲卿帮他打点好行装，朝他施了一礼，说道：

"魏大人，多谢您对焦某一片挚爱，大人且去居巢，仲卿随后便向太守请求，跟随大人回县听差。"

"别说傻话了，贬为居巢县丞，这不过是第一步而已，用不上三个月，我可能就会人头落地了。人活一世，死生有命，奸人当道，魑魅横行，魏某早已将生死置之度外。可惜原打算帮你破镜重圆，如今看来已不可能了，抱歉，抱歉！"

"大人说哪里话，是小的给大人添麻烦。好在小的家住居巢县，日后见面的机会还多。"

he found Magistrate Wang in an agony of suspense. Without any formality whatsoever, the latter pounced on the secretary:

"What did he want?" he demanded.

Secretary He, not daring to look the magistrate in the eye, uttered a long sigh. Finally, his head bowed, he said, "Sir, the matter does not affect you directly, but ... but, I don't know how young Master Ruiqi will take it."

As he listened to this opaque speech, Magistrate Wang felt as though a solid lump were growing in his heart. Although he did not fully approve of his son's attachment to Lanzhi, he was aware what she meant to him, and that if she were married off to Commander Xu's son it might be the death of Ruiqi! Yet, the commander, it seemed, was scheming to force Lanzhi into marrying his son. The magistrate was at his wits' ends.

Secretary He was in a quandary too. He knew how passionately in love with Lanzhi the magistrate's son was, but he was terrified of opposing Commander Xu in this matter. But if he obeyed the commander, and went to Lanzhi's house with his proposal, what would Magistrate Wang think of him? It's a dog's life in officialdom, he reflected, a dog's life!

In the meantime, Mounted Escort Wei was preparing to leave for his new post. Jiao Zhongqing got his baggage ready, and then went to his superior. After saluting the latter sincerely, the young man said, "Your Honor, I wish to express my gratitude for the kindness you have shown me. Now that you are to depart for a new position in Juchao County, I wish to inform you that I intend to ask the commander to allow me in due time to follow you there, and serve you as a clerk."

"What foolish talk is this, my boy?" cried the astonished Wei.

焦仲卿送了一程，与魏别驾长揖而别。

这几天的变故，使焦仲卿如堕五里雾中，他真不明白，为什么原本艰难的人世上，人与人之间还不能彼此谅解，彼此关爱。他的神思越来越恍惚，饮食也日渐衰减，府中的一些事务，处理起来也是心不在焉，时常出错。

这一日，焦仲卿觉得十分烦闷，他感到原本宽敞的厅堂如今像被压缩了一样，变得格外窄狭，好像要把他压垮挤碎一样。他实在受不了这种莫名的窒闷，撂开公务，走出厅堂，沿着郡衙前的大街信步徜徉。呼吸到新鲜的空气，见到了街边的绿柳，听到了树上的鸟鸣，他觉得心情好了一些。

突然，他远远地看到邻家张二哥骑着马正朝这边走来。他迎上前去，向张二哥打了个招呼。

张二哥也见到了焦仲卿，他翻身下马，额头上已挂满汗水。

"太巧了，在路上就碰到你，我还担心到衙门里找你，人家不让我进去呢！"

"二哥，你是来找我的？"焦仲卿有些奇怪。

"是啊，你娘病了，特地让我给你捎个信儿，叫你赶快回去呢！"

孔/雀/东/南/飞

"My transfer to Juchao is only the first step in my degradation. In all likelihood, I'll lose my head before three months are out. Life and death are matters decided by Fate. In these troubled times, with scoundrels holding sway and fiends riding roughshod over the people, I have long ceased to have any attachment to life, or any aversion to death. My only regret is that I was not able to bring you and your wife back together. There seems to be no hope of that now. Please accept my humblest apologies."

"The fact is, Sir," stammered Zhongqing, dismayed, "that I have caused you a great deal of trouble. But, luckily, Juchao is my hometown, and therefore I am sure we will have many opportunities to meet again." Zhongqing then saw Wei off on his journey, bowed deeply, and left him.

The upheavals of the previous few days had left Jiao Zhongqing feeling dazed. He really could not understand how, in this troubled world, people did not show consideration and fondness for each other. He became more and more absent-minded as the days went by, paying less and less attention to his meals, and doing his official work in such a desultory way that he started to make mistakes.

One day, Zhongqing was feeling particularly depressed. The walls of the hall where he did his work, which seemed spacious enough at ordinary times, suddenly seemed to be closing in on him, until he felt that they were on the point of crushing him to pieces. Unable to endure the suffocating sensation any longer, he pushed his work aside, and hurried out. Wandering up and down the street and gulping lungfuls of air, he relaxed somewhat, a process assisted by the soothing sight of green willow trees and the cheerful chirping of the birds perched on their branches.

"什么？"焦仲卿的心一下子收紧了，"得的什么病？要紧不要紧？"

"什么病我也不知道，是你家妹子来说的，她小小年纪也说不清楚。我去看了看，老人家躺在床上，闭着眼，也没跟我说话。我怕误事，就赶紧来了。"

"那你还有别的事吗？"

"我是来走亲戚的。"

"那你去吧，二哥，我这就回府告假。"

焦仲卿刚刚转好的心情一下子又变得坏极了。他急匆匆赶回了府衙。

王县令从郡城回来后，第一件事就是来看瑞琪。他不知如何对瑞琪说这件事，只好先聊聊别的。

"怎么样，好多了吧？"

"爹爹，你是知道孩儿心事的，我现在最怕像上回一样耽误了向刘家提亲之事，求爹爹派何主簿快些到鸳鸯集去为孩儿提亲。"

这句话正扎在王县令心里，看着如此痴情的瑞琪，他真是左右为难。

"瑞琪，何主簿不是已经去过刘家了嘛，那刘兰芝既然如此铁石心肠，你难道就不懂强扭的瓜不甜这样浅的道理吗？"

Suddenly, he spied in the distance his neighbor from Yuanyang Second Brother Zhang approaching on horseback. He hastened forward, and called out to Zhang.

The other jumped down from his horse, beads of sweat glistening on his forehead. "What a stroke of luck meeting you in the street!" he said to Zhongqing. "I was afraid they wouldn't let me into the prefectural office to see you."

"Oh, you're coming to see me?" cried Zhongqing in surprise.

"Yes, your mother's ill," Second Brother Zhang informed him. "She sent me specially to tell you that, and to urge you to return home at once."

"What?" gasped Zhongqing, as a spasm seized his heart. "What's the matter? Is it serious?"

"I don't know what kind of illness it is. It was your sister who came to inform me, and she was not too clear what it was herself. I hurried over, and found your mother lying in bed with her eyes closed. She didn't speak to me. I was afraid to delay any longer, so I came here as quick as I could."

"Have you any other business here?" asked Zhongqing.

"Yes, I intend to call on relatives," said Second Brother Zhang.

"Very well, I'll go straight back to the office, and ask for leave," said Zhongqing. Just as he had been beginning to feel better, his spirits had been cast back into the depths of gloom and foreboding. He rushed back to the prefectural office.

When Magistrate Wang got back from the prefectural capital, the first thing he did was to go and see his son Ruiqi. Unable to bring himself to broach the matter he had to inform him of, he started with small talk: "Well, how have you been? Fine, I suppose?"

"Father," interrupted the petulant youth, "you know my state

"爹爹，孩儿自知如此执拗使长辈为难，可是这情乃心中所生，不由自主啊！"

"不必如此。天下并不只有刘兰芝一个好女子，上次曾给你说的那个秦罗敷，不也是美貌大方，招人喜爱吗？"

"孩儿说不出罗敷姑娘有什么不好，可孩儿就是不能为之动情。论相貌，刘兰芝比不上罗敷姑娘，这一点我自心知肚明。只是兰芝的琴声在我心里何等震撼，爹爹你是想不出来的。"说到这里，瑞琪激动起来，"除了兰芝，我谁也不想娶！"

王县令不明白儿子为什么如此冥顽不化，心里又气又急。尽管他对儿子历来百依百顺，可这次，他却真的动怒了，不由得声调也高起来：

"这不行！你知道刘兰芝为什么被焦家休了吗？是因为她不能生育！"

"这种事谁能说得清！"王瑞琪顶了一句。

"就算是不能生育，为父也依顺了你，可是人家刘家不愿意，我总不能强抢民女吧！再说，许太守已经……"

大概王县令也是怒火攻心，一时说漏了半句。当他意识到这一点，急忙把话头截住时，已经来不及了。

瑞琪警惕起来，眼睛瞪得像要从眼眶里爆出

of mind these days. I am only afraid that you will delay like you did last time. I beseech you to hurry up and send Secretary He to arrange my marriage with Lanzhi."

These words pierced his father's heart like a knife. The sight of the lovelorn Ruiqi filled Magistrate Wang with anguish.

"Ruiqi, Secretary He has already called at the Liu household once, hasn't he?" the magistrate said, plaintively, almost pleadingly. "Lanzhi was adamant in her refusal, remember? Don't you know that melons wrenched out of the ground are never sweet-tasting?"

"Father," replied the young man, "I know that this obsession of mine will probably be the death of me. But I can't help it. It is a love that springs from the heart."

"Come to your senses, my boy," his father urged. "Lanzhi isn't the only nice girl in the world. What about that girl Qin Luofu, I talked to you about before? Isn't she a lovely, adorable creature?"

"I'm not saying there's anything objectionable about Qin Luofu, Father; it's just that I'm not in love with her, that's all," said Ruiqi. "As a matter of fact, she's better looking than Liu Lanzhi, I admit. But you don't realize, Father, how the sound of Lanzhi's lute made my heartstrings quiver." He paused, and then a passionate cry burst from his lips: "If I can't marry Lanzhi, I'll never marry at all!"

For Magistrate Wang, driven to the point of utter exasperation by his son's thick-headed stubbornness, although he had always indulged the boy's whims in the past, this was the last straw. "Don't talk such rubbish!" he yelled. "Do you know why Lanzhi was driven from her husband's home? Well, I'll tell you: It was because she can't conceive a child, that's why!"

"How can anyone know that?" rebutted his son.

来：

"许太守？许太守怎么了？"

事已至此，王县令想，索性把实情和盘托出，或许能绝了瑞琪的望，他才会回心转意，也未可知。他叹了口气，说道：

"许太守已经命何主簿去鸳鸯集，为他儿子说媒去了！"

"兰芝？"

"不错。而且是依也得依，不依也得依。"

"啊！"王瑞琪突然大叫了一声，还没等王县令定下神来，早已"哇"地吐出一口鲜血，躺倒在床上。

"瑞琪！瑞琪！"王县令见儿子昏厥过去，嘴唇发青，嘴角的鲜血还在往外流，一下子惊呆了，他双手抱住儿子的肩头，失声大叫："快，快来人！快去请郎中！快！"

再说焦仲卿听得母亲病重，赶紧回郡衙告过假，便骑马上路，向居巢县城奔去。

一路上，他心乱如麻，先是想着母亲的病，数日前身体尚且康强，怎么会忽然重病在身呢？唉，母亲也是自取其殃，如果善待兰芝，身边不还多一个伺候的人吗？如今兰芝不知怎样，此行就经过鸳鸯集，是否该去看望看望她？可自己现

"Well, anyway, even if I were willing to indulge you in this matter, Lanzhi refuses to marry you, and I can't just go around kidnapping girls off the street. Besides, Commander Xu has already...." Here, just on the point of letting the cat out of the bag, he caught his tongue. But it was too late.

Ruiqi's ears pricked up, and his eyes bulged almost out of their sockets. "Commander Xu?" he queried. "What's Commander Xu got to do with this?"

Realizing that the truth couldn't be concealed any further, and reflecting that if Ruiqi knew that Commander Xu had chosen Lanzhi as a bride for his own son he might see that there was no hope for him, and drop the matter, the magistrate decided to come clean. With a deep sigh, he said,"Commander Xu has ordered Secretary He to go to Yuanyang and ask for Lanzhi's hand for the commander's son." "Lanzhi?" "Yes, and it seems the secretary's not to take no for an answer." At this, Ruiqi uttered a piercing cry, and before his father could do anything to calm him down, fell on the bed, vomiting blood.

For a moment, the magistrate just stood there, dazed, gazing in horror at the senseless body of his son, from the blue lips of which blood ran in a steady stream. Then, gripping the boy by the shoulders, he called hoarsely for help.

In the meantime, Jiao Zhongqing obtained compassionate leave from his office, and rode like the wind to Juchao County.

On the way, his mind was in a turmoil. First he thought of his mother. He had left his mother hale and hearty not long before, so what could be the cause of this sudden illness? Upon sober reflection, he concluded that this emergency was probably his mother's own fault: If she hadn't treated Lanzhi so badly there

在以什么身份到刘家去呢？到了刘家，又如何面对兰芝母亲和兄长呢？魏别驾的仕途急转直下，使自己失去了惟一能够信赖倚恃的官长，此后的新上司是什么样的人，只有天知道。此行能否见到魏别驾？魏别驾又为何说三个月人头落地呢？这一切，焦仲卿都想不明白。他时而神情散乱，那马儿便慢下来，时而又盼着快快到家，加上两鞭，那马儿又狂奔不止。到家时，已是黄昏时分了。

"开门！开门！"焦仲卿用力摔打着门环，大声地叫。

小妹梅梅跑来开门，一见哥哥，还是满脸笑意，亲热地叫着：

"哥，你回来啦！"

"娘怎么样？"焦仲卿没有理会妹妹，牵着马径直往院里走。

"娘？啊，娘没有病，她有话要对你说，又怕你告不下假，就让我跟邻家二哥说了个谎。哥，对不起呀！"

"谁说娘没病！"焦母听到梅梅的话，从屋里迎了出来，脸上挂着一丝难得的笑容，"娘有心病，也用不着请郎中，你哥哥就能治好。"

"母亲！"焦仲卿长吁了一口气，又带着埋怨的口气说："你老人家没有病，却要说有病，把我

would have been an extra person in the house to look after her.
He toyed with the idea of paying a visit to the Lius on his way
through Yuanyang, to see how Lanzhi was getting along. But, on
second thoughts, he decided that he could not face her mother
and brother. Then he thought of his superior Mounted Escort Wei.
The latter's sudden demotion had removed the only man in an
official position he could rely on. He wondered what kind of a
person Wei's replacement would be. Would he be able to meet
Wei on this journey? Why had Wei said that his head would roll
within three months?

All these ruminations left Zhongqing mystified. Whenever
his mind wandered, his horse slowed down, and then suddenly
an impatience to be home came upon the young man, and he
whipped the horse to a gallop. Dusk was falling when he finally
reached home.

Meimei answered his frenzied knocking. She received her
brother with a radiant smile.

"How is Mother?" Zhongqing asked anxiously, leading his
horse into the courtyard.

"Mother?" Meimei looked at him blankly. Then, recollecting,
she said, "Oh, mother is not really ill. It's just that she has some-
thing important to say to you. You see, she was afraid that you
would not be able to get leave in the ordinary way, and so she
sent me to tell that lie to our neighbor. Please don't be angry."

"Who says I'm not ill?"

Zhongqing and Meimei turned to see their mother standing
in the doorway. Lady Jiao's face was graced by a rare smile. "I'm
ill all right. I've got heart trouble." the old woman said, cheerfully
enough. "But there's no use sending for a doctor. Only your brother
can cure me."

吓死了。再说，没病往身上揽病，这也不吉利呀！"

"说的是。不过娘有大吉大利的大喜事要为你办，不就把这不吉利冲掉了吗？"

焦母把儿子拉进房中，兴冲冲地说：

"你和罗敷的亲事已经议定，这次我请了合八字的先生给你们仔细地推算，你两人的命相十分相合，吉期就定在后五日。你看看，娘把新婚的东西都给你备办好了，中意不中意？罗敷姑娘那边的陪嫁也丰厚得很，不用你操心。"

焦仲卿的眼睛像是蒙上了一层薄雾，面对着摆满房间的锦被、鸳枕、幔帐、箱笼，他感到有点头昏目眩。中间那张新漆过的大方案上摆着两盏油灯。他还记得这张案子，那是自己与兰芝新婚时专门请木匠打制的。桌旁的两把椅子也重新漆过了，这两把椅子曾经是自己与兰芝共话时经常坐的。他眼前又浮现出兰芝坐在椅子上，用含情的目光与自己四目相视的情景。他迷蒙的眼里，仿佛兰芝又重新回到桌旁的椅子上轻轻坐下，以手支颐，那双柔情万种的眼睛又在注视着他，嘴角仍挂着幸福而又苦涩的笑意。唉，如今物是人非，兰芝永远也不可能再坐在椅子上弹箜篌、诉衷情、读诗书了，替代她的，将是一位十分美丽，但与自己的心相隔遥远的姑娘。兰芝呢，她怎么办？

"Mother, you scare me to death, saying that you're ill," Zhongqing chided her. "Besides, it's bad luck for a healthy person to claim to be sick."

"Well, that bad luck will be wiped out by the wonderfully auspicious big event I have planned for you," said Lady Jiao. And, with that, she pulled him into the inner room, and said, in an excited whisper:

"I've arranged for you to marry Luofu. What's more, I've already asked a soothsayer to read your horoscopes, and he finds that you two are perfectly compatible! I've fixed the wedding for five days from now. You see, I've taken care of everything. Aren't you pleased? Another thing: Luofu's dowry is going to be a very generous won, never fear!"

A mist seemed to cloud Zhongqing's eyes. Groggily, he looked around the room, and perceived that it had been furnished as a bridal chamber — with quilts, pillows, bed hangings and chests. In the middle of the room was a newly lacquered table, upon which stood two oil lamps. He remembered that the table was one which he and Lanzhi had ordered made specially for their nuptials. The two chairs which accompanied it were newly lacquered also. They were the chairs on which he and Lanzhi used to sit to chat. A vision of Lanzhi sitting in one of them and gazing at him with loving tenderness rose before his eyes, resting her cheek in the palm of her hand, and wearing that happy but wistful smile of hers. Ah, but she would never sit in that seat again, playing her *konghou*, whispering tender words and reading poetry. Instead, it would be occupied by a girl — beautiful, it is true — but far from his heart. Oh, Lanzhi, what will become of you? He thought, in anguish.

Suddenly, he awoke from his reverie.

"娘啊！"焦仲卿像是从迷惘中走回来，声音嘶哑地说："你老人家的好意我实在不能领受。我与兰芝原本如鱼似水，情投意合。从兰芝走进焦家的第一天起，我们就指天盟誓，今生今世，永不分离。可你老人家从不理解我的心思，非要把她休回家去，我的心已经死了，母亲你能看得见吗？"

焦母的脸色渐渐阴沉下来。

"儿送兰芝回娘家的时候，又发下誓言：虽然是棒打鸳鸯各东西。但两颗心永不分离。我原想劝您老人家回心转意，可您却全然不顾儿与兰芝的情意，真的与秦家订下亲事。罗敷姑娘根本不属于我，她嫁过来也不可能得到任何幸福，您这是何苦呢！"

"儿啊，你不知道，这罗敷姑娘又伶俐又懂事，等把她娶过来，生下一男半女，一家人也是和和美美。那时你就明白为娘的苦心了。"

"母亲！"仲卿打断母亲的话，"儿今生只能再娶一回，就是把兰芝重新娶进焦家！"

"办不到！"焦母再也忍不住了，狠狠地拍了一下桌子。

"兰芝何罪？罗敷何辜？"焦仲卿的情绪也更激动。"您何必非要毁了两个好女人？"

"算了算了！你今天刚进家门就把我气个半死。我现在不跟你理会，睡觉时好好想一想，娘究

"Mother," he croaked, "I'm afraid that I can't accept your kind offer. Lanzhi and I are like fish and water; we are perfect for each other. The very first day she entered this house, we swore an eternal vow never to part in this life. But you never understood my feelings, Mother. When you sent her away, my heart died."

Listening to this, Lady Jiao's face grew steadily cloudier.

The young man went on, "When you sent her back to her parents' home, we swore another oath: That whatever happened, our hearts would always be as one. I tried to get you to change your mind, but you wouldn't listen to me. And now you have arranged a marriage for me with Qin Luofu. I tell you, Mother, she cannot belong to me. No happiness can come of such a match, and then all your efforts will have been in vain."

But Lady Jiao countered with "My son, you don't understand. Luofu is a fine, intelligent girl. When you've been married for a while, and she bears you a male child, we'll all be a happy family. Then you will appreciate your mother's kindness."

"Mother!" Zhongqing interrupted her, "If I get married again, it will be to re-marry Lanzhi. I will never marry anyone else."

"That will never be!" the old woman cried, slamming her fist down on the table in exasperation.

"What crime has Lanzhi committed? And what harm has Luofu done to you? Why are you intent on destroying two fine young women?" Zhongqing was almost beside himself with anger by this time.

"That's enough!" screamed Lady Jiao. "No sooner have you set foot in the door of your own home than you abuse me half to death. I want nothing to do with you for the time being. Have a good night's rest, and think about whether your mother is trying to help you or harm you."

竟是为了你好还是在害你？"焦母气呼呼地说。

"娘，回房歇息吧。"梅梅刚才见到哥哥时的喜悦早已消失得无影无踪，她拉拉母亲的衣襟，轻声地说。

那张与兰芝共枕同眠的床，那张留给他无限春意的床，如今变得十分冰冷。焦仲卿懒得脱衣，随意地蜷缩在床上，习惯地将胳膊朝床里一搂，却搂了个空。他更感到凄凉和孤独。

在他的脑海里，两个女子的容貌交替地出现，刘兰芝充满忧愁的脸，苍白憔悴；秦罗敷灿如明月的脸，红唇皓齿。刘兰芝绝望而痛苦，秦罗敷幸福而欢快。刘兰芝渐渐地模糊了，而秦罗敷却张开双臂，向他奔跑过来。他吓得一闪身，竟真的从床上掉了下来。

他无法再睡，于是走出房门，仰望着天上的繁星。

太静了，静得让人窒息。

这时，他听到院墙角落里发出一种轻微的喷鼻声，这声音是那么亲切，他知道这是他的马发出的声音。

焦仲卿来到马房，轻轻地抚了抚马背，像是在自言自语，又像是在对马诉说：

"人为什么都要生活在痛苦之中？"

那马像是听懂了他的话，又摆摆头，发出一声

"Come away, Mother," said Meimei quietly, tugging the old woman's sleeve, her delight at seeing her brother again having disappeared without trace.

Zhongqing undressed languidly, and curled up on that cold comfortless bed of a thousand delights, where once he had shared a pillow with Lanzhi. By force of habit, he stretched out his arms — only to embrace emptiness. He felt even more lonely and desolate than ever.

In his mind's eye, pictures of two girls kept popping up alternately. Lanzhi's was careworn and haggard; Luofu's was as radiant as the moon, with ruby lips and pearly-white teeth. Lanzhi's showed despair and suffering; Luofu's showed happiness and gaiety. The image of Lanzhi then began to fade, while that of Luofu seemed to be running toward him with arms outstretched. A spasm of terror caused Zhongqing's body to quiver, and he fell out of bed.

Finding it impossible to get back to sleep, he left the house, and lifted his head to gaze at the stars.

The night was silent, silent enough to be suffocating.

Suddenly he heard a snuffling sound coming from a corner of the courtyard. It sounded like it was made by his horse. Zhongqing walked over to the stable, and stroked the animal, and said, partly to himself and partly to the horse: "Why is a man destined to lead a life of pain?"

As if it understood, the horse shook its head, and whinnied softly. Zhongqing found this strangely comforting. He hugged the horse's neck, and murmured, "Let's go. Let's go."

He unhitched the horse, and led it out of the courtyard. Zhongqing felt that only his horse could be a solace to him now. Forgetting even to close the gate, he mounted the horse, and

低鸣。这声音让焦仲卿得到了一点安慰，他搂住马头，低声说：

"我们走，我们走！"

他解开马缰，马儿顺从地随他走出院门。焦仲卿感到眼下最能给他带来宽慰的，就是自己的马。他连院门也忘记了关，翻身上马，直奔郡城而去。

何主簿又来到了鸳鸯集。这一次，他没让胡坎带路，径直来到刘家。

"何大人。"兰芝母亲认出了何主簿。一边把他让进家门，一边说："我上次不是跟大人说了吗，小女辜负了公子的美意，又劳大人跑到我们这陋乡僻壤来。"

"刘家妈妈，容我慢慢对你说。"何主簿进屋落坐，接过兰芝母亲递过来的汗巾，擦擦汗。

"我这回来，不是为了王公子。"何主簿把许太守求亲的意思原原本本地讲了出来，并暗示了这一次与上次不同，太守的命令是难以违抗的。他只是隐瞒了太守之子是个痴呆这个事实。

兰芝母亲自知做不了女儿的主，她把继宗叫来陪何主簿说话，自己匆匆来到兰芝房中。

兰芝在娘家这些日子很少出门，烦闷时，便飞针刺绣。她的心里仍旧燃着一把火，虽然忍受着时光的煎熬，但丈夫临别时的誓言却给了她希望，她

sped off in the direction of Lujiang.

Meanwhile, Secretary He had arrived in Yuanyang. This time, he dispensed with the services of Hu Kan, and went straight to the Liu house himself.

Lanzhi's mother was puzzled when she saw who the visitor was, and as she led the secretary inside, even before giving him a chance to sit down, she said, "Sir, I told you last time how stubborn my daughter was in refusing Master Wang's kind offer. I'm afraid you've had another wasted journey."

"Madame, let me explain," Secretary He said, as he mopped his brow with a towel Lanzhi's mother handed to him. "The situation this time is different from what it was before."

He then explained his mission in detail, hinting at dire consequences if Commander Xu's wish were to be thwarted. The one detail he purposely omitted was what a crass dunce the commander's son was.

Lanzhi's mother understood, and although she despaired of being able to persuade the girl to accept this new offer, nevertheless she hurried off to take the news to her daughter, leaving her son Jizong to keep Secretary He company.

For the past several days, Lanzhi had scarcely left her room, but busied herself with needlework to relieve her feelings of gloom. The agony in her heart was relieved by a glimmer of hope that Zhongqing would keep the promise he had made on parting, and in anticipation of the day they would be re-united was determined to look even more beautiful for him than when they were first married. She was embroidering a pretty new blouse.

"Who came, Mother?" she asked, as her mother entered the room. She had heard a knock at the gate, and a man's

盼望着丈夫早日来接她，那时她要把自己打扮得比初婚时更加美丽。她现在又在绣一件短襦。

"娘，谁来了？"兰芝问道，他听到了敲门声和一个男人的声音。

"是郡太守派何主簿来，为太守公子提亲的。"

"娘，我不是跟您讲过了嘛，女儿既嫁了焦仲卿，就不会再适他人。"兰芝一听说是提亲的，心里便有些烦。

"娘也是这么说呀，可这次何大人口气很硬，说是答应也得答应，不答应也得答应，没有商量。我们这种庄户人家，怎么抗得过太守大人呢？"兰芝母亲忧心忡忡地说。

"我不怕。"兰芝并无愠怒，语调坚决地说，"王县令不也是一县父母嘛，上次我们说不愿意，不也就推辞掉了嘛。"

"傻孩子，谁不知道王县令是个清廉的父母官，可郡太守就不一样了。何主簿虽然没有明说，可为娘是过来人，早就听出话外之音。若是不应下这门亲事，咱家怕是要遭殃了。"

兰芝没有立即答话，此时她心中想的却是焦仲卿准备得怎么样了，他什么时候才能把自己接回去？想着想着，她不禁在心中埋怨起仲卿来，为什么这么多天还没有音信呀？

兰芝母亲见她不说话，以为她心里活动了，继

孔/雀/东/南/飞/

voice.

Her mother came straight to the point: "It's Secretary He. Commander Xu has sent him with an offer of marriage on behalf of the commander's son."

"Mother, haven't I already told you that Jiao Zhongqing is my husband, and that I will never marry anyone else?" cried Lanzhi, pained.

"This time, it's different, I'm afraid," sighed the other. "Secretary He made it quite clear that a refusal is out of the question." She added, pleading: "We are only poor village folk; how can we go against the commander?"

"I don't care," rejoined Lanzhi, completely unperturbed. "We turned down Magistrate Wang's offer the last time, didn't we? Well, we can turn down this offer too."

"You silly, empty-headed child," her mother cried. "Everybody knows that Magistrate Wang is an honest and upright official, and that Commander Xu is completely different. The secretary didn't say so in as many words, but I know from experience how to take a hint. I'm afraid that if we disappoint the commander we will be bringing disaster on our own heads."

For a while, Lanzhi said nothing. She was wondering what Zhongqing was planning to do. When would he come for her? In her anguish, she began to feel resentment against him. Why had she heard no news from him for so long?

Her mother, thinking that Lanzhi might be softening at last, followed up what she perceived as her advantage, by saying, "Lanzhi, listen to me. A woman can't just do as she likes. I know perfectly well that there is only Zhongqing in your heart. But how can you be sure that he will keep his word?"

"I am sure that he will be faithful to his promise," said Lanzhi,

续说道：

"兰芝，女人家是没办法按自己的想法行事的，为娘何尝不知道你心中只有焦仲卿一个人，可焦仲卿的话能当真吗？"

"娘，我相信焦仲卿不会食言，不会负了女儿。"

"那他为什么还不来接你，这么多天，连个面也不露？"

"这……"兰芝语塞了。

"咣当"一声，刘继宗大步闯进来，兴冲冲地说：

"妹妹，你好福气呀！"

兰芝瞥了哥哥一眼，把头扭过去。

"怎么，你是不是又不愿意？"继宗瞪起眼睛，"妹妹，你真不识抬举，太守家的亲事，有几个人能攀得上？你糊涂到家了！"

"哥哥先别恼怒，我想问你一句，小妹这样一个被休的女子，何德何能敢登太守家的门？"

刘继宗没有想过这事，被妹妹一问，也答不上来。

"不管怎么说，县令、太守都来了，你千万不能一误再误。"

上次王县令来提亲，继宗正好不在家，回来后听说妹妹拒绝了婚事，心中好大不乐意。他想着如

simply.

"Then why has he not come to fetch you after all this time?" her mother demanded. "He hasn't as much as shown his face."

Lanzhi was at a loss how to reply to this. As she was hesitating, her brother came clattering into the room.

"Lanzhi, what a stroke of good luck for you!" he babbled.

The girl shot him a sideways glance, and turned her head away.

Taken aback, Jizong glared at her. "What? You don't mean to say you're going to turn the commander's son down, do you?" he demanded. "You don't know a Heaven-sent opportunity when you see one, that's your trouble. There are not many girls who would be lucky enough to receive such an honor. You're incredibly stupid!"

"Please don't be upset," Lanzhi begged him. "Just think: How can a girl who has been thrown out by her in-laws aspire to enter the mansion of the commander?"

The obtuse Jizong hadn't thought of this, and stood there dumbfounded for a while. In the end, he said, "Well, anyway ... you can't just keep turning down one suitor after another. First the son of the magistrate, then the commander's son...."

Jizong had happened to be out when Secretary He came with the proposal from Magistrate Wang's son. When he returned and learned that Lanzhi had spurned the offer, he had been angry. As the brother-in-law of the magistrate's son, he thought, he would not only get a government sinecure, but have all the people in the county eager to flatter him. At the very least, nobody would dare to bully him again. He couldn't understand why his sister didn't think of these things. From that time on, he had not missed a chance to intimate to her that she was the one who was stop-

果妹妹嫁给王公子，自己不但能在县里找份好差事，而且一县的人都会来巴结自己，至少也不会再受人欺负，没想到妹妹如此不懂事。从那时起，他就天天指桑骂槐，嫌妹妹耽误了自己的好事。今天太守又来提亲，那又非县令可比，继宗俨然觉得已经成了太守家的大舅哥，趾高气扬起来。

"那焦仲卿有什么好？芝麻大的小吏，什么忙也帮不上。他就是不休你，我还想让你离开他呢！如今你成了太守家的人，你哥哥我不就有了出头的日子了吗？哼，这回羞死焦仲卿和那死老婆子！"

兰芝母亲听了儿子说的这几句话，也觉得有道理。于是，也帮着继宗劝说女儿：

"兰芝，你别那么认死理，焦仲卿对你好没有用。他娘要休你，自然会给他另娶，不会老让他等着你的。"

这时继宗忽然想起刚刚何主簿说的话，抢过话头说：

"你还等着焦仲卿，那焦仲卿都快成亲了，新娘子就是咱鸳鸯集的秦罗敷！"

"你听谁说的？"连刘兰芝的母亲都感到有些意外。

"刚才何主簿告诉我的，是他亲口听说破天讲的。"

ping him making his way up the social ladder. But now, as soon as he heard of the offer from the son of the commander — who was of even more importance than the magistrate — he immediately pictured himself as part of the commander's family, strutting around and putting on airs.

"What was so wonderful about that Jiao Zhongqing, anyway? He was only a petty clerk; he couldn't help me get an official position. If he hadn't divorced you, I would have made you leave him. If you become a member of the commander's family, my future will be assured. And, moreover, Jiao Zhongqing and his mother will be green with envy!"

Lanzhi's mother saw the sense in this argument, and immediately backed her son up:

"Yes, indeed. Lanzhi, Jiao Zhongqing was not right for you. Besides, since his mother was the one who threw you out, you can be sure that she will lose no time finding another wife for him. She won't allow him to wait for you."

At this point, Jizong suddenly remembered something that Secretary He had told him, and he chimed in with, "Yes, but not only that. While you've been waiting for him, he's been busy getting another woman for himself. His bride-to-be is Qin Luofu, from right here in Yuanyang!"

This piece of news took both Lanzhi and her mother by surprise. "How do you know?" they chorused.

"Secretary He told me just now. He got it from Talk Even Heaven into Anything."

Lanzhi showed no reaction to this bombshell, but her heart felt as though it were being crushed under a great weight, and she found it difficult to breath. Even though her brother was a muddle-headed oaf, and was liable to spout all sorts of nonsense,

兰芝虽然一声没吭，一动没动，可她心里却像被铅砣狠狠地砸了一下，胸口闷得喘不上气来。哥哥虽然平常有天没日，信口胡说，但这句话她却相信。因为自己还在焦家的时候，就已看出焦母喜欢罗敷，而罗敷对焦仲卿的倾心，也是不言而喻的。难道焦仲卿真是个负心的男子？难道他真是贪恋罗敷的美貌而忘记了誓约？

"俗话说，痴心女子负心汉。"兰芝母亲也相信继宗的话，"兰芝啊，你还在这儿傻等他？何主簿既是这么说，肯定是真的了。"

兰芝心中烦乱极了，她真想奔到郡城问一问焦仲卿，又想奔到居巢县问一问罗敷，可莫说是做不到，就是真的去问了，又有什么用呢？

"你到底说个话呀，人家何主簿还等着呢！"

兰芝深知焦母的专横，她想要做的事，焦仲卿是违抗不了的。想到这里，她的心冷透了。

她抬起头，看着哥哥那副急不可待的样子，说：

"随你们的便吧！"

"你应了？"继宗兴奋起来。

"你想好了？"母亲将信将疑。

"娘！"兰芝一头扑进母亲怀里，"女儿的命为什么这样苦？"

for some reason Lanzhi felt that his words rang true this time.
She remembered that while she had been living in the Jiao
household, Lady Jiao and Qin Luofu had shown a liking for each
other. It was an unspoken affinity, but none the less real for that.
Was Zhongqing being unfaithful, after all? She wondered. Had
he fallen for Luofu's charms, and forgotten his vow?

"As the saying goes, 'When a girl is madly in love, the boy
betrays her.' " Lanzhi's mother also believed what Jizong had
said. "Lanzhi, how can you languish him like a fool, waiting for
somebody who is not going to come back for you? If Secretary
He said it, it must be true."

Lanzhi's head was in turmoil. She had an impulse to rush to
Lujiang, to confront Zhongqing. This was immediately replaced
by an impulse to rush to Juchao, to confront Luofu. But she real-
ized that this would be futile.

"Well?" said Jizong. "Secretary He is waiting for an answer."

Lanzhi knew how overbearing Lady Jiao could be. Once she
had made up her mind, there was nothing Zhongqing could do to
change it. Lanzhi's heart suddenly turned as cold as ice. Raising
her head, she said to her impatient brother: "Let it be as you
wish."

"You agree?" Jizong hooted in glee.

"Are you sure?" her mother said, in a tone of doubt.

Lanzhi threw herself into her mother's arms. "Oh, Mother,"
she cried, "why is your daughter's fate so cruel?"

焦仲卿
刘兰芝
之墓

◎第八章
两家合葬华山旁

　　许太守家里已经忙成一片，为了操办儿子的婚事，他已经两日没有坐衙了。且不说郡中大小吏役听说太守家有喜事都来送礼，就是属县令丞，也一个不缺地纷至沓来，一时间礼品堆积如山。

　　焦仲卿自从与母亲不辞而别回到郡中，终日里恍然若失。魏别驾已经离开郡衙，新别驾还没到任，他这几日倒是颇觉清闲。眼见得郡衙中来来往往不断有人送礼，他也懒得打听为什么，只是行走坐卧之间，时而觉出别人都用异样的眼光瞅他，甚至在他背后还有些叽叽喳喳的议论。初时只当是别人笑他的上司倒霉，或是议论他休妻之事，因此也不去计较。突然有一天，同衙的陈甲、陈乙兄弟来找他，说：

　　"仲卿兄弟，有件让你为难的事，本不想对你说，可这事早晚你也会知道，到那时，怕你说我们兄弟不义。"

　　"什么事？"焦仲卿无精打采地问。

　　"太守家的公子要娶亲，一郡里上上下下都去送贺礼，现在就剩下你没有表示意思了。我们若是

Chapter Eight
Buried Together at the Foot of Mount Hua

The household of Commander Xu was a hive of activity, with everybody bustling about making preparations for the wedding. Even the commander himself had not attended to his official duties for two days. Needless to say, at the news of the happy event, all the officials, high and low, of Lujiang Prefecture, as well as those of Juchao County, flocked to bring presents, until there was a pile of wedding gifts the size of a small hill.

Meanwhile, ever since leaving his mother's home so abruptly, Jiao Zhongqing had been acting like a man in a daze. Mounted Escort Wei had already left his post, and his replacement had not yet arrived, so for a few days he had little to do. Watching the steady stream of people arriving with gifts, he was disinclined to ask what the special occasion was, but in the course of his daily routine he could not help noticing the strange glances people cast at him from time to time; nor could he ignore the snatches of gossip he heard behind his back. At first, Zhongqing thought that people were sneering at the downfall of his mentor Mounted Escort Wei, or the breakdown of his marriage, so he took no particular notice. Then, suddenly one day two of his colleagues came on him. One of them said, "Brother Zhongqing, there is a matter which might distress you, and we are not sure how to broach the subject. But, since you will find out sooner or later, we are afraid that you will consider us false friends for not having informed you."

不告诉你，怕你将来有所得罪，告诉你吧，又怕你为难。"

"哦，原来如此。我又不是太守看得上眼的人，跟众位一起随个份子就行了，有何为难之处？"

"不是这个意思。"陈甲道，"因为这门亲事与你不无关系，我们怕你心中不快，故而迟迟不敢对你讲。"

"太守家的婚事与我有何相干？"焦仲卿不解地问。

"这，这，唉！"陈甲难于启齿，瞅瞅陈乙，"我就直说了吧，太守家要娶的，正是你的前妻刘兰芝。"

"什么！"焦仲卿顿时觉得如震雷轰顶，有些站立不稳，好一会儿才定住了神。他像失了魂魄一样左右顾盼了两眼，向陈氏兄弟作了一揖，说道："谢谢二位兄弟。"便跨出房门，直奔马房，解开缰绳，跨上马背，头也不回地朝鸳鸯集驰去。

大路上扬起团团黄尘，焦仲卿还嫌太慢，不时地在马背上抽一鞭子。来到鸳鸯集时还不到日晡。他在兰芝家门前跳下马，使劲地拍打着刘家的大门。

"来啦来啦！"开门的是刘继宗，他一见是焦

"What is it?" Zhongqing inquired dully.

"The commander's son is about to be married," replied the other man. "Everyone of standing in the prefecture has donated a wedding present — all except you. You have shown no interest whatsoever. We are afraid that such a breach of etiquette could land you in hot water. Please excuse my bluntness."

"Oh, I see," said Zhongqing. "Well, as my position is a lowly one, such as to be beneath the commander's notice, I suppose I'll just do what the ordinary run of people do on these occasions. I can't see any problem."

The first man objected, "It's not quite as easy as that, I'm afraid. The reason we hesitated to approach you is that this marriage is not unconnected with yourself, and the news might be painful for you to hear."

"What can a marriage in the commander's family have to do with me?" asked Zhongqing, puzzled.

His visitors exchanged uneasy glances. Finally, one of them plucked up courage to say, "The fact is Brother Zhongqing, the bride is your former wife, Liu Lanzhi."

"What!" howled Zhongqing, feeling as if he had been struck by a thunderbolt. He staggered where he stood. Regaining his composure somewhat, he gazed wildly around, made a hurried bow, and thanked the speaker. Then, he ran out to the stables, flung himself on his horse, and galloped full speed in the direction of Yuanyang without a backward glance.

Zhongqing wielded his whip all the way along the road, urging the horse on to greater and greater speed. The horse's hooves raised clouds of choking yellow dust, but the young man seemed not to notice. It was not even dusk when Zhongqing dismounted at the gate of the Liu house in Yuanyang. He commenced to beat

仲卿，脸就拉了下来，"你来干什么？"

"大哥，让我进去说话。"焦仲卿说着就往门里闯。

"哎哎，谁是你大哥！"刘继宗没好气地说，"有什么话，就在这儿说吧。快点，我还忙着呢，没功夫陪你！"

"大哥，大哥，我要找兰芝！"焦仲卿还想往里走，却被刘继宗挡在门外。

"你是兰芝的什么人？你凭什么要找兰芝？"

"兰芝是我妻子，我要找她说话，你不要拦我！"焦仲卿不由得也提高了嗓门。

"兰芝是你妻子？"刘继宗依然横着两臂，用鄙夷的口气说，"不错，我妹子是嫁过你，可你一个小小的郡吏，竟然把她休了回来！我妹子现在不是你的人了，你放聪明点吧，她现在是太守大人的儿媳了！你也不看看你这副嘴脸，还敢欺负我妹妹。咱们走着瞧！"

"我不与你歪缠。你把兰芝叫出来，我求你还不行吗！"

"她不在家。"刘继宗眼皮一翻，故意气焦仲卿。

"那岳母大人……"

刘继宗打断焦仲卿："你说话规矩点，这儿没有你岳母大人！"说罢，"咣当"一声，把院门狠

vigorously at the gate, demanding entry.

"All right, all right. I'm coming, I'm coming." It was Jizong who opened the gate.

"What do you want?" he barked, when he found himself face to face with Zhongqing.

"Let me in. I have something to say," gasped Zhongqing as he tried to force his way past Lanzhi's brother.

"If you've got something to say, say it to me," brayed Jizong. "And be quick about it. I'm a busy man; I don't have time to waste with the likes of you."

"I must find Lanzhi," cried Zhongqing, still struggling with Jizong.

"What right have you to demand to see Lanzhi?" the latter snarled, both arms stretch out to bar Zhongqing's entry.

"She is my wife," Zhongqing cried, his voice rising higher. "I must speak with her. Please don't stop me."

"What do you mean 'your wife'?" retorted Jizong. "She was your wife, you mean. But she wasn't good enough for a petty little pen-pusher like you, was she? And so you kicked her out. She's not your wife any longer. You just get it into your head once and for all that my sister's going to be the daughter-in-law of the commander. And you have the nerve to come here trying to bully her! Well, we'll see about that!"

"Please, I have no quarrel with you. Bring her here. That's all I ask."

"She's not at home," snapped Jizong, fixing Zhongqing with a baleful glare.

"What about my mother-in-law...?"

Before Zhongqing could say any more, Jizong interrupted him, with, "There's no mother-in-law of yours here." With that, he

狠地关上了。

焦仲卿气得拼尽全力拍打着大门，声嘶力竭地叫着："兰芝！兰芝！你快出来！"

门又开了，刘继宗怒睁双眼，恶狠狠地说："你吼什么！再吼我就去告你私扰民宅！"

焦仲卿绝望地牵着马离开了刘家，由这番吵嚷引来的几个看热闹的小孩子嘻嘻哈哈地指点着他的背影，笑他是疯子。他头也不回，脚步蹒跚地出了鸳鸯集。

"兰芝啊！"他心里叫着，"我们不是说好不分手吗？怎么才这么几天，你就忍心离开我呢？"他漫无目的地走着，不知要到哪里去，又不知能到哪里去。身旁的马儿像是理解主人的心思，轻嘶一声，把他带向坡下的桥边。

焦仲卿来时，兰芝与母亲就在屋里，听见仲卿的叫声，兰芝的心像被电击了一样，脱身就要出来相迎，却被母亲一把拉住。兰芝怎么也挣不脱，泪珠早已挂满两颊，她没有别的办法，只好跪在母亲面前，央求道："娘，让女儿再跟仲卿说句话，也算了却了一生心愿。"

母亲死死地攥住女儿的衣袖，她真担心女儿再见到焦仲卿，又不知生出什么故事来，所以坚决不放手。看着兰芝布满泪水的脸，她虽然心疼，但

forced Zhongqing outside, and slammed the gate shut on him.

Outside, Zhongqing hammered with all his might on the gate, and yelled himself hoarse: "Lanzhi, Lanzhi! Come to me!"

The gate flew open, and Jizong stuck his ugly snout in the aperture. "Stop that row, or I'll sue you for disturbing the peace!" he yelled.

Zhongqing turned, and disconsolately led his horse away, amid the cackles and jeers of a group of neighborhood children attracted by the fuss. Zhongqing did not even turn his head as he trudged away from Yuanyang. Echoing in his heart were the words "Lanzhi, did we not vow never to part? How could you be so hardhearted as to cast me off within the space of only a few days?" As he wandered aimlessly, his horse seemed to sense its master's anguish, and whinnied softly from time to time. In this way, the two of them came to a bridge.

Lanzhi and her mother had, in fact, been in the house when Zhongqing called. Hearing the commotion at the gate, Lanzhi had tried to run to him, but had been held back by her mother. She had then thrown herself on her knees, and, weeping copious tears, begged to be allowed to speak to Zhongqing one last time. But her mother, afraid of the consequences if Lanzhi were to see her husband again, held her in a vice-like grip. The sight of her daughter's tear-streaked face was distressing to her, and she coaxed the girl thus: "Lanzhi, it's not that I'm trying to be cruel. It's just that we waited and waited for Zhongqing. We even turned down that offer of marriage from the magistrate's son because there had been no news from Zhongqing. We couldn't wait for ever, could we? It was only when we learned that Zhongqing had got engaged to another girl that we accepted the proposal from

还是苦苦劝道："兰芝，你也替娘想一想，不是为娘狠心，我们为等他，已经回绝了县令。可他一直没有音讯，我们也不能死等呀。因为他先定了亲，咱们才许了太守家。如今他又跑来搅和，咱家的日子什么时候才能安宁下来呀！"

兰芝仰望着母亲的脸，说道：

"娘，仲卿迟迟不来，必定有他的难处。如今他既然来了，总不该连门也不让他进啊！"

"这不是进门不进门的事，若是没有与太守家的婚约，为娘还巴不得要让他把话说清楚，可现在不行！"母亲的手始终不曾松开，生怕兰芝跑出去，节外生枝。今日之事，她虽然觉得继宗粗鲁失礼了些，但不让兰芝与仲卿谋面，是绝没有错的。

兰芝的双膝跪得酸了，身子一歪，坐在地上。母亲扶她起来，边为她擦泪边说："事情已经铁板钉钉了，你要顾全体面。"

"娘，女儿一切都听您的安排，太守家的婚事也是女儿亲口所允，并不是娘与哥哥逼迫所致。我现在只求娘一件事，让我与仲卿告别一下，也不枉我们夫妻一场。"

母亲终于软下心来，说："我相信你的话。如果焦仲卿还在外面等着你，你就见他一面，赶快回来！"说完，起身拉着兰芝的手，把她送出院门，继宗想拦，母亲瞪了他一眼。

the commander's son. If Zhongqing keeps coming back and caus-
ing trouble like this, well never get a minute's peace."

Lanzhi looked up at her mother, and beseeched her: "Mother,
Zhongqing must have been delayed for some reason beyond his
control. Now that he is here, we can't just let him stand outside
the gate."

"It's not a matter of keeping him standing outside the gate,"
her mother replied. "If you weren't already engaged to the
commander's son, I would be only too pleased to have him come
in and say what he has to say. But, the situation being what it is,
that is utterly impossible." All this while, she kept a firm grip on
Lanzhi, determined not to give her an opportunity to talk to
Zhongqing, even though she thought her son's behavior toward
him had been somewhat crude.

Lanzhi collapsed on the floor, in exhaustion. Her mother
hastily held her up, and wiped her tears away, saying, "I know
it's hard on you, my child, but you must look at the wider
picture."

The girl said, "Mother, I agreed of my own free will to do as
you advised, and marry the commander's son. I did not give in to
pressure from you and my brother. Now I only have one thing to
ask of you, and that is that you allow me to bid farewell to
Zhongqing, so that our marriage can be brought to a suitable
conclusion."

This seemed to soften her mother's heart, as she said, "All
right. If he's still waiting outside, you can have a word with him.
But don't take long about it." Thereupon, she took her daughter
by the hand, and led her into the courtyard. Jizong made a half-
hearted attempt to stop them, but a glare from his mother made
him step aside.

兰芝跑出鸳鸯集，哪里还看得见仲卿的身影？她不知仲卿往哪边走了，一时没了主意，但她又不想回家，于是不知不觉，又来到那座古桥边。

此时的焦仲卿并没有上官道，这条官道，一端通向郡城，一端通向居巢县。他既不想回到郡城去忍受爱妻被人夺走的羞辱，也不想回到家中去折磨无辜的罗敷。他信马游缰，沿着这条小河不知走了多少个来回。突然，他的马长嘶一声，奋起四蹄向前跑去。他向前一望，兰芝那单弱的身影正在风中默然伫立。这一声马嘶，也把兰芝的目光吸引过来，她看见了仲卿！仲卿骑着马正朝她跑来。她不由得攥紧双手，迎着仲卿跑过去。

四目相对，刘兰芝的心像被火烧灼一样，真想扑到仲卿的怀里，再静静地听一听他胸膛的跳动，但双脚却像灌了铅，一寸也挪不动；焦仲卿也没有继续向前，在离兰芝四五步远的地方站住了。

不知过了多长时间，焦仲卿长吁一口气，恭恭敬敬地朝兰芝作了一个揖，然后扭身拉起马缰，一只脚踏在马镫上。

这却是兰芝始料未及的，眼看着仲卿上马要走，她急得高声喊道："焦仲卿，你下来！你不是来找我说话的吗？为什么一言不发就要离去！"

焦仲卿并没有回过头来，他的眼睛望着马背。他来时感到有许多话要对兰芝说，可现在真的见

Lanzhi ran out of the gate, and into the streets of Yuanyang. Zhongqing was nowhere to be seen. Flying hither and thither, the girl at last found herself at the old bridge.

In the meantime, Zhongqing had been wandering up and down the bank of the river, allowing his horse to lead him wherever it wished. He was loath to take the high road to Lujiang, where he would have to endure the humiliation of seeing his wife taken by another man. At the same time, he couldn't bear to take the road in the other direction, which would lead him home and to marriage to Luofu, whom he didn't love. Suddenly, his horse gave a loud neigh, and broke into a trot. Zhongqing looked into the distance. Lo and behold! He saw Lanzhi's frail form standing unsteadily in the wind. At the same moment, alerted by the noise from the horse, Lanzhi looked up and saw Zhongqing. The young man leaped on the horse, and galloped toward his beloved, who came tripping onward, her hands clasped in entreaty.

Their eyes met. Lanzhi's heart was like a blazing fire, and she felt an overpowering longing to throw herself into Zhongqing's arms and feel the quiet beating of his breast. But suddenly her legs seemed to turn into lead, and she couldn't move an inch further. Zhongqing too, after dismounting, for no apparent reason, found himself standing stock still, about four or five paces from Lanzhi.

After some lapse of time, the young man made a stiff and formal bow, turned, and vaulted onto his horse's back. But just as the horse was cantering off, Lanzhi called out, "Zhongqing, stop! Didn't you say you had something to say to me? Why are you going away without saying a word?"

Zhongqing reined in his horse, but did not turn his head. His

了面，他反倒不知该说些什么。"你如今已是太守家的人了，我们还有什么话说！可怜我焦仲卿磐石之心，终归敌不过荣华富贵更让人心动。"

"焦仲卿！你说这话，就不怕上天告遣吗？"刘兰芝感到天大的委屈。

"那你为什么就不能容我几日？"焦仲卿反问道。

"我在家里日日盼望，夜夜无眠，你知道吗？为了等你，我回绝了多少媒人，你知道吗？如今，一边是罗敷待嫁，一边是太守催婚，兄长又苦苦相逼，我一个弱女子，上天无路，入地无门，我是什么处境，这些你都知道吗？"兰芝说得激动起来，"我倒想问问你，你为什么就不能早几天来？为什么这么快就与罗敷定了亲？"

"这不是我的本意，是被母亲逼迫的啊！"

"你被母亲逼迫，难道我就不是被家人逼迫？同是苦命之人，你怎么能说出这样的话来！"

望着刘兰芝那充满忧愁的脸，焦仲卿不由得心疼起来，他走上前去搂住她，抚摸着她乌黑的头发。

"人都说破镜难圆，难道这话真的要在你我身上应验？"兰芝感到十分绝望。

"我既许你磐石之坚，就不会再娶他人！"焦仲卿口气坚决地说。

"那你要怎样？"

"有死而已！"

eyes were fixed on the nape of his steed's neck. All the things
that he had wanted to say to Lanzhi had evaporated from his
mind, and speech had deserted him. Finally, he muttered, "If you
are going to marry the commander's son, then there is nothing to
say. Seemingly, my constant heart is no match for wealth and
power when it comes to winning my true love."

"Zhongqing, how can you say such a thing?" Lanzhi wailed
piteously. "Aren't you afraid of Heaven's retribution?"

"Then, why could you not wait for me for even a few days?"

"I longed for your return night and day. I turned down sev-
eral offers of marriage. But finally, when you got engaged to
Luofu, the pressure from my mother and brother on me to re-
marry became too much for me to bear. I, a poor, weak woman
alone, had no way out. Don't you understand?" Lanzhi's
heartrending sobbing reached a crescendo: "Oh, why didn't you
come back sooner? Why did you rush into an engagement with
Luofu?"

"It wasn't my fault," Zhongqing protested. "My mother forced
me into it."

"Then you should be able to understand how much pres-
sure I was under," retorted Lanzhi.

Zhongqing looked at Lanzhi. Her forlorn expression moved
him deeply. Jumping down from his horse, he clasped Lanzhi to
his breast, and stroked her raven-black hair.

"They say that a broken mirror can never be put together
again," Lanzhi murmured, in the depths of despair. "I wonder if
this is going to be proved true in our case."

Zhongqing's reply to this was a stout one: "My love for you is
eternal. My heart is unyielding. I will never marry anyone else."

"But, what will you do?"

兰芝听到这话，并不感到意外，这也是她自己多次想过的结局。她之所以还没有这样做，就是还恋着焦仲卿，总想与他再见上一面。如今心愿已足，她感到十分欣慰。

"婚期定在何日？"仲卿见兰芝没有说话，又问了一句。

"就在明日！"

魏别驾在庐江郡待了两年，也与王县令打过几次交道。以他看来，王县令还算是个好人。他知道上次王县令与何主簿到郡里去，许太守已经交待了让他们寻自己的短处，以便借县令之手将自己除掉，但他又相信王县令未必是那样阴毒的人。或许正因为这个原因，魏别驾心中早已有了退隐的打算。到居巢县的第二天，他便以下官身份备礼来到县令府上。

王县令这里也是祸不单行，前几天瑞琪口吐鲜血之后，病情非但没有好转，反而日渐沉重。正在县令与夫人焦灼之际，又有熟人捎过信来，说在外为军校的二儿子瑞瑜在一次战斗中命丧沙场，夫人急火攻心，中风不语。魏别驾前来拜见时，王县令正坐在正厅发呆。见到魏别驾，没精打采地说了声："请坐。"

"下官是来向大人辞行的。"魏别驾施礼道。

"Until my dying day, I will never remarry!"

Lanzhi was not surprised to hear this; it was what she had many times hoped to hear. Her heart's desire had been fulfilled, and she felt a deep sense of contentment.

"When is your wedding day?" Zhongqing asked.

"Tomorrow."

During his two years as prefect of Lujiang, Mounted Escort Wei had had dealings with Magistrate Wang several times, and had come to regard the latter as a sound man. He was aware of the fact that when Magistrate Wang and Secretary He had visited him the last time, Commander Xu had tried to use them to ferret out the prefect's shortcomings so as to engineer his downfall. But he was sure that Magistrate Wang was not the sort of person to stoop to such low tricks. Since his demotion, Mounted Escort Wei had been thinking of retiring from official life, and on the second day of his arrival in Juchao County, he went to pay his respects to the magistrate and tender his resignation.

As they say, troubles never come singly, and this was true for Magistrate Wang too. No sooner had his son Ruiqi's illness taken a turn for the worse than a message came that his other son, Ruiyu, who had been serving as an officer in the army, had been killed in battle. The shock was too much for the magistrate's wife, who suffered a stroke which rendered her unable to speak. When Mounted Escort Wei called, Magistrate Wang was sitting in the main hall, staring straight ahead as if in a daze. Listlessly, he invited the visitor to take a seat.

"I have come to take my leave," said Mounted Escort Wei, after the usual greetings.

"What do you mean?" replied the magistrate. But before

"不知魏大人此话怎讲？"还没等魏别驾开口细说，县令家里的老仆跌跌撞撞地跑进来跪在地上，哭着禀报：

"老爷，三公子他，他……"

"三公子怎么了？"王县令顾不得失态，蹭地一下子从椅子上跳起来。

"三公子，不行了！"

"啊！"王县令大叫一声，踉踉跄跄地奔了出去。

许太守家娶亲，真让鸳鸯集的人大开了眼界。这一天前晌，一顶华丽的大花轿便来到了刘家门前，抬轿的汉子每人帽翅上都别着一朵红花，腰间都系着红腰带，这番排场，引得大半个鸳鸯集的人都赶来看热闹。

刘兰芝这次出嫁的心情与初嫁大不相同，雄鸡初啼，她就起身梳妆，对着铜镜，她仔仔细细地匀着脸，画着眉，粉黛轻施，凤钗斜插。她反复地端详着自己，直到她觉得尽善尽美，才离开妆台开始穿衣。按照母亲的意思，这次要穿一件新的嫁衣，可兰芝执意不肯。她拿出初嫁时穿的那件绣着孔雀兰的短襦，放在床上，久久地抚摸着，似乎那衣上的细褶永远也抚不平了。直到花轿来到门前，母亲再三催促，她才把绣襦穿在身上，外面又披了一件大红色的长披。母亲为她把红绫盖头盖好，拉

Wei could explain, and old servant rushed into the hall in a state of great agitation, and fell to his knees before Magistrate Wang.

"Your Honor," he gasped, "It's the Third Master.... He's...."

"How is he?"

"He's dead."

The magistrate, throwing protocol to the winds, leaped from his chair, and dashed out.

The wedding at Commander Xu's dazzled the whole population of Yuanyang. On the morning of the appointed day, a sumptuous sedan chair arrived at the Xu mansion, the bearers wearing red sashes and caps with red flowers in them. Half the inhabitants of Yuanyang came rushing to see the spectacle.

Lanzhi's feelings on this day were much different from those she had entertained on her first wedding day. She rose at cockcrow, washed, and carefully applied her makeup and placed pins in her hair before her mirror. Not until she was satisfied that everything was perfect did she leave the dressing table. Her mother had tried to get her to wear a brand-new set of wedding garments, but Lanzhi had insisted on wearing the ones she had been married to Zhongqing in. She took out the short jacket decorated with phoenix flowers, laid it on the bed, and stroked it for a long time, as if she felt that she would never be able to get the creases out of it. On top of it, she wore a long red cloak. Her mother adjusted her red gauze veil, took her by the hand, and murmured, "Lanzhi, please let this marriage work. Don't cause me any more heartaches."

着她的手，哽咽地说："兰芝，这次出嫁，你可不要再让为娘为你担心了啊。"

"母亲，兰芝早已想好，这次与您相别，就是要让您老人家永远地放宽心！"

吹吹打打的乐声响遍了鸳鸯集，接亲的队伍几十人，沿着大路渐渐远去。

这一次的婚礼，兰芝没有了羞涩，没有了激动，没有了憧憬，没有了期望，整个过程都像个偶人一样任人摆布。她既没听到三媒六证的拿腔作调，也没听到酒席宴上的大呼小叫，她已心如死灰，不知道什么是疲惫和困倦了。

不知过了多久，她才被人搀扶着进了洞房，像块木头般地墩在了床沿上。自从出了家门，那块盖头就一直蒙住她的双眼，按上次的经验，现在应当是她与新郎单独相对，新郎为她揭去盖头的时候了。可过了好一会儿，并没有人来揭她的盖头。凭着她的感觉，屋里至少还有三四个女仆在窃窃私语。她等得有点不耐烦，就自己撩开红绫，当她看到新郎那副尊容时，就明白了郡守大人为何非要娶自己了。新郎面容说不上十分丑陋，但两眼发直，即使看到盛妆的刘兰芝，依旧是表情呆滞，没有任何表示。看来，新郎是个痴儿。

然而刘兰芝并没有感到失望，许家少爷的痴

"You can be sure I will put your mind at ease, Mother," the girl replied.

Then, to the sound of gay music, the wedding procession made its way along the main street of Yuanyang.

Lanzhi endured the whole ritual of the wedding ceremony as if she were a puppet manipulated by others. She felt no shyness, no excitement, no hope, no expectation. She seemed not to hear the chanting of the wedding vows, nor the congratulatory speeches at the wedding banquet. Her heart had turned to ashes, and she felt neither fatigue nor discomfort throughout the long, tedious day.

Eventually, she was helped into the bridal chamber, and lay on the bed as stiff and unmoving as a carved wooden image. Her veil had hidden her face ever since she had left her mother's house. Now was the time, as at her previous nuptials, when the bride and groom were at last alone, for the latter to remove the veil. But when, after an extraordinarily long time, no one came to lift the veil, and it seemed that there were at least three or four maid servants whispering in the room, Lanzhi removed her veil herself.

She found herself gazing at the face of her new husband. Not only was he incredibly ugly, but his popeyed stare betrayed not a flicker of interest in his beautiful bride. The face was that of a moron.

Nevertheless, the repulsive sight did not cause her any misgivings. Although she had not expected the commander's son to be such an imbecile, the shock soon wore off. Ever since she had parted from Zhongqing for the last time by the river she had made her mind up as to what she must do. Even if her new hus-

呆固然出乎她的意料，但这惊诧在她心中并没有停留太久，因为自从与焦仲卿在河边诀别之后，她该怎么做，早已想好了。眼前的新郎纵然是个玉人，也无法使她改变初衷，只不过这个蠢物使她能有机会提前离开洞房。

"伺候公子睡吧。"她吩咐女仆道，顺势站起来，让出床铺。

女仆们应声忙给许公子脱鞋宽衣，盖上被子，然后悄悄退下。不大一会儿，公子已鼾声如雷。

刘兰芝捏着自己的红盖头，揉来揉去，望着一盏盏血红的蜡烛，望着烛影中到处贴满的阴森森的喜字，她想起了自己的初嫁，想起被焦仲卿撩开红绫后的喜悦和激动，不由自主地轻声唤道：

"仲卿，仲卿。"

她把披在外面的红衫脱下来，露出了那件绣满兰花的短襦，走出房门。外面下起了雨，噼噼啪啪地击打着窗纸。这一天一直是阴沉沉的，此刻终于下雨了，这雨水是否能洗刷掉自己的耻辱？这雨水是不是上天为她洒下的泪水？

漆黑的夜，阴冷的天，雨越下越大，太守家一座座房子像一头头猛兽，但刘兰芝心中已没有了惧怕，她在这巨兽间摸索着行走。前面是一道矮墙，矮墙间隐隐约约露出一个月洞门，她朝月洞门走去。

band had turned out to be perfect in every way, it would have made no difference to her. Luckily, since the commander's son was such a dolt, she would easily have an opportunity of slipping out of the bedroom.

Turning to the maidservants, she said, "The master wishes to sleep." With this, she arose, and started arranging the bedding.

On cue, the maidservants undressed the commander's son, put him to bed, and discreetly retired.

Before long, the bridegroom was snoring like thunder on his wedding night.

Fingering her red gauze veil, and looking around at the blood-red wedding candles, and the sad strips of paper pasted all over the walls wishing happiness to the newlyweds, which cowered in the flickering candlelight, Lanzhi thought back to her first wedding night. She remembered how overjoyed she had felt when Zhongqing had lifted her veil. She couldn't help calling softly: "Zhongqing, Zhongqing."

She took of her scarlet mantle, revealing the embroidered blouse she was wearing beneath it, and left the room. It had been cloudy all day, and at last the rain had begun to fall. The raindrops pattered on the window paper. Lanzhi wondered if this rain would be sufficient to wash away her shame. Perhaps it was Heaven's way of weeping for her?

In the pitch-black night, the rain poured down more and more fiercely from an icy sky. The various buildings which composed the commander's mansion looked like the heads of rearing beasts. Yet Lanzhi felt no fear as she picked her way through the threatening herd. She came to a squat wall, in which there was a round moon-gate. She stepped through the moon-gate.

The wind howled louder, and the rain lashed the streets.

风更紧了，雨更大了，一道闪电划过夜空。这道闪电让刘兰芝看到了她最需要的一幕：绿柳围绕的地方，是一汪清池。原来这里是太守家的后花园。她在风雨中朝池塘走去。到了，到池边了。

她坐在一块低矮的石头上，衣裙已经被打得精湿。她双手交抱在胸前，不是因为天冷，因为此时她已经感觉不到冷暖了，她只想最后感受一下自己的心跳，她要用这双手向焦仲卿证明，她这颗心直到最后，还在为他跳着。

"仲卿，我们黄泉相见了！"兰芝向这世界发出最后一声呼喊，双足一蹬，跳进池中。

焦仲卿与兰芝分别之后，回到家中，脑海里总是响着兰芝与她说的最后一句话："就在明日。"

就在明日，这四个字分明有话外之音，凭着仲卿对兰芝的了解，有一点他是拿得稳的，兰芝绝不是一个朝秦暮楚的女子，更不是一个攀结富贵的浅薄之人。河边对语之时，当自己说"有死而已"时，兰芝为什么没有劝自己，而是面露喜色？而自己问她与太守公子的婚期时，她为什么又毫无愧色，脱口而出？

焦母也已把婚期定了下来，焦仲卿到家时，母亲已经连喜酒和花烛都准备好了。那间他与兰芝共同生活过二三年的厢房也被修饰一新。焦仲卿

Lanzhi stumbled along, finding her way with the help of an occa-
sional flash of jagged lightning, until she found what she was
looking for — a pond of clear water surrounded by willow trees.
The pond was part of a park at the rear of Commander Xu's
mansion. Lanzhi walked to the edge of the water. There she sat
down on a low rock. Her clothes were soaking wet by this time.
She clasped her hands to her breast; not because she felt cold
— she was past feeling such physical sensations as cold and
warmth — but because she wanted to feel her heartbeats, to
send a message to Zhongqing that her heart was beating to the
last only for him.

"Zhongqing, we will meet again at the Yellow Springs!" With
this final call, Lanzhi threw herself into the pond.

Ever since he left Lanzhi, and returned home, Zhongqing
had been unable to get out of his head her last word — 'Tomorrow'.
Somehow, he felt that it had a hidden meaning. If there was one
thing he was sure about Lanzhi it was that she was not fickle, nor
was she a shallow person who hankered after wealth and honor.
When he had said to her at the riverside: "Until my dying day ...",
why had she not protested that he must not waste his life, but
had assumed an expression of great joy? And why, when he had
asked her when her marriage to the commander's son was to
take place, had she shown no glimmer of embarrassment, but
had told him straightforwardly?

 Meanwhile, his mother had fixed his wedding day for him.
When Zhongqing arrived home, he found all the nuptial trim-
mings set out. The room where he and Lanzhi had spent a
couple of years together had been completely refurbished. He
entered it reluctantly. Looking around the room with languid

懒洋洋地走进屋里，忽然发现兰芝临行前亲手挂起的纱帐被换掉了。他立刻返回母亲房中：

"那顶四角垂香囊的帐子呢？"

"为娘换掉了。"焦母并没有在意，随口答道。

"母亲，孩儿这辈子再求你一件事，请你把那顶帐子还给我，让我在里面再歇息几日。"

焦母明白让仲卿把刘兰芝彻底忘掉是不可能的，只要他答应把罗敷娶进家，自己也就不愿意再为这点儿小事与儿子闹气。于是勉勉强强把那顶帐子翻出来，扔给仲卿。

焦仲卿没有向母亲道谢，拿着帐子回到房中，很快把帐子换好，又轻手轻脚地把四角的垂囊整理一番，直到恢复了兰芝走时的原样，才颓唐地和衣躺在帐中。

今天是兰芝出嫁的日子，焦仲卿怎么也睡不着。

外面突然下起了倾盆大雨，这在阳春三月的庐江一带是很少遇到的事。焦仲卿刚想起来将窗户关闭，一阵狂风刮来，把案上的灯烛吹灭，接着一道闪电凌空劈下，焦仲卿心中一阵颤抖，瘫在床上动弹不得。

第二天，雨过天晴，日上三竿，仲卿还没有起床。梅梅唤了几次让他吃饭，他才不得不慵懒地爬了起来。焦母为儿子的婚事忙得晕头转向，而焦仲卿却对此事毫不关心。

eyes, he suddenly noticed that the bed drape that Lanzhi had hung up specially just before she left had been changed for a new one. He hurried to his mother, and demanded, "What happened to that bed drape with the perfume sachets at the four corners."

"I took it down, and put another one up in its place," Lady Jiao said, carelessly.

"Mother, please give it back to me," Zhongqing begged, "and let me sleep behind it for just a few days."

Lady Jiao knew that her son would never be able to forget Lanzhi completely. But, so long as he agreed to marry Luofu, she saw no point in making a fuss over this trifle, and so she went and fetched the item he so desired.

Zhongqing accepted it without thanking his mother, and took it back to the bridal chamber. He carefully arranged it until it was just as it had been when Lanzhi had left. Then, dispirited, for this was Lanzhi's wedding day, he lay down on the bed, fully clothed, to endure a long, sleepless night.

Outside, it suddenly started to rain heavily. This was unusual in the Lujiang area in early spring. Zhongqing was just about to get up and close the window, when a blast of wind blew the lamp out. Then, a jagged bolt of lightning ripped the sky apart. Aghast, Zhongqing dare not stir from the bed.

He awoke late the following morning, to find that the rain had stopped and the sky had cleared. Zhongqing was loath to rise, and it was only after Meimei had called him three times for breakfast that he finally heaved himself out of bed. After breakfast, he went back and lay on the bed, once more fully clothed. His mother was still running around making preparations for the wedding, but Zhongqing gave the matter scarcely

吃罢饭，他又回到床上，和衣倒下。刚刚闭上眼睛，就看见兰芝笑盈盈地朝自己走来，身上还穿着那件绣着孔雀兰的短襦。他伸出双臂想把她紧紧地搂在怀中，可兰芝却像一缕烟一样地消失了。

不知过了多久，焦仲卿感到胸口憋闷得很。他坐起来，又觉得头疼得厉害，只好又躺下。这时他听到院子里有说话的声音，接着有人推门进来，他以为又是梅梅叫他吃饭，所以连眼也没睁。

"兄弟，兄弟。"是邻家张二哥的声音，焦仲卿这才慢慢睁眼起身。

"兄弟，你怎么啦？"

"没什么，有点累。二哥请坐。"

"我不坐了，跟你说几句就走。"张二哥嘴上这么说，却迟疑了半天不开口。焦仲卿也不催他，屋里的气氛令人窒息。终于，张二哥憋不住了："仲卿兄弟，有句话本不该对你讲，可我肚里憋不住。再说，这事你迟早也会知道的。"

焦仲卿像是预感到什么，紧盯着张二哥。

"我刚从郡城回来，郡里出了大事了！太守家昨日娶了刘兰芝，还没等到天明，兰芝就投湖自尽了！"

焦仲卿虽然知道结局必会如此，但听了张二哥的话，他还是难以控制自己的情绪，身子摇晃了

a thought.

Zhongqing closed his eyes, and immediately he saw Lanzhi, her face wreathed in smiles, coming near to him. She was wearing the blouse which she herself had embroidered with peacock flowers. She stretched out her arms to embrace him — and vanished like a whisp of smoke.

Some time later, Zhongqing sat up, a stifling feeling in his chest and a throbbing in his head. He could do nothing but lie down again. He heard a babble of voices in the courtyard, and somebody pushed open the door and entered the room. At first, he thought that it must be Meimei coming to call him for lunch, so he didn't even open his eyes.

"Zhongqing, Zhongqing!" It was the voice of his neighbor Zhang. "Are you all right?"

"It's nothing. It's just that I'm a bit tired, that's all," replied Zhongqing, opening his eyes lazily. "Please take a seat."

"No, I won't sit down. I just have something to tell you, and then I must be off." Zhang hesitated. Zhongqing patiently waited for him to say what he had to say. The atmosphere in the room became oppressive. Finally, Zhang blurted out, "Zhongqing, I don't know how to tell you this, but I can't keep it to myself any longer. You'll find out sooner or later, anyway."

An ominous sense of foreboding came over Zhongqing, whose eyes widened as he stared at the visitor.

"I've just come from Juchao," Zhang explained. "Something terrible has happened. Liu Lanzhi got married to the commander's son yesterday, and sometime during the night she threw herself into a pond, and drowned."

Even before the words were out of Zhang's mouth, Zhongqing knew what the dreadful news would be. His body shud-

好几下，张二哥慌忙把他扶住。

又是一个阴惨惨的夜晚，风从入夜时刮起，越刮越紧。

焦仲卿屋里的灯始终亮着。

院角的青花马今夜不知为什么，不时地发出阵阵嘶鸣。

梅梅被一场恶梦惊醒。她梦见天上掉下一座大山，刚好砸在自家的院子里，房子全被砸塌了。她吓得惊叫一声坐起来，揉揉眼睛，看到自己还好端端的。她似醒非醒，想要看看母亲和哥哥的房屋是否完好。于是披衣下床，走到院里。院子里哪有什么大山，所有的房屋都好好的。只是昏暗的晓色中，哥哥房中的烛光还在闪动。她悄悄走过去，想把灯烛吹熄。当她推开门时，屋里的情景使她很纳闷：幔帐被拆下来，平平整整地叠好放在床上，却不见哥哥的身影。这几天哥哥心绪不好她是知道的，或许哥哥又早早地出去走动了？她吹熄了灯，刚刚出屋，又听见墙角那匹马使劲地刨着地，不停地仰头嘶叫，她想过去看个究竟。可当她抬起头时，却看见哥哥悬吊在老槐树上！

两家求合葬，合葬华山傍。
东西植松柏，左右种梧桐。

dered with violent convulsions. In consternation, Zhang hurried to support him.

Another gloomy night. With nightfall, a wind started to blow, stronger and stronger.

A candle burned in Zhongqing's room.

In the courtyard, from time to time, and for no apparent reason, Zhongqing's horse whinnied uneasily.

Meimei awoke with a scream from a terrifying dream, in which she saw a huge mountain fall from the sky and smash the house into a million pieces. Rubbing her eyes, she saw that she was all right, but she worried that something might have happened to her mother and brother. So, still half asleep, she crept out of bed, threw a robe around her shoulders, and went out into the courtyard. She found nothing amiss there, but she noticed that there was a light still burning in her brother's room, although dawn was near. She thought that she would go in and blow out the candle. As she entered on tiptoe, she experienced a feeling of stuffiness. The bed hanging had been taken down, and folded neatly on the bed. There was no sign of her brother. She knew that he had been depressed for the previous few days, so perhaps he had gone out for an early morning walk? She blew out the candle, and had just left the room, when she heard the horse pawing the ground and whinnying. She was just about to go to it, to see what the matter was, when she saw her brother's body dangling from the scholartree in the courtyard!

Zhongqing and Lanzhi were buried together at the foot of Mount Hua.

Pine, cypress and *Wutong* trees were planted all around

枝枝相覆盖，叶叶相交通。

孔／雀／东／南／飞

春末，正是孔雀兰开得最盛的时节。一个女子在鸳鸯集前的河边采着兰草。她怀中已经抱满了深蓝色的花。

她独自一人默默地过了古桥，又穿过官道，来到山岗之间。一座新起的坟墓，碑阳刻着隽秀的一行字：焦仲卿刘兰芝合葬之墓。

那女子捧着花束，恭恭敬敬地把它插在坟前，闭上眼睛，轻声说道：

"仲卿，兰芝，罗敷为你们送行来了。仲卿，我知道你心里只有兰芝一个人，可罗敷也是深爱你的。你我无缘，也是有缘，因为我已经与你订了婚，只是我无福消受罢了。兰芝，我的好姐姐，你本该比罗敷幸福，可你怎么也无福消受呢！"

她轻轻捧起一把土，慢慢地撒在坟上：

"你们虽然去了，可你们多么幸福！现在好了，你们终于同眠于地下，直到地老，直到天荒，永远也不分开了。可我呢？"

286 两家合葬华山旁

their grave.

In time, the branches of the trees formed a canopy over the mound, and their leaves intertwined.

As that spring drew to a close, the peacock orchids bloomed as never before. In the meadow by the river which flows near Yuanyang, a girl was picking the flowers. She already had a large bunch of the blue blossoms.

Alone and silent, she passed over the old bridge. Crossing the highway, she approached a new grave on a hillock. On the gravestone was written:

"Jiao Zhongqing and Liu Lanzhi are buried here. "

The girl reverentially placed the flowers she had gathered before the grave. Closing her eyes, she said in a low voice: "Zhongqing and Lanzhi, Luofu is here to say goodbye to you. Zhongqing, I know that Lanzhi was the only person in your heart, but I loved you dearly. But Fate decreed that we were never to be together. I was once engaged to you, but I lost you. Lanzhi, my dear friend, you once experienced the happiness that was not to be mine, but in the end you lost it too."

Scraping together a handful of soil, she lightly scattered it over the grave.

"Although you have both departed," she went on, "I know that you have found happiness, as you will sleep together below the ground, until the earth grows old and the sky melts. You will never be parted from each other. But me?"

图书在版编目（CIP）数据

孔雀东南飞：中国古代爱情故事／徐飞编著；
（英）保尔·怀特译.
－北京：新世界出版社，2002
ISBN 7-80005-923-5

Ⅰ.孔… Ⅱ.①徐…②保… Ⅲ.英语－对照读物，
故事 Ⅳ.H319 4:1

中国版本图书馆 CIP 数据核字(2002)第 091120 号

孔雀东南飞

编　　著：	徐飞	
翻　　译：	保尔·怀特	
封面剪纸：	于平　任凭	
绘　　图：	李士伋	
责任编辑：	张民捷	
装帧设计：	贺玉婷	
责任印制：	黄厚清	
出版发行：	新世界出版社	
社　　址：	北京阜成门外百万庄路24号	
邮政编码：	100037	
电　　话：	0086-10-68994118	
传　　真：	0086-10-68326679	
电子邮件：	nwpcn@public.bta.net.cn	
印　　刷：	北京京东印刷厂	
经　　销：	新华书店　外文书店	
开　　本：	850×1168（毫米）　1/32	
字　　数：	180千	
印　　张：	9.625	
印　　数：	1-5000册	
版　　次：	2003年1月（汉英）第1版第1次印刷	
书　　号：	ISBN 7-80005-923-5/I·166	
定　　价：	25.00元	